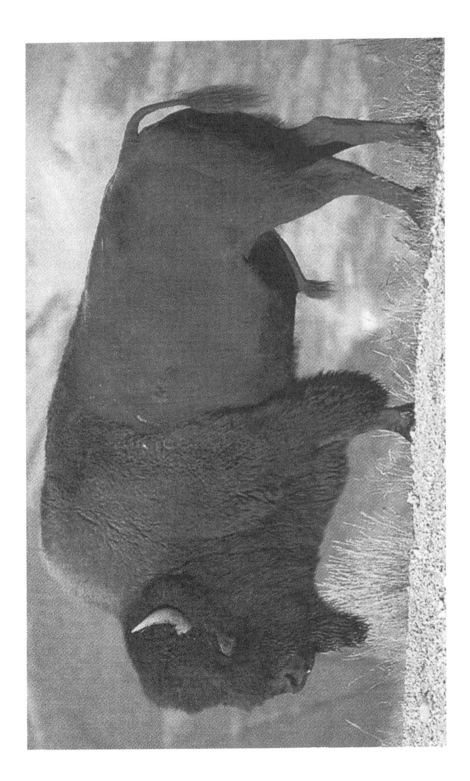

The buffalo exemplifies the rendering industry because the American Plains Indian appreciated the value of utilizing the whole animal. The buffalo is one of the many animals which when properly utilized, a wide range of products become available to society.

Dennis K Mullane

# The Original Recyclers

edited by

Don A Franco
&
Winfield Swanson

under the auspices of

The Animal Protein Producers Industry
The Fats & Proteins Research Foundation
The National Renderers Association

## Publishing Committee Members:

**Dennis Mullane, Chairman**
Taylor By-Products, Inc
PO Box 849—Route 706
Wyalusing, PA 18853

**Don Franco, Coordinator**
The National Renderers Association
801 N Fairfax Street—Suite 207
Alexandria, VA 22314

**Fred Bisplinghoff**
Fred Bisplinghoff & Associates
7150 Estero Blvd. #904—Creciente South
Ft Meyers, FL 33932

**Robert Desnoyers**
Lomex, Inc.
9900 6e Rue
Montreal, Quebec, CANADA H1C 1G2

**David Kaluzny, II**
Kaluzny Bros, Inc
1528 Mound Road
Joliet, IL 60436-9808

**Ray Kelly**
Baker Commodities, Inc
4020 Bandini Blvd
Los Angeles, CA 90023

**Bill Stappenback**
8/17/36 to 01/14/95
Baker Commodities, Inc
Rochester, NY

**Greg Van Hoven**
Van Hoven Co, Inc
PO Box 56
South St Paul, MN 55075

# The Authors

**Fred Bisplinghoff** was a practicing veterinarian before entering the rendering industry in 1956. He retired from National By-Products in 1985 and served as a consultant for Holly Farms Foods from 1985 to 1988. From 1988 to 1993 he served as President and Director of Technical Services of Fats and Proteins Research Foundation and is currently serving the rendering industry as a consultant.

**Frank A Burnham** is the author of *The Invisible Industry*, and for the past 25 years, edited and published *Render*, the national magazine of the rendering industry.

**Henry L Fuller**, Professor Emeritus of Animal and Poultry Nutrition was engaged in teaching and research at the University of Georgia for 35 years. During this time and subsequently, he serves as a consultant to the poultry and related industries including the National Renderers Association and the Fats and Proteins Research Foundation.

**Ric R Grummer** was with the Department of Dairy Science at the University of Wisconsin-Madison in 1984. In 1995 he obtained the rank of full Professor and was selected by the American Dairy Science Association as the recipient of the American Food Industry Award.

**Kenneth A Halloran** was with Proctor & Gamble Research & Development for 38 years (12 as R&D Director in International Assignments in the Far East and Latin America). Since 1991 he has been an oleochemical consultant.

**Terry Klopfenstein** is on staff at the University of Nebrask-Lincoln from 1965 to present. Currently he teaches undergraduate and graduate courses, research activity relates to growing-finishing cattle.

**Darrell A Knabe** is a Professor of animal science at Texas A&M University. His research interests focus on nutrient bioavailability and factors affecting lean deposition in pigs.

**Robert McCoy** retired from Proctor & Gamble after 37 years serving in commodity purchasing, research, and management (including purchasing group for fats and oils for technical applications).

**Timothy Miller**, principal of Process Associates in St Charles, Missouri, has 27 years experience in pet food industry research, ranging from product and process development to plant start-up to supplier inspection, approval, supplier product improvement, and product development.

**Gary G Pearl,** President and Director of Technical Services for the Fats and Proteins Research Foundation, graduated from Purdue University and pursued his veterinary career with FS Services Inc and Growmark Inc.

**William H Prokop** was the National Renderers Association director of engineering services from 1971 until 1985. Since then, he has served as an environmental engineering consultant to the rendering industry.

## The Editors

**Don A Franco** currently serves as the director of scientific services for the National Renderers Association and Animal Protein Producers Industry. His career with the Department of Agriculture began in 1968 and culminated in his retirement in 1992 as Director of Slaughter Operations, Washington, DC.

**Winfield Swanson** has written, edited, and indexed scientific material for scholarly publications since 1975. From 1984 until its demise in 1996, she was Managing Editor of the National Geographic Society's *Research & Exploration.*

For

Those who came before us

and

those who will follow,

*The Original Recyclers.*

In memory of Bill Stappenback,

former chairman,

Domestic Market Development Committee

# PREFACE

In the early '90s it became obvious to a few renderers that we needed to actively promote our industry. People in academia, the government, and the public sector—a whole new generation far removed from livestock, agriculture, and biochemistry—need to know who we are. They need to know that we renderers provide safe products, that we are environmentally aware that we are the original recyclers. Rendering can no longer afford to be the "Invisible Industry" (the title of the book the National Renderers Association produced in 1978).

We formed a committee to explore the best way to achieve this goal. From those debates emerged the title *The Original Recyclers*, and the recommendation to write a book that would draw on all aspects of the rendering industry of today and into the 21st century. Despite numerous challenges, the committee members never lost sight of the goal; each member contributed dedication and foresight.

To set a direction for the book, I reflected on my years growing up in and around the industry. The first thing that came to mind was, as a boy, showing the employees at the plant how I had learned to tie my sneakers. And the second thing I remembered was my childhood dilemma of how to answer the question, "What does your father do for a living?" Then, one day I realized that no one wanted to do what my father and grandfather did. Therefore, they had to be special people. As I got older, I realized that there were few of these special people, but that they had a tremendous responsibility. They handled much of the perishable byproducts our society produces. These people—who have kept pace with the ever growing population and the challenges of processing, transporting, and marketing goods made from these perishables—truly are the original recyclers.

# ACKNOWLEDGMENTS

On behalf of the National Renderers Association, the Animal Protein Producers Industry, and the Fats and Protein Research Foundation, I thank the following:

We would have had no book without the authors, who contributed considerable time and effort—they are the professionals in this field. Without their contributions to *The Original Recyclers* and to our industry, we as an industry would be less prepared for the challenges of the 21st century.

Lisa Truesdell devoted many hours turning draft manuscripts into camera-ready copy.

Taylor By-Products, Inc., Wyalusing, Pennsylvania, generously allowed me the time and facilities to work on this project.

Valerie Mullane contributed the design for the cover of this book.


—Dennis K Mullane

# TABLE OF CONTENTS

# 1

# The Rendering Industry: A Historical Perspective

Little more than 20 years ago, recycling was only a buzzword; by the mid-1990s it had exploded into a massive, nationwide undertaking. Citizens, companies, whole industries and institutions were saving waste paper, pasteboard, tin and aluminum cans, glass bottles, and some types of plastic to be reprocessed into usable products, instead of adding them to our burgeoning municipal waste. In 1992, for instance, we recycled 45 million tons of this material, little more than 21% of the nearly 207 million tons of waste we generated that year.

Thanks to the highly specialized rendering industry, another 15 million tons of material never entered the waste stream. Diverted before it could be considered waste, this material consists of the unused animal parts from our huge meat and poultry industry—highly perishable material that in a matter of hours can become infested with microbiological pathogens and pose a tremendous health and sanitation problem. The rendering industry, quietly and with little fanfare, has collected this potential waste and converted it into usable, in fact, essential products.

# EUROPE
## Soap-making

Although rendering as an organized and cohesive industry has been around for only 150 years, the process of melting down animal fats to produce tallow and other fats and oils probably got its start when *Homo sapiens* began cooking meat over a campfire and saving the drippings.

One of the few records of this mundane activity was written shortly after the birth of Christ. Plinius Secundus (Pliny the Elder), Roman soldier, scholar, historian, and naturalist, was a curious man, as his *Natural History* testifies. His is the first written record of a process that gave birth to today's billion-dollar rendering industry. Pliny reported a cleansing compound prepared from goat's tallow and wood ashes, the earliest record of soap and, *ergo,* the first record of rendering—the melting down of animal fat to obtain tallow.

Historians are uncertain whether the Romans adopted their tallow-making process from the chance discoveries of wandering Bedouins or from the Celts who are known to have made *saipo* by boiling animal fats and plant ashes together. Soap was evidently well-known to the Romans of Pliny's day, although it did not come into wide use for some 1800 years.

The Greek physician, Galen (AD 130 to 200), described soap both as a means of cleansing the body and as a medicament. Another physician, Theodorus Priscianus (AD 385), described its use as a shampoo; he also was the first to record the trade of *saponarius* or soap-boiler. In about AD 800, Jabir ibn Hayyan, an Arab chemist known as the father of alchemy, wrote repeatedly of soap as an effective means of cleaning. But notwithstanding an apparent general knowledge of soap at least among scholars, scientists, and physicians, soap seems to have been limited to cleaning hair and body.

As a laundry product, it did not come into general use until the mid-1800s. From the time of the Roman Empire through even the early part of the 19th century, "fulling" remained the principal method of laundering. In ancient Rome, the fullers—next to the bakers—seemed to have the largest group of tradesmen. The Roman *fullonica* or laundry, operated using what is now known as Fuller's earth. This greenish, clay-like material absorbs grease from cloth and was the fuller's chief tool. With this, and with potash obtained from the burnt wood ash and carbonate of soda, the *fullonica* would wash, beat, dry, and whiten the cloth with sulfur fumes. Even as late as the 1830s, English fullers used Fuller's earth, lye, and ammonia as the Greeks and Romans had. Soap was still an expensive and much taxed luxury.

Following the decline and fall of Rome, historians find comparatively little reference to the use of soap. Its manufacture and popular use may have been revived in Germany, but it appears to have been developed largely in Italy, England, and France. In the Middle Ages, Marseilles was the center of the growing, young industry of soap-making. The manufacturing families of the famous Marseilles soap managed to keep their process secret for many generations. Even the offer of a generous prize by the Academy of Marseilles in 1769 for the best paper on the manufacturing of soap failed to draw out the secret process. But, 5 years later a layman to whom the secret had been described by a member of the trade did submit such a paper. Just before the French Revolution, soap production in Marseilles had reached 3500 tons per year from some 34 factories. Marseilles developed a considerable export business of its soap, chiefly to America. The industry in France received still greater impetus by Nicolas Leblanc's discovery in the 18th century of a process for making soda from brine.

In England, soap was first made in Bristol toward the end of the 12th century, but the center of the industry developed in Cheapside, a suburb of London—not that there was anything cheap about soap in England from the 12th and well into the 19th centuries. Soap-makers were required to pay a duty on every ton produced. This tax, of course, was passed on to the consumer. Following the Napoleonic Wars of the early 19th century, the tax on soap rose to as high as 3 pence on every pound produced. Soap-boiling pans were fitted with lids, which the tax collector could lock at night to prevent "tax-free" soap-making under the cover of darkness. In spite of these handicaps, the use of soap—and its use of tallow—continued to spread in England. Queen Elizabeth, in the latter 16th century, is reported to have indulged in a hot bath with *sope* once a month. Finally, in 1853 under the government of Prime Minister William E Gladstone, the tax on soap manufacture was abolished, making the product available to a much larger market.

Meanwhile, new formulas that blended fat and oil stocks from tallow and seed oils, helped speed development of the soap-making industry. Chemists, such as Michel-Eugène Chevreul, were elucidating the processes involved in both soap- and candle-making.

## Candle-making

Although soap ultimately became the principal product made from tallow, soap essentially was a byproduct until the latter part of the 19th century. The main product was candles. Starting with primitive tallow dips and rushlights (the pith of rushes soaked in household grease), candle-making became a widespread house industry.

In 13th century Paris, one of the strongest guilds was that of traveling candle-makers who went from house to house practicing their trade. Later, primitive candle factories, similar to those of soap-makers, developed with a simple version of the modern-day assembly line for boiling and drawing, molding and finishing the candles.

In England, the making of candles was the business of London's tallow chandlers. Randall Monier-Williams devotes 3 volumes to the history of London's Worshipful Company of Tallow Chandlers. Even in those days, the finest candles were made from beeswax, but only for the wealthy. And, even then, tallow candles appear to have been generally used except on special occasions and in the master's quarters. According to Monier-Williams, the tallow candles were called peric or peris candles and distinguished from beeswax candles. Peric candles, he reports, were part of the regular service everywhere in the royal household except for the King's chamber.

While most of Monier-Williams' work is devoted to the establishment of the tallow chandler's trade as a recognized craft guild and the involvement of the various craft guilds in London politics over some 600 years, the author graphically describes the process itself:

> The common candle known to our ancestors as the tallow 'dip' was a simple device for providing a little artificial illumination where it was wanted after dark. At its very best, it would not light every corner of the room, but, even for the well-to-do, man-made light in the home was for centuries considered something of a luxury. That the candle was portable was its great attraction. In the winter, when the nights were long, and the need to illuminate a place in the absence of the sun was greatest, the fire gave light as well as heat, but 'the place' was constant.

> The origin of this cunning contrivance is lost in antiquity. It is indeed a matter for conjecture as to which came first—the lamp in its rudimentary form of an open saucer with a fibrous substance, which we call a wick, immersed in oil, or the candle with its wick encased in solid fat. The process by which light is produced, from the combustion of a candle or a lamp, is essentially the same, with this difference, that heat, through the wick, must first render the solid matter of the candle fluid.

> The method of making candles by 'dipping' goes back at least to the days of the Romans. They had the true candle with tallow as its combustible material surrounding a flax or cotton wick, as well as the torch, in which the fibrous matter, coated with pitch, was predominant.

> The dipping process was also used for the homemade rushlight, consisting of a reed stripped to the pith and plunged in household grease or oil, which long continued in England as the cheapest means of lighting.

> A superior type of tallow candle was made by moulding; a method said to have been introduced by a French nobleman in the fifteenth century, but moulds were not greatly used in this country until the candle-making machines of the nineteenth century were invented.

> Candles for the rich and for religious purposes were made of beeswax, an entirely separate industry. Neither moulding nor dipping was considered quite suitable for

these candles, the usual method being to ladle melted wax over the wick, and after the candle had cooled, to roll it on a smooth surface.

Tallow, by definition, is the solid oil or fat of ruminant animals, but commercially it was obtained almost entirely from oxen and sheep. According to an early eighteenth century writer, 'a tallow candle to be good, must be half sheep's tallow, and half cow's; that of hogs making 'em gutter, give an ill smell and a thick black smoak.' A century later we are told that for 'moulded candles, sheep-tallow is used with a certain proportion of the best kind of ox-tallow, that which is yielded by sheep-fat being brighter and of firmer texture than ox-tallow, which is employed with inferior pieces of sheep tallow for dips.' From other accounts it seems probable, however, that this writer failed to do the common candle justice.

For information on the changing methods of candle manufacture employed from time to time in the past, we must turn mainly to the encyclopedias, of which the earliest, for our purpose, is Ephraim Chambers' *Cyclopaedia* of 1728.

The first task was to prepare that material, which could either be performed by a 'melter' or by the tallow-chandler himself. It was known as 'rendering,' a process which the author of the article on 'Candle' in Chambers' most interesting and valuable publication describes in some detail.

Briefly, he tells us that 'the tallows'—referring to the rough fat from the butcher—were cut or hacked into pieces and thrown into a pot or boiler. When perfectly melted and skimmed, a certain quantity of water was thrown in which served to precipitate to the bottom of the vessel the impurities of the tallow that had escaped the skimmer. The melted tallow was then emptied through a sieve into a tub, having a tap for letting it out as occasion required, and was ready for use after standing for three hours. In an article on 'Chandlery' in the *London Encyclopaedia* published a century later, we are told that tallow from which all impurities had been removed was sometimes stowed away in tubs for future use, some 'superior makers' preferring to mix tallow after a twelve months' age with that which is newly rendered.

As the years passed, this rather primitive method of rendering was improved upon by employing two separate vessels. This is clear from Charles Tomlinson's *Cyclopaedia of Useful Arts and Manufacturers* published soon after the Great Exhibition of 1851. The dangerous practice of melting tallow in an open copper kettle exposed to the direct action of the fire continued, it seems, for many years. But now the membranous matters on the surface, after fusing for some time, were removed, and the melted tallow was passed through a sieve into another copper kettle where it was washed with a quantity of boiling water. The impurities settled down with the water at the bottom of the kettle, and the purified tallow was lifted out in buckets of tinned iron into a tub where it cooled and was then ready for use.

From this author and the earlier writer in the *London Encyclopaedia* of 1829, we learn that the membranous matters were subjected to the operation of a strong iron press, and the cake that was left was called greaves, or cracklings, with which dogs were fed and [according to the earlier writer] a large portion of the ducks that supplied the London markets.

Monier-Williams later adds that until the introduction of the new product known as spermaceti—derived from the oil in the head cavity of the sperm whale—about the year 1750, the only candle-making materials were tallow and beeswax. Because of its clear steady flame, spermaceti became the standard measure for artificial light, the term "1 candle power" being based on the light given by a pure spermaceti candle weighing 1/6 lb and burning 120 g/hour.

Tallow and beeswax remained, nevertheless, the chief candle-making materials for many years. That this was still so in 1829 was recognized in the article in the *London Encyclopaedia*, but by this date the age-long use of the tallow candle was steadily declining. A number of substitutes had made their way onto the London market. Palm oil in particular was much in vogue in the 1850s.

The era of the tallow chandler (as a candle-maker, that is) ended in the 1850s with the advent of paraffin wax. By this time, however, soap-making had become a growing industry on its own.

Frenchman, Michel-Eugène Chevreul, demonstrated that fats were, in fact, fatty acids and glycerine (significant for both soap- and candle-making). In 1823 he successfully separated the fatty acids from the glycerine—that is saponification—and thus established the groundwork for today's fat-splitting industry, which opened new, potential markets for animal fats.

By the mid-19th century, the market for tallow had shifted from raw material for candles, then the major source of illumination, to soap, and this market was to consume the lion's share of the world's tallow for the better part of another century; in fact, until the advent of the petroleum-based, synthetic detergent of today.

# NORTH AMERICA
## Northwest Coast Indians

American Indians also practiced a rendering-like process but to produce a foodstuff. Robert F Heizer reports that such an activity was based on the Nass River in British Columbia on the Pacific Coast:

> The lower Nass was one of the spawning rivers of the eulachon, and the Tsimshian were chief purveyors of its 'grease,' a highly prized foodstuff. As shoals of the tiny eulachon, or candlefish, silvered the surface, the Tsimshian raked them from the crests or netted them with a funnel-shaped *yakati,* quickly filling their canoes.
>
> Ashore, they emptied the fish in pits to rot and went back for more. To render the oil, they dumped the partly decomposed fish into wooden boxes, added water, and boiled them by dropping in heated stones. They skimmed off the oil as it rose.
>
> Grease was a favorite food—butter, sauce, gravy—served at festivals and given as gifts by all northwest tribes. I have tasted eulachon oil and class it one of the gamiest foods ever concocted. A beach camp where the oil was rendered in quantity could be smelled 10 miles downwind.
>
> The most important grease camps were at Red Bluff on the Nass. At trying time, groups of grease-hungry Indians—Haida with canoes and chewing tobacco, Tlingit with blankets and large copper plaques—came to trade with the Tsimshian. Red Bluff became a hubbub of haggling, enlivened by fights, like as not. The Tlingit had little use for the Tsimshian and would just as soon fight as bargain, so long as they

got the grease. By one means or another, the rank riches were distributed and dele-
gations, trailing a certain aura, paddled away.

## Soap- and Candle-making

As the wheels of Industrial Revolution began to turn in the United
States, rendering and the manufacturing of soap progressed together.
Following the Civil War, domestic consumption of soap rose tremen-
dously. The first well-known brand of soap was "German Detersive," a
cut pound-bar wrapped by the manufacturer or supplied to the retailer
with the wrappers left loose in the case. The bars were then wrapped as
they were sold. This was a considerable improvement over the usual
method of just supplying large blocks to the storekeeper who would then
have to cut off portions of the size the shopper wanted.

During this period tallow was derived primarily from the fat of sheep and
goats. Pork fat, while used in soap-making, made very poor candles.
Obviously, as the world population of cattle grew, more and more beef
tallow was produced, but it took the United States, with its voracious ap-
petite for beef and its explosive development of the cattle industry in the
latter part of the 1800s and on into this century, to propel rendering into
its current place of prominence. The cattle industry developed differently
in California than it did in Texas and throughout mid-America. In fact, in
California in the 1850s, cattle were raised mainly for hides and tallow.
Because a relatively small amount of beef was consumed, most of it
went to the coyotes and other wild animals.

In his *Cow Hides to Golden Fleece,* Reuben L Underhill recounts early
California history as derived from unpublished correspondence with
Thomas Oliver Larkin, the so-called Yankee super-salesman—who later
became the US Consul General to the then foreign state of California.
Whalers of the early 1830s told "incredible tales of the Californios with
enormous herds of cattle valued only for their hides and tallow." Hearing
this, Larkin went West, arriving on the California shores in 1832, and
subsequently became a millionaire trading in hides and tallow, sea otter
and beaver skins.

Robert C Cleland in his *March of Industry* quotes Larkin, on the eve of
the US occupation of California in 1846, as saying that the province was
annually exporting 80,000 hides and 1,500,000 lb of tallow. These exports for the most part went to Boston; many hides returned to California
in the form of shoes and other products.

During the Mexican–Spanish regime, Cleland reports, California was to
all intents and purposes the land of a single occupation—stock raising—
its chief source of wealth. Trading hides and tallow to foreigners who
arrived by ship gave California nearly all of the manufactured articles

and most of the luxuries it could not produce. Hides and tallow were its only marketable products and were commonly exchanged at greatly enhanced prices instead of being sold. In this economy, dominated by the production of hides and tallow, the rancher's income was ascertained from the number of cattle he held. The value of beef per se was nominal. A small part of the beef animal was salted down and used as a staple in the diet, but for the most part it remained a waste product abandoned on the range. The hide sold for $2 and with the tallow—2 or 3 *arrobas* (25 lb to the arroba at $1.50 the arroba)—netted the owner $5 or so.

By the 1850s, a steer was worth $12 to $13, yielding about 50 lb of dried beef and 200 lb of tallow and the hide. The cost of slaughtering, skinning, and "trying out" the tallow came to about $4.50 per animal. However, while dried beef was selling for 20¢/lb, tallow was bringing 48¢/lb. Some of the tallow was made into soap locally, but most went back East to be made into soap.

Cleland's second book on early California, *Cattle on a Thousand Hills,* gives us another look at soap-making in those early days. Reporting on the process as it was used on Isaac Williams' Rancho Chino, Cleland said:

> . . . over a durance was placed a boiler about 10 feet deep and the same size in diameter, the upper part was made of wood. This was filled with tallow and the fattest of the meat. A little water was also poured into it and then the whole was tried out after which the grease was dipped into a box about 10 to 12 feet square. The meat was then thrown away. Mineral earth was leached like ashes, the lye obtained put with the grease and boiled into soap.

The best quality soap, Cleland said, "was almost as white as snow."

Meanwhile, as the eastern part of the nation became involved in the Industrial Revolution, immigrants poured into the country; and city-dwellers' taste for beef increased. Actually, the advent of commercial meat packing in the United States predated the Declaration of Independence by more than 100 years. William Pynchon of Boston became the first commercial meat packer in America in 1662, and by 1756 Boston had become the slaughter center for most of the Northeast. Still, most animals were slaughtered on the farm and most tallow was rendered on the farm.

The nation's first combined slaughtering and meat-packing operation was established in 1838 at Alton, Illinois; in 1865 the Chicago Stockyard became the nation's leading livestock market. During the mid-1850s, the railroads drove deeper into the nation's heartland. With them came the era of the great cattle drives from the plains of Texas to the railheads in Kansas and Oklahoma. The Civil War came and went. GH Hammond, a Detroit meat packer, invented the refrigerated freight car, and Gustavus Swift brought it to reality. As cattle slaughter made the transition from the farm and ranch to the city, so did rendering. However, to a great extent rendering continued to exist in concert with soap manufacturing.

## RENDERING COMPANIES

The industry as we know it came into being with the discovery that it was easier and more profitable to produce tallow and sell it to the soap manufacturer than to make the tallow, turn it into soap, and then sell the soap. Thus, the history of the US rendering industry is reflected in the history of many of today's successful rendering companies; Baker and Darling serve as examples.

## Baker Commodities, Inc

One of the early rendering companies was Corenco, now part of Baker Commodities, Inc, one of the nation's largest rendering companies. HW Heath, son of a slaughterhouse owner and operator in Groton, Vermont, grew up with the business and by the latter part of the 1800s had developed some of his own ideas about the relationships among cattle slaughter, meat packing, and rendering. By 1883, he was managing a facility for Gustavus and Edwin Swift in Manchester, New Hampshire; under his stewardship the business flourished. Heath's approach (from the Corenco history) is typical of what was going on in many areas during that period.

Western-dressed beef had become firmly established with the consuming public as to its superior quality compared with native beef. Its distribution stabilized and became dependable, and the old-time country slaughter houses gradually went out of business. Most of these old-time slaughter houses rendered a small quantity of tallow incidental to their principal business of slaughtering native cattle. Their methods were crude and conditions caused much complaint among the public.

Heath visualized the possibilities of centralized rendering units, and persistently endeavored to interest the Swifts personally to furnish the money for this new venture, with the view of building plants at various locations. In this he succeeded and ever since, the Swifts' interest in the rendering business has been a personal one.

The first rendering unit established was located at Manchester, New Hampshire; HW Heath managed it. The original building was erected by the Swifts to conduct a slaughtering business, and for several years they averaged to kill a car of Western hogs each working day.

They also slaughtered and dressed hogs raised and brought in by individuals in the city and vicinity. The hogs, after being dressed at the plant, were put in the cooler at the Franklin and Cedar Streets building, from where they were sold.

As the Swifts became interested in larger packing plants in the East, slaughtering was discontinued at Manchester, and in December 1889 the nucleus of a rendering business was established. Before the rendering industry became established, rendering was done at country slaughter houses and small establishments throughout New England, where the population was sufficient to support it. Generally, the buildings were hardly more than windbreaks, and the processing resulted in a great deal of waste; tank water ran down the brooks; tankage was air dried on platforms outside the building and sold by the barrel for chicken feed. Population growth curbed the continuation of such plants; some of the plants were located in what was soon to be the heart of cities or towns.

The business increased gradually and although the volume was small at the beginning, stations had been established at Nashua, Concord, and Laconia. In a few years the business extended throughout central New Hampshire, and was branching out into the hide and skin business. Financial results were encouraging.

In 1893, and continuing until 1896, a financial panic was well under way, unemployment became general throughout the country, and banks failed. Nevertheless, the founders of the rendering business built a plant in Portland, Maine, and developed it as they had the Manchester plant. Branches were gradually established as far north as Rumford Falls, Maine, and as far east as Bangor, with others in the principal central cities of Maine.

In those days, the raw material was picked up by teams and brought into the "stations" and then shipped to the plant by railroad. It was not unusual for material collected on a Saturday, even from so short a distance as 25 miles away, not to arrive at the plant until the early afternoon of the following Monday.

## Darling International, Inc

In the 1890s, a Berkeley, California, hog raiser began collecting waste suet and bone from butcher shops in the growing San Francisco Bay area to supplement the diet of his animals. In a huge iron kettle on the kitchen stove, his wife cooked the scraps, skimming off the liquid fat that rose to the top of the kettle and storing it in drums. The residue, or cracklings as they were known, were used in the hog rations. When enough fat, now solidified into tallow, had accumulated, it was carted down to the Oakland port and put aboard ships bound around Cape Horn to the East Coast plants that converted the tallow into soap. That man was Nels P Peterson Sr, and the company he founded in the family kitchen was Peterson Tallow Co.

Meanwhile, soap-making plants became established on the West Coast and increased the demand for tallow. Concurrently the necessity increased to find a sanitary method of quick disposal of the ever-increasing amounts of highly perishable wastes from the growing meat packing and butchering operations. Shortly after the turn of the century, Nels Peterson moved his operation from the family kitchen to Emeryville, California, a city now part of the greater Oakland complex of East Bay communities.

During this period more and more people began to expect beef as regular fare. As the 19th century ended and the 20th began, available means of transportation became faster and more reliable; commercial manufacture of ice for use in cold rooms became more plentiful, rudimentary systems for evaporative cooling came into use, and suddenly beef for the table no longer was the byproduct of the cattle industry. Soon it became as important as hides and tallow; quickly it outstripped them both to become the cattle industry's most important product.

Nels Peterson was one of a handful of men across the country who were pioneering what today can be recognized as the first full-blown recycling industry—an industry that currently converts some 50,000 tons/day of fat, bone, and muscle tissue from the meat and poultry industries into billions of pounds of products used by both industry and agriculture.

## IN SUMMARY

From the eastern seaboard through the Midwest and on the Pacific shores, the face of a nation changed as the Gay Nineties gave way to the 20th century. Those changes were paced by the skyrocketing growth of industry. The nation's economy moved farther and farther from its agrarian beginnings as business and industry flourished.

World War I triggered still another new surge toward industrialization as the United States became the major source of the guns, tanks, ships, and airplanes that augured for an Allied victory. The influx of immigrants in the latter years of the 19th century and the early 1900s already had swelled the size of most major cities, and with the end of the First World War another trend began—young men began opting for city life as opposed to following in the footsteps of their fathers on the farms.

Where the population congregated, the need for food— bread, potatoes, milk, and of course meat—soared. Hogs, sheep, and goats—all relatively small animals with proportionately small yield of edible meat—just were not available. In fact, they could not practically be made available in sufficient numbers to meet the demand. It was during this period of great transition that the beef animal really came into its own. Notwithstanding the development of refrigeration, logistics dictated that these huge supplies of beef, as well as pork, lamb, and mutton, be slaughtered and packed for market near the consuming public. Now, not only did other major meat packing centers emerge—Kansas City, Omaha, St Louis—but almost every city of any size got its own intra-area packing industry. And, as the meat packing industry grew, so did the rendering industry. Until this point, the renderer's major contribution appears to have been the production of a useful commodity—tallow—originally for candles, later for soap; and, as oil chemistry technology developed, for glycerine and fatty acids needed by other industries.

Only about 60% of the beef animal provides edible products. The hide, bones, entrails, hooves, horns, fat, gristle, and tough membranes are, by law, not permitted to be used as food. In other words, 400 lb or more of a 1,000-lb steer is inedible. Consider also that animal tissue, once the animal is no longer alive, is perhaps one of the world's most perishable substances. As the kill rate rose in the nation's slaughter houses from tens to hundreds, even thousands, of animals per week, without the renderer the problem of disposing of these inedible byproducts of the beef industry would have become one of horrendous proportions. Certainly, the renderers of that day did not think of themselves as recyclers, especially since that term has only come into vogue since the 1970s with our emphasis on the environment. But, in retrospect, it appears that they may well have been the original recyclers, and as the growth of the rendering industry paced that of our meat industry, an automatic and invisible solution solved the problem of that highly perishable waste almost as the problem itself grew.

The contribution of the renderer today to our overall effort to maintain a clean and healthful environment is staggering. Our meat industry—and this must include chicken and turkey as well as the so-called red meats—generates some 30 billion lb of inedible surplus each year. Any city generates a million pounds or more a week. This includes not only the slaughter house and packing plant waste, but also that produced by the supermarkets, the local butchers, and the restaurants. At 30 lb/ft$^3$, each city could build one or more monoliths 10 ft$^2$ and more than 1000 ft high with each week's waste. Leave a small piece of uncooked steak out in a warm room for a couple of days and you can get some idea of the immensity of the problem.

By its very existence the rendering industry prevents a waste disposal problem of Herculean proportions. In addition, it turns otherwise unusable material into usable commodities: tallow for soap production and the manufacture of fatty acids; animal protein which is a major ingredient in livestock and poultry feed; and feed-grade animal fat which provides a high energy ingredient for livestock and poultry feed. All of these commodities touch every facet of our 20th century way of life.

The rendering industry began as a dirty and foul-smelling business. It was not a job for men with weak stomachs and it was not pleasant for those who lived downwind of a rendering plant. In fact, this olfactory obtrusiveness caused the renderer to quietly go about his business, shunning public attention and seeking anonymity. For this reason, until recent technological developments, renderers considered their industry the invisible industry.

# 2

# The Rendering Industry— a Commitment to Public Service

## William H Prokop

The rendering industry processes or "recycles" animal and poultry by-products such as animal fat, bone, hide, offal, feathers, and blood. For example, a 1000-lb beef steer produces approximately 600 lb of edible dressed meat; the remaining 400 lb are processed at a rendering plant. During 1994, rendering plants throughout the United States processed an estimated 36 billion lb of animal and poultry byproducts to manufacture beneficial commodities such as tallow, grease, and protein meals.

During 1994, renderers produced 8.4 billion lb of tallow and grease of which 2.8 billion lb were added to animal and poultry feed in the United States (Bureau of the Census 1995). Also during 1994, 90% of the 6 billion lb of meat meal, feather meal, and other protein products were used to enrich feed for cattle, hogs, and poultry (Bureau of the Census 1995). When these animals are slaughtered and marketed, the resulting byproducts are again processed, and the recycling loop repeated. (For a glossary of rendering terminology and operations, see the appendix.)

## INDUSTRY CLASSIFICATION

Rendering plants are either integrated or independent. Integrated rendering plants are operated in conjunction with animal slaughter-houses and poultry processing plants. This type of plant is integral to the slaughterhouse or meat packing operation, and processes all residual material from these operations, including offal and feathers.

Independent rendering plants collect raw material off-site, but primarily in urban areas. These renderers send specially designed trucks to collect discarded fat and bone trimmings, meat scraps, restaurant grease, blood, feathers, offal, and fallen animals from a variety of sources: butcher shops, supermarkets, restaurants, fast-food chains, poultry processors, slaughterhouses, farms, feedlots, ranches, and animal shelters. A number of these renderers collect raw material from regional areas, using a transfer station, which receives the collected material.

Rendering systems either render edible animal fatty tissue into edible fats and proteins for human consumption, or they render inedible animal byproducts into fats and proteins for animal feed and nonedible applications. Normally operated in conjunction with meat packing plants, edible rendering plants are subject to inspection and processing standards established by the US Department of Agriculture's Food Safety and Inspection Service (USDA/FSIS). Edible tallow or lard is produced from beef or swine fatty tissue, respectively.

Inedible rendering plants, operated by independent renderers, produce tallow and grease used in feed for livestock and poultry, in soap production, and in fatty acid manufacture. Inedible tallow and grease are produced in grades appropriate to the category of use. For example, "yellow grease" or feed-grade animal fat is produced from waste cooking fats received from restaurants and deep-fat fryers. This product is used as an ingredient in animal and poultry feeds and pet foods Feed rations include animal and poultry meals used as feed supplements for livestock and poultry. Rendering plants also produce blood meal and feather meal, usually of a specified protein content.

## PRODUCTION & USAGE OF RENDERED PRODUCTS

Table 1 summarizes the quantities of rendered products manufactured in the United States, their domestic usage and amount exported during 1994. The discrepancy between the amount produced and the sum of the amount consumed domestically and the amount exported—particularly for inedible tallow and grease, and also for edible tallow—is probably due to exclusion of inventories and export shipments in transit.

**Table 1.** Production, Consumption, and Export of Rendered Products, United States, 1994

| PRODUCT (million lb) | PRODUCED | DOMESTIC CONSUMPTION | EXPORTS |
|---|---|---|---|
| Inedible tallow & greases | 6366 | 3259* | 2,666 |
| Edible tallow | 1513 | 557 | 295 |
| Lard | 559 | 422 | 137 |
| Meat meal & other proteins | 6043 | 5491 | 552 |
| Other inedible product | 1855 | | |
| **Totals:** | **16 336** | **9729** | **3650** |

\* = 2,186 million lb feed products, 634 million lb fatty acids, 301 million lb soap, 128 million lb lubricants & other products
*Source:* Bureau of the Census. 1995.

# RAW MATERIAL IMPACTS UPON INDUSTRY

The meat packing industry during the past 20 years has converted its meat-production facilities almost totally from an animal carcass to a "boxed beef" and "boxed pork" operation (DPRA 1980). This has resulted in more fat and bone being trimmed at the slaughterhouse and less raw material being available to the independent renderer.

Therefore, during the past 15 years or more, the number of independent rendering plants has been reduced significantly, so that now only an estimated 135 independent rendering plants are operating in the United States. This consolidation also applies to integrated rendering; there are now in the United States an estimated 80 meat packing and 40 poultry processing plants, which include rendering operations (NRA 1995). Of Canada's 20 rendering plants, 17 are independent renderers.

Since 1965, the fat content of steers and hogs has changed significantly (Table 2) as a result of improved breeding and nutritional feeding of fat to livestock. Meanwhile, the yield of butcher shop fat and bone has decreased because of the production of boxed beef and pork. Thus, more of the available fat is trimmed at the packing house. These operations have reduced not only the quantity but also the quality of animal by-products available to the independent rendering industry. Concurrently, production of edible tallow and grease produced at beef and pork processing plants has increased significantly. Unfortunately that increase entails a corresponding decrease in the raw material for the independent rendering plants.

This reallocation of raw material has required the independent rendering industry to seek other sources of raw material. For example, within the past 20 years independent renderers have developed other sources such as waste cooking fats (restaurant grease) obtained from restaurants and fast-food establishments. The processing of restaurant grease increased from some 2.25 billion lb in 1987 to 3.18 billion lb in 1994.

**Table 2.** Composition of Raw Materials for Inedible Rendering

| Source | Tallow/grease wt % | Protein solids wt % | Moisture wt % |
|---|---|---|---|
| Packing house offal and bone | | | |
| Steers | 30-35 | 15-20 | 45-55 |
| Cows | 10-20 | 20-30 | 50-70 |
| Calves | 10-15 | 15-20 | 65-75 |
| Sheep | 25-30 | 20-25 | 45-55 |
| Hogs | 25-30 | 10-15 | 55-65 |
| Dead stock (whole animals) | | | |
| Cattle | 12 | 25 | 63 |
| Calves | 10 | 22 | 68 |
| Sheep | 22 | 25 | 53 |
| Hogs | 30 | 28 | 42 |
| Butcher shop fat and bone | 31 | 32 | 37 |
| Blood | none | 16-18 | 82-84 |
| Restaurant grease | 65 | 10 | 25 |
| Poultry offal | 10 | 25 | 65 |
| Poultry feathers | none | 33 | 67 |

*Source:* DPRA 1980

The availability of raw material for processing is probably the most significant problem facing the independent renderer. The slaughter of animals and poultry in the future is anticipated to increase only slightly. Other sources of raw material must be found if we are to use the evaporative processing capacity of the current rendering facilities.

## ECONOMIC AND ENVIRONMENTAL BENEFITS

The rendering industry is processing animal and poultry byproducts that have no intrinsic value. In fact, this perishable material becomes a liability if not processed within 24 hours, especially during the summer. Incineration would seriously pollute the air and consume large amounts of energy. Deposition in landfills could allow the emission of odors and the contamination of ground water. Regulatory agencies would be unlikely to permit either method of disposal.

Rendering this material is advantageous not only environmentally, but also economically, due to the production of animal and poultry fats and proteins. These products are sold on the open commodity market in competition with other sources of animal fats, vegetable oils, and proteins worldwide. The availability of the renderers' products to be sold in this market provides a balance by which the ultimate consumer benefits by not having to pay higher prices for meat and poultry products due to increased feed prices.

Another vital factor concerns the pricing of the renderers' fat and protein products. Many industries, including chemical and petroleum, increase the prices of their products when costs increase. The rendering industry cannot do so. Since the renderers' products are sold on the open commodity market in competition with other worldwide sources of fats, oils, and proteins, increased costs due to the installation of pollution-control equipment or higher energy prices cannot be passed on to the customer.

US exports of fats and proteins to other countries totaled 3650 million lb during 1994 (Table 1). These exports yielded a favorable balance of payments of $639 million returned to the United States (DOC 1995). This figure is particularly relevant in view of the current US deficit which includes $166 billion annually for imports exceeding exports.

A particularly important service provided by the renderer is the pick up and processing of animals that have died on farms, ranches, and feedlots. Federal and state agriculture and public health departments have worked closely with the independent rendering industry to provide prompt collection of fallen animals that likewise are processed into useable products.

In summary, the rendering industry is committed to providing a service of both economic and environmental benefit to the public.

## REFERENCES

Bureau of the Census. 1995. M2OK series for Fat and Oils, Production, Consumption, and Stocks. US Department of Commerce.

[DOC] US Department of Commerce. 1995. Export Declarations for 1994.

[DPRA] Development Planning & Research Associates. 1980. US Production, Consumption, Trade, and Stocks of Tallow    Grease, Lard, and Animal Protein Meals; Estimates and Projections, report no P-318. USDA Foreign Agriculture Service, Washington, DC.

[NRA] National Renderers Association. 1995. Listing of Member and Non-member Plants, NRA, Alexandria, VA.

# 3

# Technological and Environmental Impacts on the Rendering Industry

## William H Prokop

This chapter describes edible and inedible rendering systems in current use (Prokop 1985). These include the batch cooker, Dupps continuous, and Stord waste heat dewatering systems for inedible rendering. The Sharples Trim-R process is described for edible rendering. In these descriptions, reference is made to the degree of odor emitted from the rendering process.

Also, this chapter describes the odor control technology developed by the industry to treat the odor emissions from the rendering process and from within the rendering plant. In addition, technology to treat waste water from the plant effluent is described. Pollution-control equipment required to comply with federal, state, and local regulations to prevent air and water pollution poses an economic challenge for the rendering industry.

## PROCESS DESCRIPTION
## Edible Rendering

The current edible rendering process is continuous and consists of 2 stages of centrifugal separation. A typical feedstock of beef fat trimmings from USDA-inspected meat processing plants consists of 60 to 64% fat, 14 to 16% moisture, and 22 to 24% protein solids.

With the Sharples Trim-R Edible Fat Process (Figure 1), fat trimmings are ground through a Weiler grinder and belt conveyed to a melt tank equipped with an agitator and steam-heated jacket. The melted fatty tissue at 110°F is pumped to a Reitz disintegrator to rupture the fat cells. A Sharples Super-D-Canter Centrifuge separates the proteinaceous solids from the melted fat and moisture containing a small percentage of solids or fines.

A second-stage centrifuge is required to "polish" the edible fat, which is first heated to 200°F by a shell-and-tube heat exchanger with steam. The Westfalia De-Sludging Separator makes a 2-phase separation where the polished edible fat discharges from the top and the water fraction containing the protein fines is discharged as sludge from the bottom. The edible fat is pumped to storage, whereas the sludge from the centrifuge is either transported to an inedible rendering plant or passed through a primary treatment system for waste water.

A similar feedstock of pork fat trimmings can be processed by the same edible rendering system to produce lard. For the beef material, the product is known as edible tallow.

Since no cooking vapors are emitted from current edible rendering processes, and heat contact with the edible fat is minimal, odor emissions from these rendering plants are perceived as insignificant. This also is due to the freshness of the raw material being processed and the plant sanitation and housekeeping practices that have been established by the US Department of Agriculture, Food Safety & Inspection Service (USDA/FSIS).

## Wet Rendering vs Dry Rendering

Wet rendering is defined as a process of separating fat from raw material by boiling with water. This is normally accomplished by boiling the raw material in a tank of water. The products of wet rendering are fat, sticky water containing glue, and wet tankage (protein solids). The water added to the raw material must be evaporated, thereby increasing fuel costs to generate additional steam for moisture removal.

The wet rendering process is no longer used in the United States because of the high cost of energy and because of its adverse effect on fat quality. Instead, it has been replaced by dry rendering, a process for releasing fat by dehydrating raw material in a batch or continuous cooker. After moisture removal in the cooker, the melted fat is separated from the protein solids. No excess water or live steam is added to the raw material.

## Raw Materials for Rendering

The integrated rendering plant for an animal slaughterhouse or poultry processor normally receives only one type of raw material. This simplifies the control of the processing conditions, which usually require only minor adjustments. Also, the raw material is relatively fresh, undergoing little or no noticeable deterioration. Conversely, the independent renderer often processes a variety of raw materials that require either the operation of multiple rendering systems in parallel or significant changes in operating conditions for a single system.

## BASIC RENDERING PROCESS
## Batch Cooker Systems

Batch cookers (Figure 2) are multiple units arranged in a row or series of rows, depending on the size and layout of the rendering plant. Each cooker consists of a horizontal, steam-jacketed cylindrical vessel equipped with an agitator. This vessel is known as a batch cooker because it follows a repetitive cycle: The cooker is charged with the proper amount of raw material, the material is cooked under controlled conditions, and, finally, the cooked material is discharged.

The raw material from the receiving bin is screw conveyed to a crusher or similar device to reduce the size of its pieces. For batch cookers, the raw material is reduced to 1- or 2-inch pieces for efficient cooking, which normally requires 2 to 3 hours. The raw material varies, depending on the source, and cooking time and temperature may have to be adjusted. The final temperature of the cooked material ranges from 250 to 275°F, depending on the type of raw material.

The cooked material is discharged to the percolator drain pan, which contains a perforated screen that allows the free-run fat to drain away from the protein solids, which are known as tankage. After approximately 1 hour of drainage, the protein solids still contain about 25% fat and are conveyed to the screw press to complete the separation of fat from solids. The final protein solids have a residual fat content of 10%.

The solid protein material discharged from the screw press is known as cracklings. It is normally screened and ground with a hammer mill to produce protein meal that essentially passes a 12-mesh screen. The fat discharged from the screw press usually contains fine solid particles that are removed either by centrifuging or filtration.

The primary odor emissions from the batch cooker rendering process consist of:   noncondensables from the condenser (either air-cooled finned tube or water-cooled shell and tube), vent from the percolator pan, and vent from the screw press.

These emissions result from material being heated to a temperature of 220°F or higher.  Since they have a relatively high odor intensity, these emissions should normally be treated by odor control equipment.

## Continuous Rendering Systems

During the early 1960s, Baker Commodities in Los Angeles was instrumental in developing the concept of a continuous cooking process. Since then, a variety of continuous rendering systems have been installed to replace the batch cooker systems.  Continuous rendering is synonymous with continuous cooking.  The raw material is fed continuously to the cooker, and the cooked material is likewise discharged at a constant rate.

A continuous rendering system normally consists of a single continuous cooker, whereas the batch cooker system consists of multiple cooker units.  A continuous system usually has a higher capacity than the batch cooker system it replaces.  This increased capacity provides for more efficient processing of the raw material by processing more material in less time.

Continuous rendering also has a number of other advantages over the batch system.  The continuous system occupies considerably less space than a batch cooker system of equivalent capacity, thus saving construction costs.  A single-cooker unit is inherently more efficient than a multiple-cooker unit in terms of steam consumption, which achieves a significant savings in fuel usage by the boilers. Likewise, less electric power is consumed for agitation in the single continuous cooker unit.

The Dupps Continuous Rendering System (Figure 3) (Dupps Co, Germantown, Ohio) is designed to operate similar to the batch cooker.  The Equacooker is a horizontal steam-jacketed cylindrical vessel equipped with a rotating shaft to which are attached paddles that lift and move the material horizontally through the cooker. Steam also is injected into the hollow shaft to increase heat transfer.

The feed rate to the Equacooker is controlled by adjusting the variable-speed drive of the feed screw, which establishes the production rate for the system.  The discharge rate for the Equacooker is controlled by the speed at which the control wheel rotates.  The control wheel contains buckets, similar to those used in a bucket elevator, that pick up the cooked material from the Equacooker and discharge it to the drainer.

The drainer performs the same function as the percolator drain pan in the batch cooker process. It is an enclosed screw conveyor that contains a section of perforated trough for the free melted fat to drain through to the crude tallow tank. The protein solids containing residual fat are then conveyed to the pressers for additional separation of fat. The pressers and other components of the Dupps continuous system are similar to those used for the batch cooker system. A central control panel consolidates the instruments required to control the process.

A typical, computerized rendering plant contains a process control center located inside an environmentally controlled room. It features the process control panel which provides a schematic flow diagram of the entire process. Indicator lights show on the panel whether individual equipment components are on or off. Process microcomputer controls inside the panel perform all start/stop operations in an interlocking sequence, adjust the speeds of the key equipment parts and control various process elements to optimize plant operation.

Process indications at the panel include electrical loads in amperes for certain equipment, speeds in RPM, temperatures, liquid levels, control valve settings, and equipment on/off status. A computer screen provides instantaneous indications of all of the above. Operating parameters are color coded and an audible alarm is sounded when they are exceeded or below normal.

Commands can be keyboarded into the program computer to alter control of the process. The data acquisition system collects all desired process data and stores it for recall to be used as a diagnostic and trouble-shooting tool. A printout from the computer plots this information against time to provide trend or deviation outputs.

The odor emissions from the continuous systems are similar to those from the batch system, except that batch cookers are open to the atmosphere when they are filled with raw material or when they discharge to the percolator pan. The hot, cooked material from the batch cooker not only releases odor, but also fat particles, which tend to become airborne and are deposited on equipment and building surfaces within the plant. The continuous systems are essentially enclosed and can confine the odors and fat aerosol particles within the equipment.

## Continuous Systems of Reduced Energy Usage

Although the rendering industry is small compared with the chemical or petroleum industries, the rendering process is energy intensive. Fuel is required to evaporate moisture from the raw material and to condition it for proper separation of the fat from the protein solids.

Fuel costs have been the rendering plant's single largest operating cost, exceeding that of labor. For the average rendering plant, fuel costs represent 30 to 35% of the total operating cost (not including capital). Electricity would add another 10 to 15%, so that energy accounts for nearly 50% of the total.

During the early 1980s, considerable effort went to developing new rendering systems that use cooking vapors from either a batch cooker system or a continuous rendering system to remove additional moisture. Most of this new rendering technology has evolved in Europe, where energy costs have been significantly higher than in the United States.

The Stord waste heat dewatering (WHD) system (Figure 4) is manufactured by Stord, Inc in Bergen, Norway. It consists of a preheater, twin screw press, and evaporator in addition to a conventional cooker/dryer and crackling press.

In this system, raw material is fed to a prebreaker for coarse grinding. This ground material passes through the preheater, which is a horizontal, steam-jacketed, cylindrical vessel with a rotating shaft and agitator to move the material through the vessel continuously. This heating step is necessary to melt the fat and condition the animal fibrous tissue for subsequent pressing.

The twin-screw press separates the heated and ground raw material into a press cake of solids containing fat and moisture, and a liquid mostly behind containing the melted fat and water. The solids are screw conveyed to a cooker or dryer, which is steam heated to remove the moisture. Final separation of the fat from the solids is completed with a screw press.

Liquid from the twin-screw press is pumped from the feed tank to the evaporator, a tubular heat exchanger mounted vertically and integrally with the vapor chamber. The vapors from the cooker or dryer provide the heating medium for evaporation. The liquid pumped to the evaporator enters at the top of the heat exchanger and flows by gravity through the tubes discharging into the vapor chamber, which is maintained under a vacuum of 24 to 26 inches of mercury provided by a vacuum pump. The temperature of the liquid ranges from 160 to 200°F at which point the moisture is evaporated. The water vapor from the vapor chamber is condensed with a shell-and-tube condenser through which cooling water circulates.

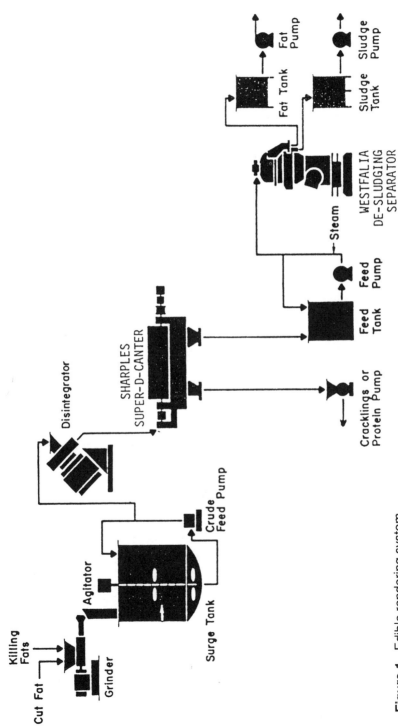

**Figure 1.** Edible rendering system

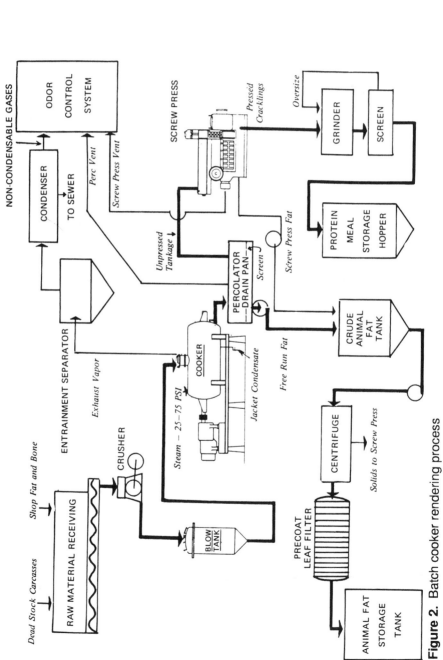

**Figure 2.** Batch cooker rendering process

The basic concept of the Stord WHD system is to use the waste heat in the vapors from the cooker to evaporate the moisture from the liquid removed by pressing the raw material, thus providing a rendering plant with a 2-stage evaporation system. The Stord WHD system can reduce fuel costs by 30 to 40%.

These new systems incorporate microcomputer controls that perform essentially all start–stop sequences, monitor process elements, and record process data to provide trend or deviation outputs. If the system malfunctions, the controls automatically shut down key operating elements that otherwise could cause serious damage or loss of production.

## Other Rendering Processes

Whole blood received from animal slaughterhouses contains 16 to 18% total protein solids. Of this amount, approximately 70% of the total protein is recovered as blood meal after steam coagulation and drying. The soluble protein fraction remains in the serum water. In the continuous blood process, whole blood passes through an inclined tubular vessel into which steam is injected to coagulate the blood solids. This slurry is pumped to a horizontal, solid-bowl centrifuge, which separates the blood solids from the blood serum water. The blood solids at 50 to 55% moisture are fed into a continuous drying system, either a gas-fired, direct-contact ring dryer or a steam tube, rotary dryer.

With the Dupps Ring Dryer, coagulated blood solids enter the dryer through a hammer-type mill and are air conveyed through the "ring" duct at a temperature of 200°F to the manifold. At this point, the moist product is separated from the dried product and is recirculated back to the ring duct for further drying. The dried product is separated from the exhaust air by twin cyclone collectors with rotary valves. This dryer is furnished in 4 different models, evaporating water at a rate ranging from 1000 to 4000 lb/hour.

In the Anderson 72 Tube Rotary Steam Dryer (Anderson International Corp, Cleveland, Ohio), the moist feed material cascades over the rotating, steam-heated tubes. Fresh air passes through the dryer across the steam-heated tubes and exits the dryer with the moisture released from the solids. The 72-tube unit is the only model available; its water evaporation capacity is estimated to be 650 lb/ hour.

Poultry feathers and hog hair consist mostly of keratin, which is a long-chain, highly cross-linked, relatively indigestible protein. The rendering process converts the keratin by chemical hydrolysis, combining with water at elevated temperatures (280 to 300°F), into shorter-chain, more

digestible amino acids.  This hydrolyzation is accomplished by processing the feathers or hair in a batch cooker with an internal cooker pressure of 40 to 50 psi maintained for 30 to 45 minutes.  The moisture
content after hydrolyzation is approximately 50%.  The drying operation
normally is conducted with either the Dupps Ring Dryer or Anderson
Rotary Steam Tube Dryer.

The recent growth of the restaurant business, and of fast-food chains in
particular, has made the recycling of restaurant grease an important part
of the rendering industry.  In the past, 55-gallon drums of grease were
picked up at restaurants and unloaded manually by plant employees for
processing.  Currently, much of this grease is bulk loaded into specially
designed and constructed vehicles that transport and discharge it directly to the grease-processing system without any manual labor.

The melted grease is screened to remove coarse solids, then heated to
200°F in vertical processing tanks, and stored for 36 to 48 hours to separate the grease from the water and fine solids by gravity.  Four phases of
separation normally occur:  solids, water, emulsion layer, and grease
product.  The solids settle to the bottom of the processing tank and are
separated from the water layer above.  The emulsion is centrifuged in 2
stages:  a horizontal, solid bowl type to remove solids, and a vertical
disk type to remove water and fines.  The grease is pumped off the top.

## AIR EMISSIONS TO ATMOSPHERE

Odor is the primary air pollutant emitted from the rendering process.  In
a few instances, dust could become a problem, such as in the exhaust
from the Dupps Ring Dryer when processing blood or feathers.  However, proper control equipment, such as cyclones and venturi scrubbers,
is normally adequate to abate emitted dust.

No federal regulations control the emission of odors from rendering
plants.  Instead, state and local air pollution control agencies are responsible for their regulation.  Usually these agencies invoke a nuisance
regulation to prohibit the emission of odors perceived to interfere with
the enjoyment of life or property.  Some agencies list numerical limits for
ambient odors in the atmosphere around the plant.  A few have numerical limits for emissions from point sources such as stacks.  A more recent concept of odor regulation stipulates that a community nuisance is
established when a given number of complaints have been received and
validated by the agency within a given period; then the source is required to conduct a compliance program.

# Points of Emission

The perishable nature of the raw material being processed inherently results in odor emissions from rendering plants. As discussed, the primary sources of high intensity odors from the rendering process include the noncondensables from the cooker exhaust and the emissions from the screw press. In addition, the processing of blood or poultry feathers normally results in high odor levels. Other sources of high intensity odors include dryers, centrifuges, tallow processing tanks, and the percolator pans which are open to the plant atmosphere and receive the discharge from the batch cookers.

The raw material is another source of odor, but it normally is not significant when the material is processed without delay. However, the age of the raw material is important because older material that has deteriorated will generate substantially more odors during cooking and pressing. Also, the type of raw material being cooked is a significant factor. For example, dead stock tend to result in the emission of high or higher-intensity odors from the rendering process.

# Composition of Rendering Odors

Odor emissions from rendering plants are relatively complex mixtures of organic compounds. Samples of rendering plant odors have been analyzed by a combination of gas chromatographic and mass spectrometric methods, and 30 or more odorous compound were identified (Burgwald 1971).

Further research identified the odorous compounds in rendering plant emissions, and improved analytical techniques provided a more complete list of components. The major compounds include organic sulfides, disulfides, aldehydes, trimethylamine and other amines, and organic acids. Compounds of less significance include alcohols, ketones, aliphatic hydrocarbons, and aromatic compound. Odor panel tests were conducted to relate odor intensity to the various important peaks identified by gas chromatography (Snow & Reilich 1972).

Some of these compounds have extremely low odor threshold levels and can be detected at concentrations as low as one part per billion (ppb) or less. This requires relatively high-efficiency odor control systems to treat these emissions and reduce their individual concentrations to levels low enough to avoid valid complaints from the community.

## Odor Emission Data

It is essential that accurate odor emission data be available in order to design an odor control system that successfully abates the emission. To obtain such data, it is necessary to be able to quantify the strength of an odor emission. The National Renderers Association through the Fats and Proteins Research Foundation recognized this need during 1972 and initiated a project with IIT Research Institute in Chicago to develop an odor sensory method of measurement.

As a result, a dynamic olfactometer was designed (Dravnieks & Prokop 1975) to measure the odor dilution to threshold ratio (D/T) of a sample of odorous gas by diluting this sample with non-odorous air at 6 different dilutions and presenting the diluted odor stimulus to a panel of 9 people. At each dilution level, each panelist is instructed to sniff 3 glass ports: 1 contains the diluted odor stimulus and the other 2 contain non-odorous air. The panelist is required to choose the port that contains the odor.

The judgments of each panelist are combined to obtain an average result, the odor dilution to threshold ratio (D/T). Threshold is defined as the dilution level at which 50% of the panel detects and 50% does not detect the odor of the diluted sample. For example, D/T = 100 means that a volume unit of the odorous gas must be diluted to 100 volume units with non-odorous air to reach the panel's threshold level.

The IITRI dynamic olfactometer has been used to obtain odor sensory data that characterize emissions from the rendering process, as well as to measure the odor removal efficiency of various methods of control. For example, a number of Dupps Series 1800 continuous systems have been evaluated to quantify the high intensity odors emitted from the process. These emissions include the noncondensibles from the Equacooker, the drainer, the centrifuge, and other sources of odor. Samples were taken of the noncondensibles alone and also of the total odor emissions from the Dupps system. These tests were conducted with varying types of raw material, including that from a beef slaughterhouse, shop fat and bone, and restaurant grease (Table I). The data shown in this table includ D/T/ rations and volumetric emission rates ($ft^3$/min).

No odor sensory data are available for the new energy-efficient continuous systems. However, odor emissions from the rendering process in these plants have been observed to be of lower intensity. This no doubt can be attributed to the lower processing temperatures used, particularly in the evaporator where the liquid from the twin-screw press is under vacuum for moisture removal.

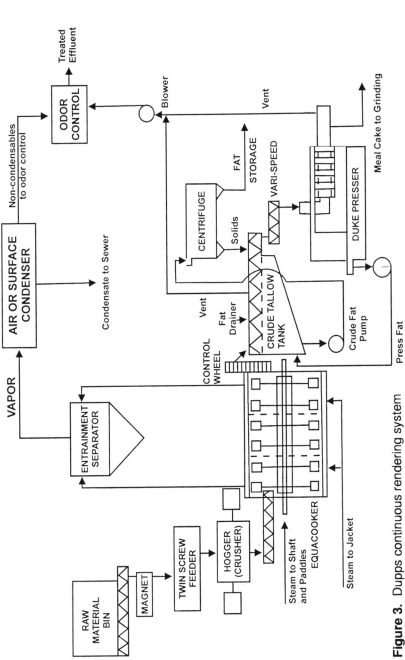

**Figure 3.** Dupps continuous rendering system

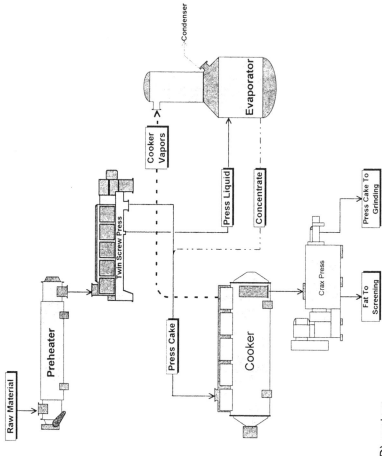

**Figure 4.** Waste heat dewatering (WHD) system

Table 1.  Odor Emissions from Dupps Continuous Systems

| Plant | Category of Renderer and Material | Type of Emission | Odor Dilution[a] to Threshold | Emission Rate ft³/min |
|-------|-----------------------------------|------------------|-------------------------------|-----------------------|
| A | Integrated - beef slaughterhouse | Noncondensibles Total process | 20,000-50,000 39,100-43,200 | 450 1,500 |
| B | Independent - beef slaughterhouse & restaurant grease | Noncondensibles Total process | 24,400-62,700 56,000-138,000 | - - |
| B | Shop fat and bone | Noncondensibles Total process | 11,000-16,700 7,600-13,200 | 665 1,200 |
| C | Independent - beef slaughterhouse & restaurant grease | Noncondensibles Total process | 36,100-39,800 21,600-73,700 | 800 1,700 |
| D | Independent - meat scraps & beef slaughterhouse | Noncondensibles Total process | 59,400-93,800 28,100-59,200 | 600 2,600 |

[a]IITRI dynamic olfactometer

# AIR POLLUTION CONTROL

Rendering plant operation and maintenance considerations are of basic importance in developing odor control measures.  Raw material received at the plant is processed with a minimum of delay.  Cooking and pressing are conducted so as to prevent the processing material from over-heating and burningl.  Start-up and shutdown procedures ensure that all odor control equipment is operating properly.  Daily plant cleanup normally follows shutdown of the rendering plant.  Sanitation practices are crucial.  A substantial amount of odor may be generated from within a building whose walls and ceiling have become permeated with fat aerosol.  For a discussion of odor control equipment used in the rendering industry, see Prokop 1992.

## Boiler Incineration of Process Odors

Capital investment and fuel costs usually preclude the installation and operation of afterburners or incinerators solely for pollution control.  Currently, boiler incineration of high-intensity process odors is a regular practice throughout the United States, since all rendering plants require the generation of steam for cooking and drying.

The odorous air can be introduced into the boiler either as primary combustion air (that mixed with fuel before ignition) or as secondary combustion air (that mixed with the burner flame to complete combustion).  Cooker noncondensibles have the highest odor intensity and are the most pervasive of the process emissions. They can be successively used as primary combustion air, provided that precautions are taken to remove moisture and particulate matter that may interfere with the operation of the burner and controls. This is accomplished with a combination scrubber and entrainment separator (Figure 5). For this application, the boiler size and burner capacity must be compatible with the amount of odorous air to be incinerated. The boiler is equipped with suitable burner controls to ensure that the minimum firing rate is sufficient to incinerate the volume of odorous air passing through the firebox, regardless of the steam demand, and to maintain a temperature of 1200°F or more in the firebox.

Table 2 illustrates the odor removal efficiency achieved by boiler incineration for the same plants used for Table 1. The odor dilution to threshold values shown were obtained with the IITRI dynamic olfactometer. These results clearly show that boiler incineration is a very efficient method of treating the high-intensity odors from the rendering process.

**Table 2.** Boiler Incineration of Rendering Process Odors

| | | | Odor Dilution to Treshold Values[a] | | |
|---|---|---|---|---|---|
| Plant | Fuel Used | Fire Box Temperature, °F | Boiler Inlet | Stack Exhaust | Odor Removal % |
| B | No. 6 oil | - | 56,000-138,000 | 234-650 | 99.5 |
| B | Natural gas | - | 7,600-13,200 | 88-128 | 99.0 |
| C | No. 6 oil | 1,400 | 21,600-73,000 | 76-157 | 99.6 |
| C | Natural gas | 1,250 | 28,100-59,200 | 202-356 | 99.3 |

[a]IITRI dynamic olfactometer

# Wet Scrubbing of Process Odors

Multistage scrubber systems for treating the high-intensity odors provide an alternative to boiler incineration when the latter approach may not be feasible because the boiler plant is remotely located or for other reasons. These multistage systems have been successfully applied to rendering plant emissions since the early 1970s.

A wet scrubber, known as a packed-bed scrubber (Figure 6), contains plastic packing of different geometric shapes and sizes to allow intimate contact between the upflowing odorous air and the downflowing scrubber solution. A chemical oxidant such as sodium hypochlorite is added to the scrubbing solution which is recirculated through the scrubber to conserve water and minimize chemical and waste water treatment costs. The caustic soda is added to control the pH of the NaOCl solution.

Wet scrubbing systems for treating process odor emissions contain a preconditioning device, such as a venturi or spray scrubber, to remove particulate matter before passing on to the packed-bed scrubber with the chemical oxidant solution. A typical wet scrubbing system for this application consists of 3 stages: a venturi scrubber and 2 packed-bed units in series. These systems normally process 4,000 to 10,000 cfm of high-intensity process odors.

The high-intensity odors enter the throat of the venturi scrubber which removes the particulates and cools the air stream. A de-mister screen removes entrained droplets from the air before it passes upward through the first-stage, counterflow packed-bed scrubber. Acid solution is recirculated through this stage to remove amine-type odors and NaOCl solution is recirculated through the second stage to remove sulfide-type odors. This system has an odor removal efficiency of about 99%.

## Wet Scrubbing of Plant Ventilating Air

Wet scrubbing of plant ventilating air provides a more complete solution to an overall plant odor problem. Fugitive odors within the plant can be captured and treated uniformly with this type of scrubber. It is particularly suited for rendering plants near sensitive populations, such as residential or commercial areas. For this application, it is essential to have adequate distribution and flow of air throughout the plant in order to pick up and capture in the ventilating air fat aerosols and other particles emitted from the rendering process.

In addition to controlling odor, these scrubbers ventilate the plant operating areas, thereby maintaining satisfactory working conditions for the employees. It is important that sufficient ventilating air pass through the operating area during the summer. Otherwise, doors and windows will be opened because of the heat, and allow the plant odors to escape from the building instead of being treated by the scrubber system. A slight negative pressure is maintained within the rendering plant.

Current practice for designing wet scrubbing systems to treat both the high-intensity process odor and plant ventilating air is to combine both types of scrubbers into a single system. A 3-stage scrubber system is described (Frega & Prokop 1981) that consists of the following:

1. A venturi scrubber in series with a vertical countercurrent packed tower to treat the high intensity odors. The scrubbing solutions consist of fresh water circulated through the venturi and sulfuric acid at 2 pH recirculated through the packed tower. This 2-stage scrubber system treats 6300 cfm of odorous air.

2.  A horizontal, cross-flow, packed-bed scrubber that receives the exhaust from the 2-stage scrubber system described above and the plant ventilating air.  Sodium hypochlorite solution at 9 pH is recirculated through this packed-bed scrubber and its capacity is 70,000 cfm.

The overall reduction of the high-intensity odors by 3 stages of scrubbing (venturi, small packed tower, and large packed bed) exceeds 99%.  The plant ventilating air scrubber's odor removal efficiency ranges from 90 to 95%, depending on the inlet odor level.

## Biofiltration

Biofilter technology developed during the past 15 years in Europe and elsewhere has been applied to the treatment of rendering odors.  Biofilters consist of large beds of porous media capable of absorbing odorous gaseous compound and reducing them by aerobic microbial action to nonodorous components.  They are less expensive to operate than wet scrubbers because they require no chemicals and less electricity than other scrubbers.  Furthermore, they require less initial investment.

Two basic types of biofilter media influence flow rate.  Compost, peat moss, bark, and other fibrous material, because of their greater porosity, allow high air flow rates ranging from 2 to 10 $cfm/ft^2$ of bed surface.  This category of biofilter is analogous to the plant ventilating air scrubber described above.  It is currently used in rendering plants in the United States.

Soil bed systems are another type of biofilter.  Less porous media such as soil result in lower air-flow rates ranging from 0.1 to 0.5 $cfm/ft^2$ of bed surface.  Such a system for a soil bed with a surface area of 4500 $ft^2$ and a bed depth of 24 inches can treat 650 cfm of Dupps Equacooker noncondensibles (Prokop & Bohn 1985).  Two series of odor sensory tests were conducted 14 months apart.  In both, odor removal efficiency exceeded 99.0% based on testing with the IITRI dynamic olfactometer.

Pine bark has been used as the bed medium in 2 biofilter systems to treat high-intensity odor emissions from poultry rendering plants (Prokop & Archer 1992).  Each filter has a surface area of 130 ft x 100 ft.  One unit has a bed depth of 5 ft and treats 40,000 cfm of high- intensity odor whereas the other unit has a depth of only 3 ft and treats 90,000 cfm of which 50% is plant ventilating air.  Odor sensory tests of the biofilter having the 5-ft bed depth resulted in an odor removal efficiency of some 90%.  Certain deficiencies in operation with this biofilter suggest that even higher efficiency is attainable

## Economic Impact of Odor Control Technology

Wet scrubbing systems to control odor emissions require considerable capital expenditures. Depending upon the plant size and specific control requirements, the capital cost of these control systems may vary from $200,000 to $1,000,000, excluding the cost of a building enclosure. Annual operating costs for chemicals, electrical power, repairs, and labor may vary from $50,000 to $300,000.

Biofiltration systems for controlling odor emissions also require large expenditures. The capital cost of these control systems may vary from $100,000 to $500,000. Annual operating costs are estimated to be approximately half those for wet scrubber systems.

## WASTE WATER DISCHARGES TO CITY SEWERS OR STREAMS

The plant effluent from an independent rendering plant usually derives from 3 major sources: condensate from the cooking vapors, wash water to clean the plant and the raw material pickup trucks, and blowdown discharge from the wet scrubbing system.

Waste water treatment is classified as primary, secondary, and tertiary. The type and degree of treatment required depends upon whether the effluent from a treatment plant discharges to a city sewer, to a navigable stream, or to land for crop irrigation.

Local municipal water pollution control authorities establish surcharge rates for discharging to sewers based on the flow and pollutant loadings to be processed by the municipal treatment plant. Also, the authorities may impose certain effluent limits on discharges from industrial plants, for example, on oil and grease.

Federal and state water pollution control agencies establish water quality standards that must be complied with for discharges to streams. Usually, these stream standards result in effluent limits being established for specific pollutants based on the maximum concentration of a pollutant (mg/L) or the maximum load (lb/day) discharged to a receiving water.

The design and operation of waste water treatment systems and equipment are discussed elsewhere (MOP 1990, 1992).

## PRIMARY WASTE WATER TREATMENT

Biochemical oxygen demand is the oxygen required for the biochemical oxidation of organic matter in waste water. Total suspended solids are solids that are removable from waste water by filtration (includes protein solids).  Oil and grease are fatty matter that can be extracted by a specific organic solvent (tallow or grease).

The concentration of pollutants, biochemical oxygen demand, total suspended solids, and oil and grease in waste water is usually expressed in milligrams per liter (mg/L).  These are easily converted to lb/day by multiplying the concentration in mg/L by the waste water flow in million gal/day times a factor of 8.33 (lb water/gal).

The purpose of primary treatment is 2-fold: to remove total suspended solids and oil and grease, and to reduce biochemical oxygen demand. Primary treatment reduces loadings of biochemical oxygen demand, total suspended solids, and oil and grease for secondary or tertiary treatment; reduces user charges for industrial discharges to municipal sewers; and recovers fats and protein solids for processing in the rendering plant.

It is more economical to reduce total suspended solids and oil and grease loadings by primary treatment rather than by secondary treatment.  For example, depending upon initial loadings and system capacity, grease and protein solids can be removed by primary treatment for 10¢ to 40¢/lb of dry substance recovered compared with 40¢ to $1.00/lb for secondary treatment.  This includes costs for operation, maintenance, chemical addition, and depreciation.

All renderers discharging to a city sewer periodically review their user charges and consider the feasibility of installing a primary treatment system to offset these costs, if one is not in place.  In order to confirm the user charges, the total flow of the plant effluent is measured and representative samples of the effluent are obtained for analyses of biochemical oxygen demand, total suspended solids, and oil and grease.

Recovery of grease and protein solids for processing in the rendering plant is an additional incentive for installing a primary treatment system. However, it is essential that the moisture content of these recovered materials not be ignored.  Otherwise, fuel costs could be excessive for cooking this material.  Another factor to consider is maintaining the quality of the tallow and grease being produced.  Recovered grease and solids from primary treatment should be carefully evaluated before being recycled to the rendering process.

## Rendering Plant Operation

Two objectives in operating the plant are to reduce the volume of plant effluent and to minimize the amounts of biochemical oxygen demand, total suspended solids, and oil and grease in the effluent.  Reuse of fresh water is an important consideration.  Loadings of grease and solids in the plant effluent can be minimized by repairing equipment leaks promptly and using dry cleanup of grease and solids spills before applying hose water.

## Equipment for Primary Treatment

For primary treatment rendering plants use screens, catch basins, and dissolved air flotation (DAF) systems (Figure 7).

Vibratory screens such as the Sweco Separator are used, although in recent years, a Rotating Drum Screen has successfully removed solids. This type of screen has a self-cleaning feature that tends to minimize binding of the screen.  The rotating bar screens used in these cases have a range of openings from 0.020 to 0.040 inches.

Catch basins are an important part of any primary treatment program for the rendering plant.  These units are normally rectangular and have a ratio of length to width of 3:1 or more.  They are usually sized to provide 30- to 40-minute retention and to have a surface flotation area of 1 ft$^2$/ gpm of flow.  Each unit is equipped with mechanical skimming and scraping devices for continuous removal of settleable solids and floatable grease.  These recovered materials are usually discharged directly to the raw material pit.

When designed and operated properly, a catch basin is an effective method for removal of solids and grease, particularly at high concentrations.  Consideration should be given to their use when total suspended solids range from 1000 to 1500 mg/L or higher and when oil and grease range from 500 to 1000 mg/L or higher.  Catch basins can reduce total suspended solids by 60 to 80% and oil and grease by 75 to 90%.

Dissolved air flotation systems have become more prevalent in rendering plants in recent years.  The dissolved air flotation system consists of a high-pressure pump, a pressurized tank for air injection, and the flotation cell.  Either influent waste water or recycled dissolved air flotation-clarified effluent is pumped to the pressurized tank where air is injected and forced into solution under a pressure of 40 to 80 psig.  When the waste water enters the flotation cell, the pressure is relieved and tiny air bubbles attach themselves to fat and solid particles which rise and float to the surface.  This float material accumulates and is continuously swept from the surface for recovery.

Dissolved air flotation systems are operated with (or without) the addition of coagulants and polymers to improve removal of fats and solids.  Dissolved air flotation systems reduce total suspended solids by 75 to 90% and oil and grease by as much as 95% or more.  Polymers and flocculants, added to improve dissolved air flotation removal of fats and solids, tend to increase moisture content of the float material and to decrease quality of the fat present in the float material.  This float material is pumped to the aerobic digestor instead of being recycled through the rendering process (Figure 7).

## Economic Impact of Primary Treatment

Primary treatment of plant effluent, either to a city sewer or to a secondary or tertiary treatment system, requires significant expenditures of capital. Depending upon the plant size and specific control requirements, the capital cost of these treatment systems may vary from $250,000 to $1,250,000, not including the cost of a building enclosure. Operating costs for chemicals, electrical power, repairs, and labor may vary from $60,000 to $250,000 (in 1995 dollars).

## SECONDARY & TERTIARY WASTE WATER TREATMENT

An example of both secondary and tertiary treatment is shown as a flow diagram in Figure 8. Secondary treatment refers to removing organic matter by biological action. Examples of secondary treatment include activated sludge systems and lagoons.

Tertiary treatment refers to removing nitrogen, phosphorus, or other pollutants below concentrations that are achievable by primary and secondary treatment. An example of tertiary treatment includes nitrification where nitrogen, present as ammonia ($NH_3$), is oxidized to nitrite ($NO_2$) and nitrate ($NO_3$).

## SECONDARY TREATMENT

Secondary or biological treatment reduces the biochemical oxygen demand concentration of the waste water after primary treatment. This biochemical oxygen demand consists of soluble biochemical oxygen demand (dissolved organic solids) and biochemical oxygen demand present in the suspended solids as organic matter. Microorganisms present in the waste water or in the solids feed upon the organic matter.

Aerobic processes (oxygen is present) are more prevalent than anaerobic processes (oxygen is not present) in secondary treatment. The oxygen present in the waste water is known as dissolved oxygen and it is a very important parameter in the operation of aerobic processes. Aerobic systems provide oxygen for the biological oxidation of biochemical oxygen demand which is converted into a biological floc, known as sludge. After its formation, this sludge must be removed and separated from the supernatant liquid which either passes on to the next stage (tertiary treatment) or discharges from the waste water treatment system to a navigable stream, if the stream water quality limits are satisfied.

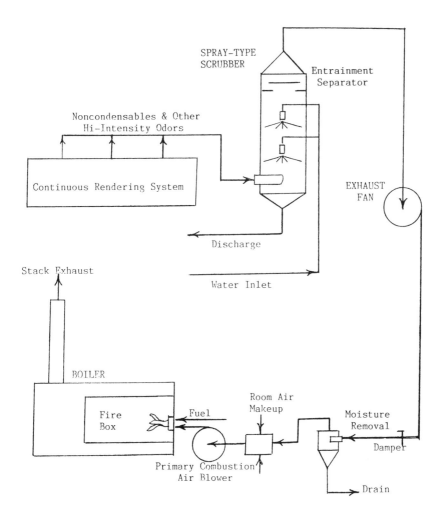

**Figure 5.** Boiler incineration of rendering process odors used as primary combustion air. A 2-stage spray scrubber with tangential inlet and entrainment separator is shown.

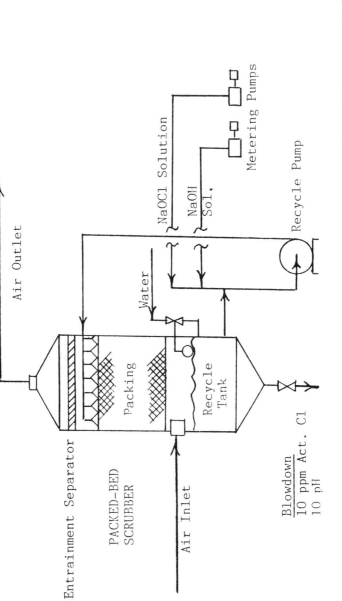

**Figure 6.** Packed-bed scrubbing of plant ventilating air. A typical plant ventilation air scrubber is this single-packed tower through which NaOCl solution is circulated. These scrubbers have capacities ranging from 40,000 to 80,000 cfm.

## Activated Sludge System

The biological floc known as sludge is referred to as activated sludge because it constantly increases in quantity as the organic matter is oxidized. Also, this sludge is biologically active since the microorganisms continue to grow. Activated sludge is contacted with the incoming waste water from primary treatment in the aeration basin (Figure 8). Sufficient oxygen is supplied by 5 surface aerators and 200 air diffuser units to provide a minimum disolved oxygen concentration of 2.0 mg/L. This step in the treatment process is followed by the secondary clarifier which allows the solids to settle and separate from the supernatant liquid.

To ensure an adequate supply of the preformed floc, a certain proportion of the activated sludge must be returned to the aeration basin. This sludge is known as the recycle or return activated sludge. The excess sludge that results is known as wasted sludge and is discharged to the aerobic digestor. The function of the aerobic digestor is 2-fold: to stabilize the sludge by oxidizing any remaining organic matter, and to increase the concentration of the sludge solids to optimize further sludge handling. This sludge is applied to neighboring farm land as a fertilizer.

Electricity requirements for activated sludge systems are high because the systems must provide sufficient oxygen to convert the organic matter, provide adequate hydraulic flow to maintain the activated sludge solids in suspension, and provide enough mixing action for the activated sludge to come into complete contact with incoming waste water. The 5 surface aerators with vertical shaft-mounted impellers have a total connected horsepower of 180 hp (Figure 8). Two 60-hp rotary blowers deliver compressed air to the 200 air diffuser units located 1 ft from the bottom. This amounts to a total of 300 hp for 1 million gal of retention capacity in the aeration basin.

The activated sludge system shown in Figure 8 can achieve the following removal efficiencies and outlet concentration levels:

98% removal of biochemical oxygen demand with 15 mg/L outlet
80% removal of total suspended solids with 40 mg/L  outlet
80% removal of oil and grease with 10 mg/L outlet

This activated sludge system can also achieve tertiary treatment since nitrification occurs where the ammonia concentration is reduced significantly. To comply with a very stringent NPDES permit limit for ammonia of 0.5 to 1.5 mg/L, the activated sludge system can reduce the ammonia concentration of approximately 300 mg/L in the effluent from primary treatment to below 1.0 mg/L at discharge from the secondary clarifier. However, to achieve this degree of nitrification, it is necessary to provide a dissolved oxygen concentration no less than 3.0 mg/L in the aeration basin.

## Lagoons

Lagoons, also known as stabilization ponds, are relatively simple and inexpensive methods of secondary or biological treatment and are widely used in the rendering industry.  They normally are rectangular and are constructed by excavating soil to a depth of 6 to 12 ft, allowing a free board space of 2 to 3 ft above the liquid level.  They may be used as part of the secondary treatment process, for storage of waste water during winter in a northern climate, or for evaporation of waste water in an arid climate.  Each type of lagoon, whether it be aerobic, facultative, or aerated, has a particular type of predominant biological life that must be nurtured and monitored for optimum growth.

Unaerated lagoons (no mechanical aerators) are shallow ponds with a liquid depth of 3 to 6 ft are either aerobic or facultative.  An aerobic lagoon is usually 3 to 4 ft deep and its biological action takes place in the presence of dissolved oxygen supplied by wind-induced turbulence.  Also, algae in the form of green plants generate oxygen in the presence of sunlight.

A facultative lagoon with a liquid depth of 4 to 6 ft has oxygen near the surface but bacterial action at the bottom of the lagoon takes place in the absence of dissolved oxygen where settleable solids accumulate over the entire bottom and decompose anaerobically.  Both the aerobic and facultative lagoons have retention times of 30 to 60 days and can reduce biochemical oxygen demand by 70 to 90%.  However, they are not usually capable of nitrification, whereby ammonia is oxidized.

Aerated lagoons, unlike aerobic or facultative lagoons, do not depend on algae and sunlight or wave action to furnish dissolved oxygen for biochemical oxygen demand reduction.   Instead, they use mechanical aerators or air diffuser systems.  Lagoons using mechanical aerators usually have a liquid depth of 10 ft or more.  These lagoons have a retention time of 10 to 25 days and can reduce biochemical oxygen demand by 50 to 80%.  They are normally incapable of nitrification.

## Economic Impact of Secondary Treatment

Secondary treatment of primary effluent requires significant expenditures of capital.  This particularly applies to the activated sludge system shown in Figure 8.  The capital cost of this treatment system (including aeration basin, clarifier, and digestor) is estimated to be $2,000,000 in current dollars.  Depending upon the plant size and specific control requirements, the capital cost of lagoon systems may vary from $250,000 to $1,000,000. A lesser lagoon cost would apply where the waste water discharge from a lagoon could be used for crop irrigation. This, of course, depends upon the specific degree of treatment required, based on the criteria specified by the water pollution control agency to prevent ground water contamination.

Annual operating costs for chemicals, electrical power, repairs, and labor for the activated sludge system shown in Figure 8 are estimated to be $300,000. Annual operating costs for lagoon systems would be considerably less, varying from $50,000 to $150,000.

## TERTIARY TREATMENT

The only tertiary treatment shown in Figure 8 is provided by a granular media filtration system consisting of 2 filter cells. This system is required to remove fine suspended particles in order to be in compliance with the NPDES permit limit of 20 mg/L total suspended solids for discharge to a stream. Each filter cell has sufficient capacity to process the waste water flow while the other filter is being backwashed or is out of service for repairs. Each filter is backwashed 3 times each day to prevent an accumulation of fine solids from plugging the filter media, thus increasing pressure drop and decreasing flow. Backwashing is accomplished by passing fresh water up through the filter media, whereas the filter is normally operated with a downward flow.

After filtration, the waste water passes through a chlorination contact chamber to eliminate pathogenic microorganisms such as fecal coliform. A dechlorination system is required to minimize the chlorine concentration in the discharge to the stream to protect aquatic life.

The many other types of tertiary treatment include activated carbon absorption for removal of organic compound, precipitation for phosphorus removal, and ion exchange for removal of inorganic dissolved solids. Denitrification, a tertiary process that uses bacteria in the absence of oxygen to convert nitrite ($NO_2$) and nitrate ($NO_3$) into nitrogen gas ($N_2$), is often combined with nitrification as a 2-step process to remove organic nitrogen from the waste water.

## Economic Impact

The capital investment cost of the 2-cell filtration system and the chlorination–dechlorination equipment shown in Figure 8 is estimated to be $700,000 in current dollars. Annual operating costs are estimated to be $50,000. These costsl vary significantly depending upon the type of tertiary treatment required.

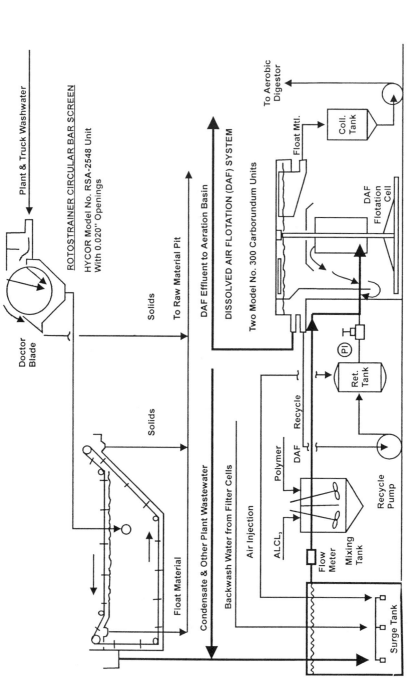

**Figure 7.** Primary treatment of rendering plant waste water

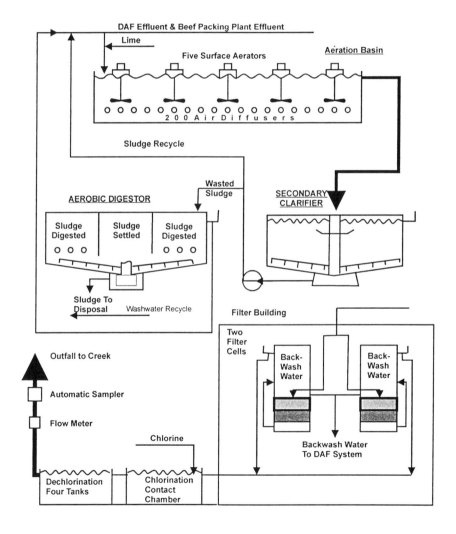

**Figure 8.** Current operation of secondary and tertiary treatment system. An activated sludge system consists of an aeration basin and a secondary clarifier for secondary treatment. The 2-cell filter system for removal of fine total suspended solids exemplifies tertiary treatment.

## REFERENCES

Burgwald TA. 1971. *Identification of Chemical Constituents in Rendering Industry Odor Emissions,* project no C8172. IIT Research Institute, Chicago.

Dravnieks A & Prokop WH. 1975. Source emission odor measurement by a dynamic forced-choice triangle olfactometer. *JAPCA* 25(1):28–35.

Frega V & Prokop WH, 1981. "Wet scrubbing of multiple source odors in a rendering plant" (paper 81-39.2), presented at the annual meeting of APCA, Philadelphia.

[MOP] *Manual of Practice,* 1990. *Operation of Waste water Treatment Plants,* no 11 (3 vol). Water Environment Federation, Alexandria, VA .

[MOP] *Manual of Practice,.* 1992. *Design of Waste water Treatment Plant,* no. 8 (2 vol). Water Environment Federation, Alexandria, VA .

Prokop WH. 1985. Rendering systems for processing animal by-product materials. *J Am Oil Chem Soc* 62(4):805–811.

Prokop WH. 1992. Rendering plants, in chapter 13, Fish, Meat and Poultry Processing. *Air Pollution Engineering Manual* (revised), Van Nostrand Reinhold.

Prokop WH & Archer NR. 1992. "Biofiltration of high intensity odors from poultry rendering plants" (paper 92-115.01), presented at annual meeting of AWMA, Kansas City.

Prokop WH & Bohn HL. 1985. Soil bed system for control of rendering plant odors. *JAPCA,* 35(12):1332–1338.

Snow RH & Reilich HG. 1972. *Investigation of Odor Control in the Rendering Industry,* project no. C8210. IIT Research Institute, Chicago.

# 4

# Biosecurity and Hazard Analysis Critical Control Points (HACCP) in the Rendering Industry

## Don A Franco

Biosecurity is one of the novel terms that is currently in vogue to describe controls of processes that could affect safety and health. It has been introduced into the quality assurance regimen of a broad range of industries and serves as a systematic managerial resource to assure compliance with regulatory or voluntary guidelines and standards. Although the traditional use of "bio-" suggests an associative link to life or a living organism, it with the suffix "-security," will be used in the broadest sense in this chapter to include other than control of living organisms, and will embrace most of the significant spheres that relate to the good manufacturing practices observed by the rendering industry. Biosecurity also promulgates the directional trend of an industry in transition. The realization that the constructs of quality procedures and principles is the sole responsibility of the industry has developed over the years as the operational model. The role of governmental agencies to mandate standards is no longer considered with disdain, provided that the government's regulatory proposals are based on science. The present thinking is that in an era of diminution and scarce government resources, it is in the industry's best long-term interests to progressively develop voluntary programs that conform with the philosophy of regulators. In essence, a bilateral working relationship that heightens and complements the mutual interests of government and industry; thus, the genesis of the concept of hazard analysis critical control points (HACCP) as the major initiative of the industry.

## Historical Background

The rendering industry has always been involved with processing procedures and practices to ensure product safety—biosecurity. Biosecurity in the industry was first associated with anthrax, a potentially fatal disease of antiquity transmitted to humans by contact with infected animals. It was the first human disease to be attributed to a specific pathogen. Contact with hides, pelts, and hair of the carcasses of infected livestock, including skinning of infected carcasses, made this disease a significant industrial dilemma. Thus, anthrax emerged as the disease prototype for the industry, and mandated a responsible program of prevention and control. The incidence of anthrax in industrialized nations has declined sharply in the 20th century. This decline is a direct result of—and the disease a direct cause of—the early establishment of controls within the livestock and rendering industries.

Anthrax was an unusual challenge to the rendering industry from the inception, because of the high incidence of the disease during the early 1900s, and even today remains an insidious threat because of occasional small-scale sporadic outbreaks. Equally important is the causative agent of the disease: *Bacillus anthracis* can form spores that resist heat, cold, chemical disinfectants, and desiccation and can survive for years in contaminated soil, hide, hair, wool, bone meal, and dried blood. Therefore, the focus of research, as exemplified by the early work of Murray in 1931 at Rutgers University, Brunswick, New Jersey, was to evaluate time–temperature inactivation of spores of anthrax. The initial research findings by Murray and associates was considered an authoritative guide for disease control officials, and ultimately became a consideration for the rendering industry to emulate and use as a guide.

As a result, the rendering industry, already cognizant that enough heat and time was needed to transform raw material into finished rendered products enjoyed both the consolation and added satisfaction that their manufacturing procedures employed a time–temperature range that was lethal to bacteria, even organisms that formed spores and were comparatively heat resistant. That knowledge remains a source of comfort to the rendering industry to the present day.

The early history of *Salmonella* "circumvented" the feed and rendering industries until 1948 when the organism was first isolated from animal feed at the University of Kentucky Experimental Station in Lexington. This initial isolation gained retrospective relevance and renewed significance in 1967 when Commissioner Goddard of the Food and Drug Administration (FDA) expanded the meaning of adulteration, hitherto limited to human food, to include food for animals. Therefore, articles used in food for animals are included within the definition of food in section 201(f) of the Federal Food, Drug and Cosmetic Act. Furthermore, *Salmonella* contamination of animal feeds that can infect and cause disease in animals must be regarded as an adulterant within the meaning of section 402(a) of the act: hence, the genesis of the regulatory implications and the pertinence of *Salmonella* contamination of animal feed.

In 1969, the National Academy of Sciences published the findings of a comprehensive study that described the *Salmonella* problem in the United States. The results clearly identified the complexity of the challenge and the need to combine the diverse resources to pursue a workable initiative to counter and limit the different sources of transmission and contamination. Concurrently, federal and state disease control agencies were conducting surveillance programs of animal byproducts to assess the incidence of *Salmonella* contamination. The results of the various studies were compiled and examined, but never heightened the degree of the problem because of the complex epidemiology associated with the data.

Equally important at the time was the limited knowledge of the behavior and ecology of the genus, the infectious dose, the pathogenicity of different serotypes and the subsequent meaning of apparent differences, and some of the difficulties associated with the isolation of the organism. Thus, in spite of emerging information of the prevalence of *Salmonella* in foods of animal origin and rendered animal byproducts, there was no consensus on the comparative relevance of incidence or prevalence to disease causation. Nonetheless, the public health awareness had been clearly established, and control and prevention strategies were beginning to evolve in many phases of livestock agriculture.

In 1984 members of the rendering industry first met and formed a nonprofit organization, the Animal Protein Producers Industry to develop a voluntary *Salmonella* education program intended to reduce contamination. The Animal Protein Producers Industry was established in response to the concerns of the rendering industry, and the perceived benefits that could ensue from an organized system for testing, surveillance, education, and prevention.

The components of the Animal Protein Producers Industry program are:

1) A *Salmonella* reduction and education program that provides training to accomplish 3 major objectives:
   - Train workers in practices that will reduce *Salmonella* recontamination of finished material (protein meals).
   - Plan and assign priority to changes and expenditures that will reduce *Salmonella* recontamination of finished material.
   - Alert consumers to a plant's participation in the *Salmonella* testing and reduction program.

2) Finished product testing:
   - Establish a voluntary program to reduce the incidence of *Salmonella* in animal proteins.

- Perform the testing program during a specified 3-consecutive-month period in the winter and summer.
- Take one sample weekly from finished products as they are loaded into a truck or other vehicle.
- Include in the sampling requests all standard instructions and recommendations for proper handling, and emphasize the need to limit any contamination during sampling to assure accurate testing results.

3) Continuing education symposia:
- Hold symposia at different locations throughout the country to update plant supervisors and other personnel on different disease-related entities (*Salmonella,* bovine spongiform encephalopathy, scrapie, etc) and quality control and biosecurity programs (HACCP) of interest to the rendering industry.

In September 1990, the Center for Veterinary Medicine (CVM)–FDA, announced a goal of zero *Salmonella* contamination in animal feed ingredients and finished feed. Since that initial announcement there has been widespread misunderstanding of the pronouncement and how it was to be interpreted. At industry–government meetings, the discussions highlighted the concept of zero in the same context as none, and the point-counterpoint continued unabated until the meaning of zero was clearly defined to reflect FDA's regulatory intent. Since that initial objective, staff specialists of CVM–FDA have been meeting with industry and other organizational representatives to heighten their position and establish a working agenda for attainable controls. The CVM staff goes beyond sampling finished products for *Salmonella* contamination and recommends integrating quality control standards for general sanitation, processing, handling, and transportation to produce and maintain a microbiologically and chemically "clean" rendered animal byproduct.

CVM staff members suggested that these preventive controls could be realized by applying the principles of HACCP to the production process. Significantly, the Food and Drug Administration published in the *Federal Register* in August 1994, an advance notice of proposed rule making, "Development of Hazard Analysis Critical Control Points for the Food Industry," to ensure that all foods shipped in interstate commerce are not contaminated or otherwise adulterated. And, this is what the industry has embraced and is working on to enhance quality and ensure safety.

Bovine spongiform encephalopathy was first recognized clinically in Great Britain in 1985 as a fatal degenerative disease of the central nervous system of cattle. The disease belongs to a group of related neurologic diseases commonly known as the transmissible spongiform encephalopathies characterized by a long incubation period and a causative agent that has not been identified. The disease has been described as the bovine equivalent of scrapie in sheep.

The prevailing hypothesis is that the disease resulted from cattle's consumption of meat and bone meal that contained a scrapie-like infectious agent. As a result of bovine spongiform encephalopathy, the rendering industry in the United States developed a voluntary program for handling sheep byproducts published by the Animal Protein Producers Industry and distributed to its membership in the United States and Canada for policy compliance. This fascinating and complex disease became an important matrix for international dialogue and has worldwide ramifications in the trade of cattle and meat exports and their byproducts from affected countries. Unaffected countries like the United States and Canada started surveillance programs to assess the epidemiology and take preventive measures to preclude outbreaks, as exemplified by the Food and Drug Administrations' proposed rule, published in the *Federal Register* (vol 59, no 166, August 29, 1994), "Substances Prohibited from Use in Animal Food or Feed; Specified Offal from Adult Sheep and Goats Prohibited in Ruminant Feed; Scrapie."

## HAZARD ANALYSIS & CRITICAL CONTROL POINTS (HACCP)

The pathway and concept of hazard analysis and critical control points (HACCP) started with the Pillsbury Company in 1959 in cooperation with The National Aeronautics and Space Agency (NASA), the US Army Natick Laboratories, and the US Air Force Space Laboratory Project Group. The objective was to assist Pillsbury to produce a food that could be used under zero gravity conditions in the space program. The most challenging aspect of this initiative was to approximate 100% assurance that the food products intended for space use would not be contaminated with chemicals, toxins, or bacterial or viral pathogens. In essence, this coalition was charged with a mandate hitherto never attempted in food quality control technology. And, for good reason. A food-related hazard to astronauts could result in an aborted or catastrophic space mission. Traditionally, quality assurance programs were developed by segments of the food industry based on individual experience and lacked uniformity, consistency, and infrastructural planning or commitment. Therefore, the scientific community embraced the new theories of quality assurance contained in HACCP.

HACCP introduces the principle of a preventive system of quality control. It outlines measures for extensive evaluation and control of raw material, process, environment, personnel, storage, distribution, monitoring, and traceability. In retrospect, the proper use of the system can control any area or point in the production sequences that could contribute to a hazardous situation, regardless of cause (contaminants, pathogenic microbes, chemicals, physical objects, raw material, etc).

Food-producing plants in this country have used HACCP for more than 20 years. But not until 1985, when the National Academy of Sciences recommended that such a preventive system was an essential adjunct to the control of microbiological hazards, was the system enthusiastically embraced by the food industry for broad application.

It is easy to modify HACCP systems, and undoubtedly refinements can be made to adjust the generic concepts and controls to different processes. Nevertheless, HACCP will succeed only in an atmosphere of total commitment. It has to be an ongoing and attitudinal process. Every person within an organization must be an active participant to promote the HACCP philosophy.

The traditional quality assurance programs in the food, feed, and rendering industries have been generally based on what the quality assurance manager believes to be a good program. In the past, most programs lacked uniformity or even consensus within a company as to what constituted an effective program. In retrospect, although many contributed to degrees of quality improvement, and doubtless improved upon previous procedures, there was a lack of planned, collective objectives to ascertain consistency of results. Additionally, many quality programs heightened the concept of end-product testing and acceptance in lieu of an active, coordinated preventive system of process controls; in lieu of a systematic approach that evaluates and validates all the production sequences to ensure compliance of established quality standards, a program like HACCP.

The successful HACCP program requires that the company begin with a firm commitment from the top down, and maintain a thorough knowledge of the processing and production systems, planning, use of personnel resources, training, and follow-through. A HACCP program that is poorly structured and supported may be worse than no program at all, because it gives the company a false sense of security.

The HACCP guidelines for the rendering industry recognize the site-specific nature of the program's concept and principles. Each plant is unique and requires the development of a plan that corresponds to the plant's layout and equipment, location, production, complexity, personnel, and corporate philosophy.

## PRINCIPLES OF HACCP

The basic principles of HACCP are:

1) Assess hazards associated with all sequences of the process (raw materials, processing (time–temperature controls), storage, etc).

2) Determine the critical control points (CCP) required to control the identified hazards (procuring raw material, handling, processing, etc).

3) Establish the critical limits that must be met at each CCP. Critical components associated with a CCP are factors critical to safety, factors where failure to provide sufficient control may result in a safety hazard. A CCP may have multiple factors or components that must be controlled to assure product safety.

4) Establish procedures to monitor critical limits. Webster defined monitoring as "watching, observing or checking especially for a special purpose." To effectively conduct monitoring procedures, 6 questions must be answered: WHAT? WHY? HOW? WHERE? WHO? WHEN? Monitoring is not the same as continuing observation. Monitoring requires management action.

5) Establish corrective action to be taken when a deviation is identified during monitoring of CCP. Corrective action involves 4 activities:
   - Use the results of monitoring to adjust the process and maintain or regain control.
   - If control was lost, deal with the noncompliance product.
   - Correct the contributing cause of noncompliance.
   - Maintain records of the corrective actions taken.

6) Establish effective record-keeping systems that document the HACCP plan. Records are an integral part of a working HACCP system. The act of keeping records assures that this written evidence is available for review and is maintained for the required length of time. Records give evidence of product safety with regard to procedures and processes, and ease of product traceablility and process review.

7) Establish procedures to verify that the HACCP system is working correctly. Verification is a mandate in a successful HACCP program. It confirms through documentation that the HACCP plan has been followed as outlined and assures that the HACCP program is achieving the established objectives of process conformance.

## THE REGULATORY PERSPECTIVE AND RATIONALE

Section 201 of the Food, Drug, and Cosmetic Act defines food as "articles used for food or drink for man or other ANIMALS." Under section 402 (a) (4) of the act, a food is deemed adulterated if it has been "prepared, packed, or held under unsanitary conditions whereby it may have become contaminated with filth, or whereby it may have been rendered injurious to health." This section of the act does not require proof that a food is actually contaminated or otherwise hazardous to establish adulteration. Instead, such adulteration requires only a showing that the conditions under which food is prepared, packed, or held create a "reasonable possibility" of contamination. The important consideration for the rendering industry is whether current practices of quality assurance and control employed by companies producing rendered animal byproducts could assure a safe finished product that is not contaminated or otherwise adulterated.

The Food and Drug Administration, which is responsible for food safety assurance programs and regulates the activities of the rendering industry, has strongly recommended requirements to ensure safety and has proposed that such a program be based upon the principles of HACCP (*Federal Register*, vol 59, no 149, August 4, 1994). The HACCP concept is a simple, logical, and specialized system of controls designed to prevent the occurrence of hazardous or critical situations during the process of rendering. The concept is predicated on the ability of plant management to analyze potential or existing hazards, establish and characterize control points important to good manufacturing practices, and determine points of the process that are critical to finished product integrity.

Thus, the difference between a control point and a critical control point is its degree of relative impact on the production or manufacturing processes that influence product safety. The system establishes a corrective response when a process is out of control, but most importantly embodies a working philosophy and environment that prevents and controls dysfunction.

The success of the HACCP concept is based on site specificity and, each time it is implemented, it must be planned by a team of committed employees on location. Establishment of HACCP guidelines must recognize that the effort is by definition limited to generic principles. This will permit a broad degree of flexibility to modify or alter the recommended guidelines to suit individual plant layout, equipment, and production and manufacturing practices to tailor an individualized initiative. The HACCP system is intended to provide optimal control of the rendering sequences so as to ultimately assure the production of safe, high-quality rendered products in an effective working environment. It also serves as an assurance to users of animal proteins and fats that an integrated system of in-plant controls has become an established practice of the rendering industry.

## THE *SALMONELLA* COMPLEX

More than 2,300 serotypes comprise the genus *Salmonella;* each has simple requirements for growth and can multiply under a wide variety of conditions. The organisms are not highly resistant to either physical or chemical agents and can be killed at 55°C in 1 hour, or at 60°C in 15 to 20 minutes. These ubiquitous organisms favor moist conditions and an optimal growing temperature of 37°C, the normal human body temperature. Standard cooking procedures and pasteurization readily destroy them; so would commonly used disinfectants. Freezing decreases *Salmonella* numbers but does not eradicate them. The organism survives desiccation well, and can survive in rodent feces for 5 months, in cattle feces for nearly 3 years, and in contaminated earth and pasture for about 8 months. Under optimum conditions, with no limits on food and space, one cell can divide every 20 minutes. At this rate, after 7 hours, one cell can give rise to more than 2 million bacteria. That is why prevention and control of *Salmonella* are so challenging. The organism has been reported to survive in meat meal fertilizer for 8 months, and in manure oxidation ditches for 47 days. It also has a prolonged survival time in water.

Salmonellae are a resourceful and defiant group of microorganisms that parasitizes a broad range of hosts including insects, reptiles, amphibians, birds, and mammals. *Salmonella* serotypes possess distinctive host ranges, and unique patterns of virulence and geographic distribution that complicate their epidemiology and control. The problem of asymptomatic carriage by animals and birds, and environmental contamination by rodents and other vectors magnify the challenge. In reality, the diversity of the *Salmonella* complex taxes our ingenuity and serves as a constant reminder that no single group can do it alone. We must combine resources to pursue a workable initiative to counter the different avenues of contamination.

The most important aspect of *Salmonella* control and prevention is the importance of serotype in disease causation, because the pathogenicity and virulence vary with the serotype. Although other factors are implicated in virulence, it is accurate to say that serotype plays a most significant role. In the review of laboratory results, we remain conscious of the potential for any *Salmonella* serotype to cause disease, however, the reality is that of the 2,300+ different serotypes, only 30 to 40 are routinely reported of clinical pertinence in animals and people. The persistent question that we face in the rendering industry is to what degree, based on serotypic comparisons, does meat and bone meal contribute to clinical salmonellosis in livestock and poultry, and ultimately humans?

A comparison of the major serotypes isolated from meat and bone meal matched with isolates from livestock and poultry and humans indicate limited or no support for disease causation. In reality, the major serotypes isolated from meat and bone meal are relatively innocuous and not routinely isolated other than from meat and bone meal. In essence, the classic postulates of validation of a causal association between meat and bone meal and clinical salmonellosis are lacking.

Another pertinent factor for consideration is that laboratory findings of Salmonellae in meat and bone meal reveal very low numbers in an assessment of most probable number, ranging from 4 to 7 organisms per gram. This, added to the usual inclusion rate of meat and bone meal to complete rations in livestock and poultry feeds of only 3 to 5%, indicates that despite the ubiquity of these organism, they pose no real threat.

Nevertheless, the rendering industry, adopted the principles of HACCP, not only to preclude bacterial contamination, but to enhance total quality improvements.

## BOVINE SPONGIFORM ENCEPHALOPATHY— IMPLICATIONS FOR THE RENDERING INDUSTRY

The world of science has reacted to bovine spongiform encephalopathy (BSE) based on the hypothesis that the disease resulted from cattle's consumption of meat and bone meal that contained a scrapie-like infectious agent. The hypothesis is not conclusive; it is suppositional. But, no single factor can account for the sudden appearance of BSE in Great Britain. According to epidemiologists who reported on a possible cause, several circumstances could have contributed and appear pertinent:

- the significant increase in the sheep population since 1980;
- an increase in the prevalence of scrapie-affected flocks;
- the increased use of sheep heads in rendering material;
- modifications in rendering technology that reduce time and temperature in a continuous rendering process;
- a decline in the use of hydrocarbon solvents for fat extraction in the rendering process.

Together, these changes appeared as the only common factor in the majority, if not all, of the investigated outbreaks of BSE.

Because scrapie has existed in sheep for at least 200 years, an important and logical question is: Why would a disease like scrapie, which is endemic worldwide, now cross a species barrier into cattle? In spite of extensive research in most of the industrialized world, the cause of scrapie remains to be determined. In fact, an analysis of the factors associated with the emergence of BSE still causes epidemiologists, clinicians, researchers, and disease-control officials to wonder why it happened when it did, that question remains unanswered.

The new knowledge of BSE is based on extensive research in molecular biology and transgenetics of central nervous system degeneration in humans and animals performed by Prusiner in San Francisco, who proposed the name prion disease. The discovery of fibrils similar to scrapie-associated fibrils in detergent extracts of BSE-affected brain confirms that BSE is a scrapie-like disease. Scrapie-associated fibrils are pathologic aggregates of a prion protein, which is a neuronal membrane protein. A protease-resistant form of prion protein is a molecular marker of scrapie-associated fibrils, which are found in brain extracts of all animal species affected by scrapie or other transmissible spongiform encephalopathies, such as BSE.

In the United States, it was readily recognized that extant risk factors for a BSE outbreak are not the same as they are in Great Britain. In spite of that knowledge, the rendering industry established a voluntary program based on the sheep scrapie theory to reduce the risk:

1) Renderers should refrain from picking up diseased, dying, disabled, and dead sheep until further notice.
2) Veterinarians should certify that a given flock is scrapie-free; picking up lambs from such a premise would pose minimal risk. Sheep older than 1 year should be avoided since they present a greater risk.
3) Renderers and packers who process sheep offal from slaughtering facilities should divert the rendered sheep protein to feeds other than dairy or beef cattle feed.
4) Renderers servicing locker plants should only pick up sheep offal under the following circumstances:
   • When the renderer can process the sheep offal from a locker plant or small packing house separately, store the finished protein separately, and sell this product into other than cattle rations.
   • If the animal's owner, locker plant operator, or inspector will certify that slaughtered lambs, younger than 1 year, came from a scrapie-free flock, then their offal, except heads, could be processed with other raw material.
   • If the route pick-up driver cannot determine whether the offal originates from lambs or sheep at locker plants or small slaughterhouses, then no heads should be picked up from these facilities, regardless of certification.

The media in both Europe and North America speculated on the public health implications, and whether BSE could be transmitted to humans by eating meat of infected animals. Several "authors" indulged their biases in the popular press by accusing the research and regulatory authorities in Great Britain of covering up the facts and implying that, indeed, a human health risk is real. Some of that type of journalism surfaced in the United States and Canada in spite of authoritative research publications to the contrary. As a result, a complex and challenging disease fell victim to the emotional outbursts of unsubstantiated statements in the press. But, the principles of science prevail. The government officials in the United States and Canada responded with conviction, that based on current knowledge, there were no apparent public health concerns. The obvious question is: Why, after the use of meat and bone meal in the United States for more than 100 years, have we not had a case of BSE?

Notwithstanding the current knowledge of the disease, the Food and Drug Administration proposed a rule in the *Federal Register* on August 29, 1994, to prohibit specified offal from adult (older than 12 months) sheep and goats for use in ruminant feed.

FDA is proposing this action because the specified offal may contain the agent that causes scrapie, a transmissible spongiform encephalopathy (TSE) of sheep and goats. . . . Because FDA cannot positively rule out a direct association between scrapie, BSE, and human TSEs, FDA is proposing this action to protect the health of animals and humans.

I gave FDA detailed comments on behalf of both the National Renderers Association and the Animal Protein Producers Industry. The summary highlights my convictions:

> Scrapie/BSE are complex diseases that defy ready answers. I doubt whether a rule would change the status. There is ongoing research that could provide 'light' to the entire scrapie transmission. Same has been conducted by the Agricultural Research Service's staff at Ames, Iowa. This is known by all with an interest in these diseases. Equally important is the fact that in spite of emotional pronouncements by some of a pending 'outbreak,' nearly a decade has gone by since the initial report from the United Kingdom. . . . We remain an advocate of all the contributions that the Center staff has made to assure public health, and plan to continue working with the dedicated staff to assist their initiatives and improve their programs. It is possible to continue our efforts without resolving to a rule. I envision more science. We can work together.

## THE NEW CHALLENGES

The rendering industry must continue to examine the many variables or combinations of factors that can contribute to disease emergence—for example, the 1985 occurrence of bovine spongiform encephalopathy in the United Kingdom—and recognize that newly emergent infectious diseases may result from changes or evolution of existing organisms. This necessitates an expanded organizational infrastructure for the Association of Protein Producers and the National Renderers Association. Such infrastructure should include:

1) Surveillance
   - Coordinating with the industry, governmental agencies, and allied groups for the early detection, tracking, and

evaluation of emerging infections of livestock, poultry, and humans in the United States and Canada.

- Improving the international network with Canada, Mexico, the European Union Renderers Association (EURA), and the Australian Renderers Association (ARA), for the anticipation, recognition, control, and prevention of potential problems.

- Strengthening communication and coordinating nationally and internationally to share information relative to new initiatives like HACCP and new technology.

2) Applied Research
- Integrating the Animal Protein Producers Industry's laboratory findings to expand epidemiologic and prevention effectiveness. In essence, use *Salmonella* incidence to highlight an effective control program.

- Evaluating the applicability of organic acids in a research environment that will reduce and control *Salmonella* and be approved by the FDA for use by the industry.

- Encouraging laboratories that serve the rendering industry to develop diagnostic tests, reagents, improved methods, and state-of-the-art technology to meet the changing demands of the industry.

3) Prevention and Control
- Establishing the mechanisms and partnerships needed to ensure rapid and effective implementation of preventive measures through planning and working with allied groups, coalitions, and regulatory agencies.

- Using diverse communication methods, including publications and press releases when applicable, for more effective delivery of critical messages.

- Coordinating with the industry's technical resources, regulatory agencies of government, academia, and allied groups to assist disease prevention and control initiatives.

4) Infrastructure
- Strengthening the industry's infrastructure and communication capability to support surveillance, disease-related research, and prevention and control initiatives to ensure prompt implementation of planned startegies.

Ensure the ready availability of professional expertise to help the industry to better understand, monitor, and control potential problems.

•  Providing training and continuing education programs to support the established objectives of the industry.

Because we are a construct of the food/feed industry cycle of production, we must live in an era of constant vigilance of the potential for the emergence of "old" pathogens and the genesis of new or unusual syndromes. A special analysis of the relevance of this perspective is the *E coli* O157:H7 foodborne disease outbreaks due to the consumption of improperly cooked hamburger, predominantly in the western United States. Although an evaluation of the epidemiology does not implicate the rendering and feed industries, we must be conscious that there are always crusaders who insist on guilt until innocence is proven. Thus, the rendering industry needs to improve its infrastructure to conduct surveillance and research that will assist in the control and prevention of potential microbial threats.

There are also non-microbial threats to the animal production cycle. Rachel Carson, in her thought-provoking book, *Silent Spring,* published in 1961, first sensitized the American public, and indeed most of the world with an environmental consciousness, that there was an impending "ecological disaster" if use of pesticides such as DDT was not curtailed. The impact of Carson's message, plus the development of a proactive environmental movement, had much to do with the regulatory actions and subsequent changes that have occurred in the use of pesticides. A retrospective comparison is pertinent. In 1906, the United States enacted the Pure Food and Drug Act, which perhaps was influenced more by the writings of a sociologist-journalist, Upton Sinclair, in his reform-seeking book, *The Jungle,* than by toxicologists. Indeed regulatory initiatives and changes in law are definitely not the sole domain of professional bureaucrats and politicians. The rendering industry, therefore, not only must keep abreast of current technology, but must be forerunners in the process and maintain a public relations demeanor within agriculture and the broad realm of environmental health. That is our rationale in advocating biosecurity and HACCP principles in the rendering industry.

Recyclers have to consider the potential harmful effects of chemicals, including pesticides, herbicides, and antimicrobials and other drugs on livestock and poultry, and the possibility of acute or chronic toxic effects that these may elicit due to contamination of animal byproducts. Although the possibility of contamination is remote, based on the recorded literature in the annals of toxicology, nonetheless exposure to toxic substances is a unique feature of agriculture, and preventive systems must be established to preclude the inadvertent transmission of toxins.

Therefore, any HACCP program must factor into the plan a sampling profile to control chemical residues.

The criteria for a chemical may vary widely among countries, but the US Department of Agriculture uses the following determinants to assess the likelihood that harmful residues will appear in the food supply:

- amount of chemical actually or probably used;
- conditions of use as related to residues at slaughter;
- potential for misuse to result in harmful residues;
- metabolic patterns of the chemical in animals, plants, or the environment, including the bioavailability and persistence of residues; and
- toxicity of the residues.

Every HACCP plan must identify the potential hazard that must be controlled for each product manufactured, and must extend beyond the narrow limits of microbes to include pesticides, from the all-inclusive use of the term, chemical contaminants, extraneous material, etc. The HACCP concept is the establishment of preventive measures at every stage of the process to assure a safe product.

## DISCUSSION

The rendering industry, cognizant of the realities of the times, has been able to keep abreast of the rapid changes in technology, government regulatory requirements, and the new environmental impetus. This progress was not accomplished by a compulsive need to satisfy any particular group or faction, but by a planned response to adjust to change and pursue a structure that will meet present and future demands. Historically, the industry has been resilient, being able to modify production practices to meet the needs of consumers and changing trends. Thus, we witness over the years, new or changing uses of animal byproducts. An outstanding example would be the increased use of fat in recent years as a source of energy in livestock, poultry, and pet rations. But, just as pertinent would be the emergence of protein-rich byproducts like blood meal, feather meal, meat and bone meal, and poultry meal as invaluable feed supplements to enhance nutritive value for all classes of livestock and pets. A highlight of the applicable use of animal proteins is the new commercial opportunities for rumen-protected amino acids to improve efficiency for growth and lactation by maximizing microbial amino acid flow to the intestine of ruminants.

The response of the industry in the past 10 years to format programs of self-regulation is most commendable. The Animal Protein Producers Industry program for *Salmonella* reduction and control is exemplary.

This initiative has grown to a level that has made the Animal Protein Producers Industry a recognized and respected leader in movements to ensure the safety of animal proteins.  Equally relevant is the Animal Protein Producers Industry's guidelines and policy for the processing and subsequent use of sheep offal in concert with government "thinking" to prevent the occurrence of BSE in the United States and Canada.  Also relevant is their progressive trend to expand their role to more than strictly disease-related issues and to include the preventive elements of the HACCP principles to heighten biosecurity as an industry initiative.

## CONCLUSION

The rendering industry's basic functions are directly associated with risk assessment, risk characterization, and risk management.  The activities, therefore, mandate the need for provisions within the production phase that will establish a system of controls that preclude hazards that could compromise the safety of the materials produced.  This will result in the practice of quality assurance offered by the incorporation of a HACCP program to heighten the concept of biosecurity.  HACCP and biosecurity are the wave of the future, and a part of the global movement to institute a formal program to control hazards within companies.

The HACCP concept has expanded to include new applicability and is now used in areas hitherto never considered.  For example, HACCP and biosecurity are integral to progressive on-farm livestock- and poultry-rearing operations.  It will serve the rendering industry equally well.  Equally important, HACCP has been promoted by government agencies as the "answer" to meet customers' needs in providing a consistent safe product, and a self-imposed industry-controlled regimen that would be an obvious improvement over the current regulatory structure.

# 5

# Fats and Oils—a Global Market Complex

### Robert J McCoy

Fats are one of numerous triglycerides produced from animal, marine, and plant sources. Generally referred to as fats and oils, many are produced in conjunction with high protein meals, which are important nutritional sources of amino acids in poultry and animal products.

The fatty acids in triglycerides are essential to good nutrition. Also, triglycerides are one of the most economical sources of calories, an important factor in lower income countries. The low per capita consumption of fats and oils in developing countries typically increases as per capita income increases—both in food products and in nonfood applications such as soap, shampoos, and household and laundry cleaning products. Further increases in living standards result in demand for numerous industrially manufactured products containing oleochemicals derived from animal fats and other triglycerides. Examples include synthetic rubber and various plastic products. The following comparison of India, China, the United States and the balance of the world illustrates the differences in consumption growth during the recent decade.

Tallow and grease are important commodities, comprising about 8% of the total of the 17 major fats and oils (Tables 1 & 2). If lard is included, the total of about 15% makes meat fats the third largest commodity behind soybean oil and palm oil. The United States produces a little over 50% of the world's tallow and grease and exports almost 40% of its production. Australia, Canada, and New Zealand are the next 3 largest exporters with a combined total about half of the US volume. A significant share of the Australian and New Zealand tallow is from sheep and has different quality characteristics.

**Table 1.** Consumption of 17 Major Fats and Oils

| Country | Consumption (Million Metric Tons) | | 10-Year Increase | |
|---|---|---|---|---|
| | 1985 | 1995 | Mil. Tons | Percent |
| India | 5,778 | 7,820 | 2,042 | 35 |
| China | 6,178 | 12,570 | 6,492 | 105 |
| United States | 9,306 | 11,959 | 2,653 | 29 |
| Rest of the World | 40,266 | 60,163 | 19,897 | 49 |
| World Total | 67,306 | 92,512 | 25,206 | 37 |

*Source:* Oil World, ISTA Mielke GmbH, Hamburg, Germany

## COMMODITIES

Commodities differ from manufactured materials in that they tend to be large volume, fairly homogeneous materials that are bought and sold freely in markets where neither the buyer nor the seller has a negotiating advantage. A buyer can typically buy an additional increment of supply, and a producer sell, without affecting the price level. Agricultural commodities are often subject to price volatility, reflecting their tendency toward demand inelasticity and the difficulty in adjusting production in the short run. The historical price pattern of soybean oil, the largest vegetable oil commodity serves as a reference for other fats and oils (Figure 1). Tallow prices (Figure 2) have somewhat less short-term volatility but similar percentage swings from cyclical lows to highs.

Another characteristic of commodities is that the cost of transportation, storage, and financing of inventory are significant to the final delivered cost at time and place of actual usage. Thus, logistical management is an integral part of marketing and purchasing of commodity raw materials. Also, the risk of changes in the market price must be well-managed because the magnitude of short-term changes in the values can severely affect not only profit margins but the financial survival of a firm. Forced bankruptcy of companies involved in commodities is not uncommon. Risk management in commodities involves the use of a number of sophisticated hedging and risk-limiting tools but few are foolproof.

**Table 2.** World Fats and Oils Usage (17 Major Fats and Oils; Calendar 1995)

| Commodity | Usage (Mil. Metric Tons) | Percent of Total |
|---|---|---|
| "Soft Oils" | | |
| Soybean | 20.3 | 21.5% |
| Canola & Rapeseed* | 10.6 | 11.1% |
| Sunflower | 8.6 | 9.2% |
| Groundnut (Peanut) | 4.3 | 4.6% |
| Cottonseed | 3.9 | 4.2% |
| Olive | 1.9 | 1.9% |
| Corn | 1.8 | 2.2% |
| Sesame | 0.7 | 0.7% |
| **Subtotal:** | 52.1 | 55.4% |
| Palm Oil | 15.2 | 16.2% |
| Lauric Oils | | |
| Coconut | 3.3 | 3.5% |
| Palm Kernal | 1.9 | 2.1% |
| **Subtotal:** | 5.2 | 5.6% |
| Tallow & Grease | 7.6 | 8.1% |
| Butter (as fat) | 5.7 | 6.1% |
| Lard | 5.8 | 6.2% |
| Fish Oil | 1.1 | 1.2% |
| Linseed Oil | 0.7 | 0.7% |
| Castor Oil | 0.5 | 0.5% |
| **TOTAL:** | **93.9** | **100.0%** |

* Canola is low-erucic varieties; H.E. Rapeseed is high-erucuc varieties.
*Source:* "Oil World"

Tallow is one of the more difficult commodities on which to limit exposure to price risks. As a result, most transactions at a fixed price are for shipment or delivery within 1 or 2 months—versus as long as a year or so in other commodities where long-term hedging tools are available; for example soybean and soy product futures contracts on the Chicago Board of Trade.

## WORLD TRENDS

The world consumption of fats and oils has been in a relatively consistent uptrend of 2 to 3% annually. This compound growth rate has resulted in world consumption (and therefore production on a running average, since what is produced is consumed) increasing from 46 million metric tons in 1975 to 92 million in 1995. This growth is a combination of expanding population and rising per capita consumption, with forecasts by ISTA Mielke of Hamburg, Germany, the world's leading source of data on fats, oils, oilseeds, and proteins, shown in Table 3.

**Figure 1.**

**CRUDE SOYBEAN OIL PRICE
(DECATUR CASH BASIS)**

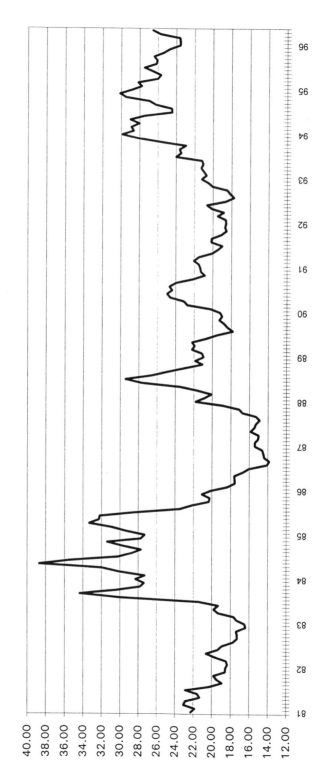

**Monthly Average**

**Figure 2.**

## TALLOW: BFT* PRICES
### Chicago

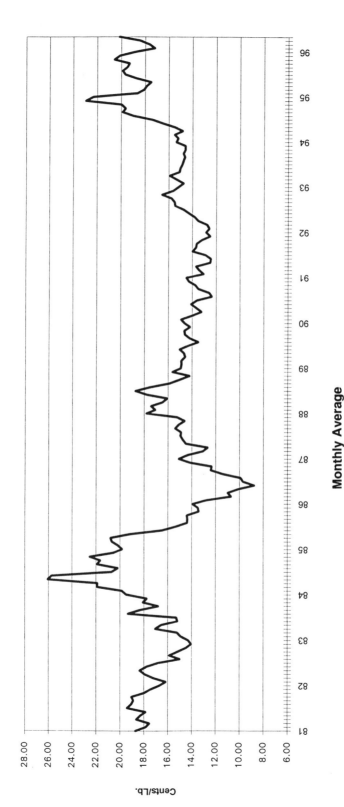

**Monthly Average**

*Bleachable Fancy Market Price

An important variable for future fats and oils markets is the growth rate in world consumption. There is a viewpoint that the rate may accelerate from the historical trend. An example of a recent increase that apparently reflects the country's economic growth and dietary changes, is in China. Over 2 recent years (beginning with the 1993/94 statistical crop year), consumption increased from 10.9 to 13.4 million tons. The growth was a copmbination of population growth of 95 million people and an increase in per-capita consumption from 9.2 to 11.0 kg.

**Table 3.** World Fats and Oils Consumption (Averages for 5-year Periods)

| 17 Major Fats and Oils | | | | |
|---|---|---|---|---|
| 5-Year Period | World Population (million) | Capita Usage (kilos) | Total Usage (mil. tons) | Total Tallow Usage (mil. tons) |
| 1973-77 | 4078 | 11.23 | 45.8 | 5.6 |
| 1978-82 | 4451 | 12.72 | 56.6 | 6.3 |
| 1983-87 | 4856 | 13.93 | 67.6 | 6.5 |
| 1988-92 | 5296 | 15.15 | 80.2 | 6.8 |
| 1993-97* | 5760 | 15.71 | 90.5 | 7.0 |
| 1998-02** | 6228 | 16.84 | 104.8 | 7.4 |
| 2003-07** | 6688 | 17.65 | 118.1 | 7.7 |
| 2008-12** | 7149 | 18.5 | 132.2 | 8.1 |

* Partly Forecast
** Forecast
# Of the 6.8 million metric ton usage, the U.S. used 2.0 million tons.
U.S. production was 3.3 million, of which 1.3 million tons was exported.
*Source:* "Oil World"; Population Data from United Nations

The declining share of tallow simply reflects the faster growth rate in vegetable oil supplies. Production of the latter are relatively easy to increase through expanded crop acreage, whereas byproduct animal fat production is relatively unresponsive to its demand and price. An important economic incentive for their production is the disposal of the slaughter byproducts and the trimmings of the fat from the carcass as it is broken down into portions for the final consumer. Their conversion into fat and protein products via the rendering process represents an effective, efficient, environmentally-sound disposal operation.

As tallow's share of total fats and oils supply continues its expected decline, its pricing may be at a smaller discount to the vegetable oils; i.e. less of a price discount is needed to "clear the market."

## PRODUCTION AND CONSUMPTION DYNAMICS

The market dynamics of the production and consumption of fats and oils are one of the more complex of any group of agricultural commodities. The supply is subject to the vagaries of the weather; the competition for cropland from non–oil-bearing crops; cycles in the livestock and poultry industries; consumer and industrial demand as affected by business cycles; and changes in world political events and trade policy. Adding complexity are two other factors: production dynamics and consumption dynamics.

Production consists of a combination of byproducts, co-products, and primary products. While tallow and grease may be perceived as byproducts of meat production, they are equally, or greater, a byproduct of an environmental disposal service. Table 4 categorizes the production mode of the major fats and oils. One analogy of the mix of production modes may be the hydrocarbon complex of intermediate feedstocks derived from petroleum and natural gas. Some of these petrochemicals could compete with oleochemicals from the "natural" fats and oils; eg, in surfactants and, in a limited way, lubricants.

Consumption dynamics involve numerous types of substitutability. There are varying time lags and degrees of price and non-price incentives in changing the total quantity used and substitution of one material for another.

The "consumption" of fats and oils in human food products occurs in two forms. One is the actual ingestion as part of the diet. The second is as a mechanism in food preparation for heat transfer and for imparting desirable flavors. Fats discarded from the cooking process (called "restaurant grease") in commercial activities, to be replaced by fresher material, are generally recovered for use in non-food products; for example in poultry and animal feeds and oleochemicals.

## Weather Factors

Examples of the more critical weather variables in the world that affect the major vegetable oil crops are August rainfall in the United States and January rainfall in Brazil and Argentina for soybeans; the Indian monsoon for the groundnut (peanut) and rapeseed crops; summer rainfall and absence of early freezes in Canada and Russia for the canola and sunflower crops, respectively. The commodity markets are sensitive to these and other potential threats and are quick to anticipate, frequently prematurely and excessively, potential crop damage.

For livestock and poultry, extreme heat or cold can accelerate death losses or slow weight gains.

Table 4. Major Sources and Uses of Triglycerides and Their Fatty Acids

| | Fatty Acid Chain Lengths (No. of Any Double Bonds) and Name | | | | | | |
| Major Source As: | C8/10 Capric/ Caprylic | C12/14 Lauric/ Myristic | C16 Palmitic | C18 Stearic | C18 (1) Oleic | C18(2)/(3) Linoleic/ Linolenic | C20/22 Arachidic/ Behenic |
|---|---|---|---|---|---|---|---|
| Primary Product | Coconut and Palm Kernal | Palm (whole) | Palm (whole) | Olive; Canola; Groudnut | Sun; Canola | Rape (high-erucic) | |
| Co-Product | | | Palm Stearine Butter | | Soy Butter Palm Olein | Soy | Fish |
| By-Product | | | Tallow | Tallow | Tallow | Cotton Corn | |

## Supply and Demand for the Protein and Fat/Oil Sectors

The terms "surplus" and "scarcity" are often used. In theory, supply and demand are always in balance at some given price level; however there can be a time lag in achieving the balance. In some cases, artificial impediments (government price programs) to the mechanics of free markets may disrupt the balance supply against demand.

The production of by- and co-products may have little or no responsiveness to price—or to the immediate volume needs of customers. For example, the price of cottonseed oil has little effect on the amount of cotton grown. Conversely, with coconut oil, more than 80% of the total product value derived from the production of coconuts for the oil market, is from the oil itself.

Most of the year-to-year changes in the production volume of fats and oils is the result of variation in vegetable oil output. There are 2 components of the change:

1. The production of the oilseeds (including coconuts and the fruits of the oil palm tree), ie the size of the crops.

2. The rate of processing (or crushing) the available oilseed supplies into the oil and meal products; eg, if all of the crop is not needed within the marketing year, the unneeded oilseeds are held in inventory for later processing.

For example, the crushing (conversion into oil and meal) of soybeans, the largest source of vegetable oils, is generally driven by the demand for soybean meal, a high-protein supplemental feed for animals and poultry. Infrequently, when the supply of fats and oils is low, crushing will be driven by the oil demand, with meal the byproduct.
Conversely, the crushing of high–oil-content oilseeds such as sunflower, canola, or groundnut, with their 40% or more oil content (versus about 18% for soybeans) and lower protein content in their meal, is influenced more by the oil price.

Table 4 summarizes the factors affecting production and processing rates of the major vegetable oils.

In normal market conditions, the supply/demand balance of the protein meal products is aligned reasonably well with the balance in the fats and oils sector. Supplies are neither burdensome nor tight; price levels and price differentials between related materials are close to historical norms. A common measurement of the relative condition of these two sectors is a simple calculation based upon the relative value of the products of a 60-lb bushel of soybeans: about 11 lb of oil and 48 lb of meal.

The calculation is:

[oil price/lb X 11] X 100 = soybean oil's percent of product value
—————————————————————————————————————————————
[oil price/lb X 11]  +  [meal price/lb X 48]

The percentage share provided by oil in normal markets tends to be between 30 and 40%. In unusual conditions it has been as low as 20% (oil supplies in surplus and/or meal in tight supply) and over 50%. (oil supplies tight and/or meal in surplus).

Once one of the sectors gets out of balance, supply/demand forces react to restore a balance; for example changes in the acreage of annual oilseed crops. The reaction can over-correct or new developments can arise to cause an over correction to an opposite extreme. A dramatic example of the potential for extremes occurred in the early 1970s and provides a case study of the interaction among the related sectors.

## Case Study

The extreme example of volatility in production and prices of agricultural commodities involving fats and oils occurred in the early 1970s as a result of an unusual sequence of production shortfalls. The sequence, with their impacts on fats and oils, including tallow, were as follows:

1.  The Peruvian anchovy catch, and therefore production of high-protein fish meal, was radically reduced by an "El Nino" weather condition which warmed the ocean water temperature along the Peruvian coast and caused the fish to move away. World prices for protein meals skyrocketed, with US soybean meal (Decatur, Illinois freight basis) rising from about $50 per short ton to a temporary peak of $400. All available oilseed supplies were crushed to replace the shortfall in fish meal supplies. Vegetable oil output expanded far above prevailing consumption rates, causing inventories to build and prices to decline.

2.  A series of major yield shortfalls in feed grain crops led to very high prices which, in fact, were needed to reduce consumption rates to match available supply. Restricted feed supply forced reduction in the number of cattle and hogs fed grain, with some cattle marketed at lower weights and therefore with less recoverable fat for rendering into tallow. The limited supplies of meat became a consumer and political issue. Less-tender ""grass-fed" beef cuts

(which produced less byproduct tallow) were marketed. Restrictions were placed on US exports of certain agricultural commodities that were in short supply.

Tallow prices increased, and there was insufficient supply to maintain normal usage rates.   The tire manufacturing industry was concerned about adequate supplies of oleic fatty acids needed to make tires.

3.   The fewer animals on feed reduced the consumption of protein meal, and the abundant oil and low meal supply imbalance was reversed.   There was strong demand for soybean oil—much greater than the demand for soybean meal.  Soybeans were "crushed for oil," and meal inventories increased.  (Large quantities of meal are far more difficult to store than large quantities of oil.)

4.   This whipsaw effect lasted until late 1975 when large crops were harvested, easing the supply tightness.   This series of events was unusual in timing and severity.

The probability of the events of the early 1970s recurring exactly the same way are remote.  However, severe dislocations are undoubtedly inevitable given the vulnerability of supply to weather.  Also, with less involvement of the US government in maintaining reserve inventories of grains can add to the possibility of greater price reaction to production shortfalls.

## Balancing World Supply and Demand for Fats and Oils

Historically, the world-wide supply–demand balance has tended to cycle irregularly, and largely unpredictably, from large price-depressing supplies (relevant to prevailing consumption) to tight balances which often trigger extreme upward price volatility.  In some cases, prices must go high enough to force reduction in usage rates to match available supply.

A frequent cause of production shortfalls is reduced yields per acre of oil crops as a result of adverse weather conditions.  For example, drought can reduce the US soybean crop 15 to 25%.  Planted acreage may be low as a result of government planting restrictions, or prices for the crop being too low relative to other crops competing for the same acreage.  Biological cycles cause yield variations of coconut and oil palm crops.

Price advances triggered by actual or potential shortfalls in agricultural commodity crops are often overdone, driven by speculative enthusiasm. The higher prices can lead to larger-than-needed increases in production The latter can be compounded by unusually favorable weather coincidentally producing above-normal yields in annual crops. And the biological processes of tree crops, such as oil palm and coconut, often compensate for a year of low yields (caused by drought or other stress) by above-normal yields in the following year.

## Tallow Price Dynamics

The price of inedible animal fats, typically at the low end of the fats and oils complex because they are limited to the non-food use, is usually affected by higher-priced vegetable oils creating a ceiling. This relationship is reflected in Figure 3 which tracks the price of the inedible bleachable fancy grade of tallow versus crude soybean oil. The affects at the high and low phases of the overall price cycle can be described as follows:

**Large Supplies and Low Prices**—With inedible prices unable to maintain parity with vegetable oils (except briefly), the latter represents a price ceiling.

**Limited Supplies and High Prices**—As vegetable oil prices increase, the price ceiling is lifted to higher levels, and demand for tallow increases as users who can substitute switch to the lower cost tallow.

An example is when soybean oil is 15¢/lb (Decatur, Illinois, basis, prompt shipment), tallow prices will typically be in the 10 to 13¢ range (delivered Chicago). Conversely, soybean oil at 30¢/lb allows tallow prices to be in the mid 20s if the tallow supply/demand balance can support that price level. Tallow prices have never held at soybean oil prices for an extended period.

When extremely large supplies of fats and oils depress prices, the use of tallow in livestock and poultry feed can increase, thereby increasing the total offtake of fats and oils. For example, in the mid 1980s, tallow prices declined to less than 10¢/lb, delivered Chicago. (The equivalent price at a producing plant in the Great Plains would have been about 8¢/lb.) At that level, it became economical to feed tallow to beef cattle in feedlots. (The cost analysis basically evaluates the value of the caloric energy in the tallow to the cost of alternative feedstuffs, eg, corn. The rule of thumb is that tallow is worth about 2-1/2 times the price of corn, possibly somewhat more.) A beef animal on feed for 4 to 5 months can consume as much tallow (at about 1 lb/day) as the animal will yield upon slaughter and processing. Conversely, high price levels will cause a partial reduction in the amount fed as feed formulations are changed.

In other words, the tallow production industry contains within itself one of the major supply-adjustment mechanisms for the world fats and oils complex.

Low tallow prices have limited effect in reducing production. The raw material from which it is rendered must be disposed of in an environmentally acceptable manner--and rendering is the most economically efficient.

## TALLOW AND GREASE PRODUCTION

The production of animal fats is a function of the number of animals (mainlly cattle and hogs) slaughtered, the amount of fat on the animals and the amount of fatty tissue trimmed and recovered for rendering into fat and protein meal. The economic drivers are as summarized in the following table.

1. Number of Animals Produced
   a. Feeding profitability (mostly a function of the price of live animals, cost of feed and feeding efficiency).
   b. Consumer demand for meat.
   c. Market Psychology; e.g. anticipated feeding profitability.

2. Amount of fat on animal
   a. Long term: genetic design of animals (guided by consumer preferences).
   b. Feeding practices; i.e. how long fed. Additional weight adds disproportionately more fat than lean. This is done if profitable or anticipate higher live animal prices through delayed sale of animals.

3. Percentage of Body Fat Trimmed off
   a. Consumer preference for leaner retail cuts.
   b. Processing and retail merchandising practices.

4. Percentage of Trimmed Fat Rendered
   a. Processing practices; trimming more fat at slaughtering plant Tallow and Protein Meal increases amount recovered for rendering.
   b. Price of tallow and protein meal; e.g. when prices extremely low and renderers charge for hauling away raw material, small amounts may not be rendered.

## Competitive Materials for Tallow

The alternative raw materials for tallow vary by geographic area. Obviously, there is less competition near the place of large-volume production such as the middle of the United States. Tallow faces more competition in countries that are net importers fats and oils. An example is Egypt where tallow from the United States competes with palm oil stearine from Malaysia.

Competitive cost analysis must incorporate the total delivered cost at the point of usage. For example, even in the United States, the delivered cost of palm oil stearine at an ocean portside plant can be competitive against certain qualities of tallow that must be shipped from mid-United States. Figure 4 provides price comparisons for tallow and palm oil stearine. Note that any price comparison must be based on specific grades and qualities. For example, there can be 2 to 4 ¢/lb difference between the price for bleachable fancy tallow and edible tallow, a top grade increasingly used for non-food applications.

The production of palm oil stearine can be a byproduct of the production of palm oil olein for cooking oil purposes (in competition against soy and other "soft oils"). The demand for olein varies and therefore the production of the stearine and the degree it must be price discounted to displace tallow and other materials in order to dispose of the inventory. If the demand for palm olein is low, and the demand for stearine is high, the price of the now-primary-product stearine can escalate sharply.

Another alternative to tallow is coconut oil in those producing countries. Government or religious restrictions can also be a factor. India prohibits the importation of tallow for soap making. Byproduct C16-18 fractions from the production of C12-14 alcohols and methyl esters from the major plant expansions in southeast Asia are relatively new competition for tallow. These plants use coconut oil (about 19% C16/18) and palm kernal oil (about 26% C16/18) as feedstocks.

## THE PETROCHEMICAL-OLEOCHEMICAL ALTERNATIVE

The major substitution alternative between natural fats and oils and hydrocarbon feedstocks has been for the $^{12}$C-$^{14}$C surfactant intermediates. The "synthetic" alternative is made from ethylene or benzene which are derived from natural gas. The development of the Ziegler process provided a hydrocarbon-based feedstock alternative to coconut oil which then was the vegetable oil alternative. The latter was noted for its weather-vulnerability and relatively narrow geographic supply base which spawned periodic price spirals. (Prior to the early-mid 1980s, palm kernel oil supplies were inadequate to be competitive in large non-food applications.)

The potential for alternative choices between tallow and oleochemical feedstocks is addressed in other sections of this book.

## ENVIRONMENTAL ISSUES

Beginning in the 1970s, environmental questions arose relative to the biodegradability of "natural" surfactants derived from fats and oils versus the "synthetics." Also, the coincidental price spirals in petroleum markets, and fears of petroleum cartels interfering with supply availability, shifted attention to the potential longer-term of "renewable" agricultural raw material supplies versus the ultimately finite supply of fossil fuels.

Subsequent holistic studies of the environmental effect of "natural" versus "synthetic"alternatives indicate that neither provides a clear advantage overall.  And the return to relatively stable hydrocarbon supply and prices, along with the end of predictions of imminent supply shortfalls and cartel withholding, tempered the move toward "naturals," with decisions being made on the basis of shorter-term economics.

The tallow interface with petrochemicals has been limited.  High petroleum prices created temporary interest in using tallow derivatives as fuel in internal combustion engines.  More recently, the Clean Air Act of 1995 created a possible opportunity to use natural fats or oils as one method to meet tighter emissions requirements in diesel engines in specified metropolitan areas with air pollution problems. The impact of these regulations is, as yet, unclear.

**Figure 3.**

**TALLOW/SBO: PRICE DIFFERENTIAL**
**Chicago BFT vs Decatur SBO**

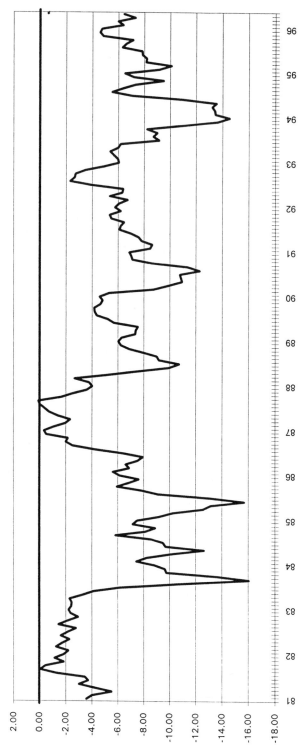

**Monthly Average**

Bleachable fancy tallow versus crude soybean oil (decatur); SBO baseline (Chicago)

**Figure 4.**

# PRICES: BFT & PALM OIL STEARINE

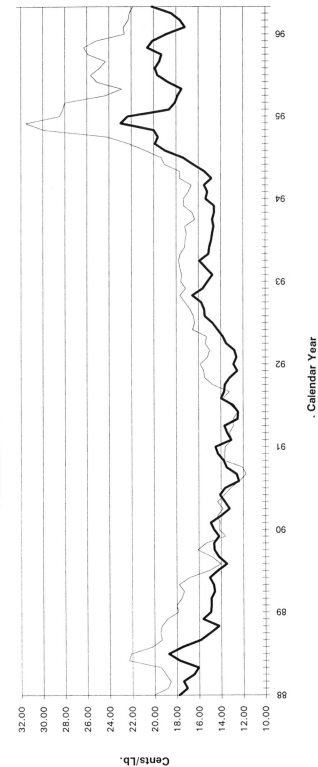

BFT: Bleachable fancy tallow (Chicago) Palm Oil stearine: Refined, bleached, deodorized (RBO) C/F U.S. Gulf/East coast ports

**Table 5.** Main Causes of Variation in Production of Major Vegetable Oils

- - - - - - - - **Sources of Production Variation** - - - - - - - -

| Crop | Oil Source | Oilseed Production | Crushing (Convert to Oil and Meal) |
|------|-----------|--------------------|-----------------------------------|
| Soybean | Soybeans | - Acreage (competition from alternate crops for land)<br>- Yields per acre | - Demand for meal (number of consuming-animal units and feeding rate/unit) |
| Canola & Sunflower | Canola & Sunflowers seeds, respectively | - Same as soybeans (but usually different competitive crops) | - Demand for oil |
| Cottonseed | Cottonseed | - Cotton acreage (price of cotton and competing crops, such as soybeans) | - Demand for oil; competition from feeding whole cottonseed |
| Palm* | Oil Palm Fruit (pulp portion) | - Acreage of producing trees<br>- Fruit yield (function of rainfall, sunlight, multi-year yield cycle, seasonality) | - No variation as fruit, must be processed within a few days after harvest--which cannot be delayed |
| Palm Kernel* | Oil Palm Fruit Kernel | - Same as palm oil (kernel oil is by-product in oil palm fruit; 11-12% of palm oil volume) | - Demand for oil; kernals can be stored and crushed up to about one year later |
| Coconut | Copra (dried coconut meat) | - Similar to oil palm but not as sensitive to low sunlight | - Demand for oil; copra can be stored for several months |

* Palm oil (from the pulp portion of the fruitlet of the oil palm tree) and palm kernel oil (from the kernel, or seed, in the fruitlet) are distinctly different vegetable oils in chemical composition, usage application and, typically, the higher price for the kernel oil. Palm oil is high in the C16 and 18 fatty acids, while the kernel oil is high in C12 and 14, and is similar to coconut oil.

# 6

# Tallow Usage and Oleochemicals— Soap Products and Fatty Acids

## Kenneth A Halloran

## ANIMAL FATS— ORIGINS, HISTORY, AND COMPETITION

From the time mankind began slaughtering animals to produce food and clothing, animal byproducts have played a role in our culture. Principal among these byproducts was the fat that resulted from cooking the meat.

Today the industry commonly uses the term "rendering" to describe the process whereby the fatty or oily materials in meat is melted away from the solid protein in an animal carcass. Quite likely the term arose from the sacrifice of animals to "render thanks to God." Thus our current rendering industry may have been divinely inspired millennia ago.

In this text I use the term tallow for all animal fats. However the fats of commercial importance are beef (bovine) fat and mutton (ovine) fat, which are true tallows. A third major commercial catgegory is hog (porcine) fat which is normally referred to as grease or lard. If other ruminants (goat, camel, llama, deer, and so forth) were ever to become commercially attractive, the hardness (higher melt point) of their fat would designate them as tallows, as well. The industry's primary distinction between a tallow and a grease remains their relative "hardness." This is measured by a melt point type test called the titer. A true melt point is not achievable on these fats since they are a mixture of chemicals. Temperature of liquefaction can only be approximated. The greases in general are softer.

Hardness or softness is just one of several key quality characteristics of animal fats that determines their suitability for use as a chemical raw material. Since tallows are used as raw material precursors across a broad spectrum of product applications, their actual chemical compositions become very important. Soaps and candles may be the first products to come to mind for tallow usage. However, today, their application ranges from rubber, paints, cosmetics, plastics, and pharmeceuticals to explosives and beyond. Several of these will be addressed in detail to illustrate the importance attached to physical and chemical characteristics when planning their usage in a product application.

## COMMERCIAL PROSPECTS FOR TALLOWS

Tallow has been used probably since mankind lived in caves. In today' competitive environment however just 2 considerations illustrate the current and future commercial aspects of tallow utilization:

- Tallow is a byproduct of a primary industry (animal slaughter).

- Tallow has significant competition both from other naturally derived oils and fats (oleochemicals) and from petrochemicals.

As a byproduct, disposing of tallow becomes a marketing opportunity if its consumption is to be sustained long term at the best possible financial return. Such a return should cover the cost of production and give a reasonable profit—an ever-increasing challenge as the decades go by.

As in most other aspects of our society, the 20th century has produced more changes, more rapidly to the rendering industry than occurred in the preceding 1900 years. The early 1900s through the early post-World War II years witnessed a vast growth in both the meat packing and the rendering businesses. Most of this was in the small business category including many "mom and pop" businesses. Evolution from the 1950s through the 1980s was so radical as to be almost a revolution within these industrial bases.

Pork led the way into centralization of the slaughtering operation much earlier than beef. Providing ready-to-cook or ready-to-eat products was a key point. The Iowa Beef Processors' introduction of "boxed-beef" in 1962 was a concept that shook the beef-packing and tallow-rendering industries. Coupled with this was the introduction and massive installation of high capacity, continuous rendering plants for both edible and inedible operations. This completed the industry transition around 1990.

By the mid-1980s independent renderers in North America numbered fewer than 5% of those who had been in business in 1960. The local butcher shop that supplied the raw material to the renderers is now a rare commodity, too. It is also hard to find a talented butcher at a supermarket anymore. As the industry continues into portion packs and ready-to-eat items the raw material fat trimmings used by the local renderers will be virtually gone, and the industry will basically have consolidated at the packing plant level.

The regional and local business for the remaining independent renderers is now predominately the collection and recycling of "restaurant grease" from fast-food outlets. This recycling process requires no cooking or rendering, per se, since these fast-food frying oils are 99% vegetable oils, and mostly soybean-derived. The volume for this restaurant recycle grease is nearing 2 billion lb annually. The use of vegetable oils exclusively by the fast-food industry began in the 1990s when the largest, McDonalds, stopped using edible tallow for potatoes in its response to public concern about animal fats, cholesterol, and heart problems This is an issue not fully understood technically or medically even today.

## TALLOW USAGE IN BAR SOAPS

The modern era in bar soap products began around the turn of the century. Mass production techniques soon followed the introduction of Ivory Soap. Beef tallow was to become the mainstay of bar soap formulation and in general continues to this day on a global basis. Formulations center around 70 to 80% tallow and 20 to 30% lauric oil (coconut) blend. The active surfactant that produces the soap lather is the sodium—neutralized fatty acids contained in the oils. Neutralization was accomplished by simply boiling the blended tallow and coconut oil with a dilute caustic solution, usually sodium hydroxide, in a large kettle. Eventually soap was boiled in 300,000-lb (150-metric ton) kettles. "Art" came into play with the need to control the boiling operation to keep the kettle contents "rolling"from top to bottom to complete the chemical reaction without the soap overflowing the kettle. Every kettle operator has stories of the last kettle boil—over.

The kettle soap operation involved the use of salt, water, and minor additives, along with the tallow/coconut oil fatty blend, in fairly precise quantities. Live steam was injected into the kettle bottom as a source of heat and agitation. Maintaining temperatures in the 190 to 205°F range was essential for the process to proceed. Additional heat was provided by closed steam coils in the bottom third of the kettle. After the chemical reaction was completed, and at least 98% of the fat was saponified or neutralized, 2 additional finishing steps were required to achieve final quality limits.

The first step was to produce a "grainy soap" in the kettle. The excess water and salt used in the reaction phase would be settled out over several days and then removed. This settling and decanting step increased the "real soap" from about 50% to 65%. The balance was mostly water with small amounts of unreacted fat along with some salt and glycerine.

Settling was a very important step since most impurities in the fat were essentially removed with the water/glycerine phase. Then a finishing step followed to"smooth out" the neat soap before further processing.

Glycerine is a valuable byproduct of the soap manufacturing process. Fats and oils occur in nature as triglycerides. The glycerine is a polyol containing 3 carbon atoms with a hydroxyl group attached to each carbon. The triglyceride consists of a triester with a fatty acid attached to each hydroxyl group. Saponification of a natural fat or oil splits the fatty acid from the glycerine backbone and produces the sodium salt of each fatty acid, the active sudsing and cleaning chemical in soap. Glycerine is of course the byproduct of soap making and is produced at a purity of more than 99% by distilling the water/glycerine/salt mixture settled out of the kettle operation.

The boiling and settling operation is a very good purification process that removes most of the noxious impurities that could come in with the fatty material feedstock, particularly the animal fats. The continuous saponification soap making plants that were primarily developed and installed between 1960 and 1980 were not as efficient in removing impurities. Thus, it became necessary that these fatty impurities not be introduced to these continuous processes. By the 1980s, to prevent the introduction of impurities, soap makers began to replace inedible grades of tallow (bleachable fancy and top white tallow) with edible tallow. By the 1990s virtually all bar soap manufacturers in the United States were using edible tallow as their only tallow feed stock simply because  continuous soap-making operations now predominate. Today's consumers also do not tolerate minor odor and color impurities. Then edible tallow became available at attractive prices for inedible uses, such as soap, when it became unpopular to use it at fast-foot outlets to deep-fry potatoes.

Meat packers supply edible tallow, since the material feedstock to rendering comes from the meat-cutting floor under government supervision. The rendering process is government regulated, as well, and is a continuous operation in stainless-steel equipment designed for easy cleaning and sterilization. This type of equipment was originally installed by meat packers to meet 2 market demands, both of which justified the capital outlay. Bony solids from edible rendering were a gelatin feedstock for photographic film emulsions—a growing demand in the 1970s and 1980s. Additionally, the edible tallow was the "special flavor" component for McDonald french fries and others.

The shift of edible tallow from fast-food outlets to soap manufacturers provided an outlet for the fat and avoided capital cost outlays by the meat packers. They would presumably have had to increase inedible rendering if all these rendering feedstocks had to be diverted to their inedible side. In recent years, a price premium in the $0.03/lb range for edible tallow has met both the producers (meat packers) and consumers (soap makers) requirements at a cost-effective level for both.

These factors continue to be important in addressing future marketing opportunities for the tallow industry.

## QUALITY REQUIREMENTS FOR SOAP TALLOW

The American Fats & Oils Association (AFOA) standards have been used to define the physical limits of the technical grades of tallows and greases (Table 1). The AFOA is a trade industry association that standardizes the trading rules and arbitration aspects for marketing these materials. In the past the AFOA dealt principally with the animal fat categories. But in recent years they have added rules for several other categories.

Soapers in the 20th century have formulated bar soap products around the use of bleachable fancy tallow. However, in the early 1950s Procter & Gamble initiated a quality improvement agenda with the independent renderers to obtain a step-wise improvement in bleachable fancy tallow quality. This was the genesis of the top white tallow quality level for tallow which AFOA later recognized and incorporated into grading rules.

**Table 1. AFOA Trading Guidelines—Better Grades of Animal Fat**

| Grades | Titer Min C | Free Fatty Acid % | Color FAC ** | RB Color Max. Lovibond | MIU* |
|--------|-------------|-------------------|--------------|------------------------|------|
| Edible | 41.0 | 0.75 | 3 | none | *** |
| Top White (Top White Tallow) | 41.0 | 2.0 | 5 | 0.5 | 1.0 |
| Packer Beef | 42.0 | 2.0 | — | 0.5 | 1.0 |
| Extra Fancy | 42.0 | 2.0 | 5 | — | 1.0 |
| Bleachable Fancy | 40.5 | 4.0 | — | 1.5 | 1.0 |
| Choice White Grease | 36.0 | 4.0 | 13-11B | — | 1.0 |

\*   Moisture, impurities and unsaponifiables
\*\*   Fats analysis committee method
\*\*\* Moisture maximum expected -- 0.10%; insoluble impurities maximum—0.05%

Between buyer and seller, a common practice is to specify the limits for the moisture, insolubles, and unsaponifiables separately with an expected moisture maximum of 0.3% for a top white tallow or equivalent quality. Other characteristics such as the iodine value (measures unsaturation) and the rate of filtration are important in some applications. Rate of filtration is important in order to avoid emulsification problems in the high-pressure hydrolysis process to make the fatty acids.

In the late 1930s, Procter & Gamble, developed a continuous soap making operation to increase making capacity for granular laundry soap products for the emerging washing machine market. "Goodbye" to hand laundry using soap bars and wash boards."Hello," Chipso, Oxydol, and Duz soap granules.

Rather than build more soap kettles to boil soap, which would have required enormous acreage and a 7-day per kettle cycle, P&G installed continuous fat-splitting equipment called hydrolyzers operating at pressures of 700 psi and temperatures of 495°F. A fat/water mixture, without caustic could be used to "split" a fat into its fatty acid and glycerine components. This allowed a continuous feed and offtake of both products. After distillation the fatty acid was fed into a continuous in-line neutralizer for saponification with dilute sodium hydroxide to make the sodium soap of the fatty acids. Other stabilizing agents were also added along with the lye. The crude glycerine produced, containing 70 to 80% glycerine (versus about 12% from a kettle boil), is sent to the glycerine recovery operation.

This continuous splitting and neutralizing process could produce a kettle of soap in one day versus the 7 days required in the most efficient counter-current flow kettle process. World War II slowed some consumer applications of these technologies in favor of an emphasis on the war effort.

Glycerine production to manufacture explosives was mandatory and tallow availability of any quality was emphasized. Nevertheless, by 1946 Procter & Gamble was using more than 1 billion lb of tallow annually for both soap granules and bars. But, in late 1946, the world of tallow was forever changed with the introduction of synthetic detergents for laundry products used in the new automatic washing machines. Tide revolutionized laundering and nearly eliminated tallow usage in the laundry process by 1950.

The use of tallow was then focused on synthetic rubber production, automotive tire compounding, plastics, paints, etc. Today its major consumption is in the oleochemicals industry.

Parallel with development of the Procter & Gamble hydrolyzer process was the competitve introduction of the Colgate/Emery continuous splitting process, a non-catalytic operation. Procter & Gamble used a zinc oxide catalyst that enabled through-put rates 3 to 4 times faster than the non-catalytic process. The zinc oxide catalyst entailed additional handling and disposal problems which were dealt with separately.

At Procter & Gamble, the Ivory Bar soap adapted well to the hyrolyzer process while using bleachable fancy tallow quality. However, Camay, introduced as Procter & Gamble's first milled bar toilet soap in the 1920s, was not so forgiving. The more delicate perfumery aspects of the competitive milled bar markets, as well as color and odor stability on shelf aging required new emphasis if Camay were to be made by the continuous splitting and neutralization process. The overwhelming success of synthetic laundry products left a lot of fatty soap plant capacity available. The successful conversion of Camay soap from kettles to hydrolyzer depended on Procter & Gamble's ability to reduce the color and odor impurities in the tallow feedstock, and to partially hydrogenate ("touch harden") the fatty acid produced to improve odor and color stability by reducing the aldehydes and ketones (carbonyls), the precursors to instability arising via this continuous process.

Touch hardening was installed by 1954 at the Camay production plants using a fixed-bed nickel catalyst continuous in-line process, fed with distilled fatty acids to avoid catalyst poisoning.

The tallow rendering process was improved only with the excellent co-operation of hundreds of independent renderers across the United States and Canada.  The result was the establishment of a top white tallow grade in sufficient volume to meet the needs of not just Camay milled bars but all subsequent Procter & Gamble milled bar introductions, as well as some competitive brands.  These improvements in color and impurities were achieved at the renderers principally through their improved feedstock selection, use of batch rendering for the first dozen years or so, and careful control of the rendering process variables.  Total segregation of the tallow produced was most important as well.  This decades-long program is just one example of teamwork in a customer-multisupplier total quality approach (TQA) program long before teams and TQA appeared in the industrial lexicon.

From the mid-1950s until the early 1980s when soapers started to use edible tallow, top white tallow was their feedstock of choice.  By 1996 very little top white tallow was produced nor was there economic incentive to do so.

## EDIBLE TALLOW IN SOAP FORMULATION TODAY

The execution of a complete milled bar formulation has been treated in a variety of ways over the years by myriad competitive companies worldwide.  The situation described above was just one of the major successful interactions between the rendering industry and the soap manufacturers.

A most significant development in the last few decades was the adoption by most multinational soap manufacturers of the continuous neutral fat saponification process (ConSap; Figure 1).   In the ConSap process a tallow/lauric oil blend is saponified directly with a dilute caustic solution. The resulting soap/glycerine/water mixture is then centrifugally separated into its component parts.  The soap phase contains about 65% real soap and the water phase about 30% glycerine.  The soap phase is then vacuum-dried to 12 to 15% water content and formed into dried noodles by a plodder.  Subsequent processing through mixers adds color, perfumes, or deodorants.  A final milling step produces the appropriate crystalline soap phase changes to achieve lathering and solubility performance. All of this is done in-line continuously with the stamping, wrapping, and casing operations.

Figure 1.

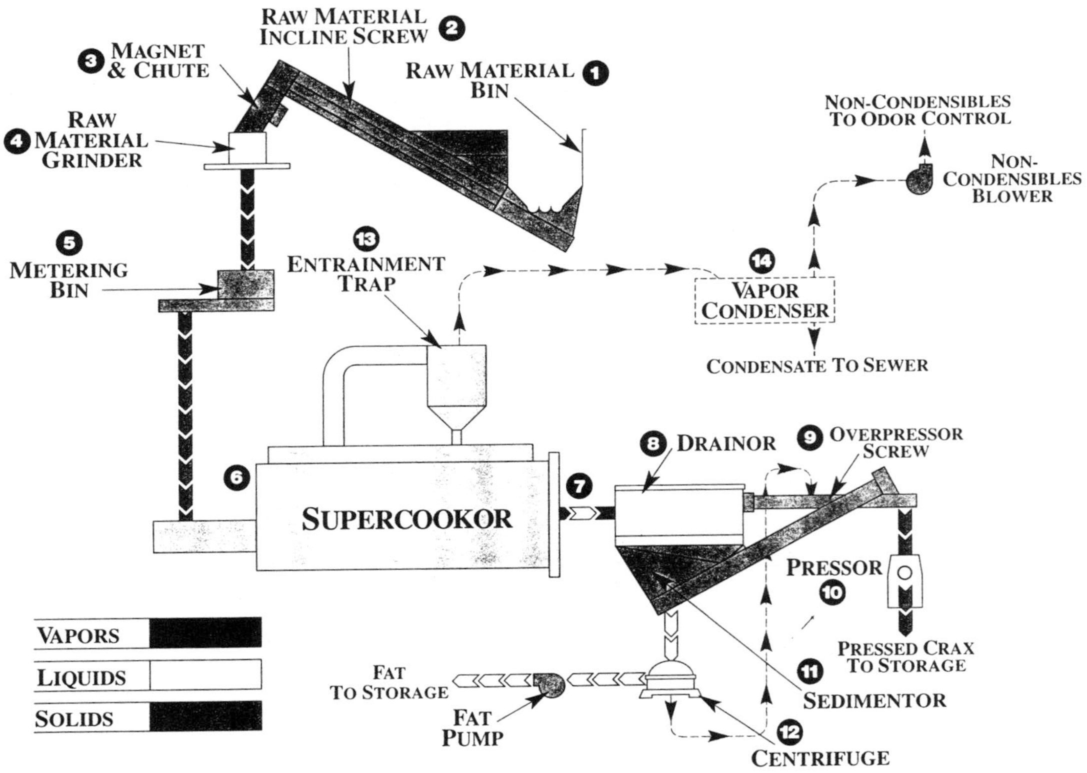

RAW MATERIAL BIN ❶
RAW MATERIAL INCLINE SCREW ❷
MAGNET & CHUTE ❸
RAW MATERIAL GRINDER ❹
METERING BIN ❺
ENTRAINMENT TRAP ❸
SUPERCOOKOR
DRAINOR ❽
OVERPRESSOR SCREW ❾
PRESSOR ❿
PRESSED CRAX TO STORAGE
SEDIMENTOR ⓫
CENTRIFUGE ⓬
FAT PUMP
FAT TO STORAGE
VAPOR CONDENSER ⓮
CONDENSATE TO SEWER
NON-CONDENSIBLES TO ODOR CONTROL
NON-CONDENSIBLES BLOWER

| VAPORS |
| LIQUIDS |
| SOLIDS |

The Mazzoni ConSap approach along with their compatible   drying, glycerine refining, mixing, stamping, and packaging protocol represents many of the early and continuing commercial installations.  A number of other companies also serve this growing market segment.  For a more detailed description see the references at the end of this chapter.

The ConSap equipment is nominally sized in the 5-thousand- to 10-thousand-lb/hour range of finished product.  Thus it has found broad acceptance among small producers, in small countries as well as with large multinationals.  Increased product demand is normally met by installing multiple units, particularly after the vacuum drying operation.

ConSap equipment suppliers usually have unique recommendations on how best to use their equipment.  It is of value here to note however that, at least in the North American market, when it comes to tallow quality the soap manufacturers in 1996 are predominately using edible grade.  We would expect this trend to continue into the next century, including hydrolyzer-made bar soaps.

Coupled with this, the lauric oils used (coconut or palm kernel) have been preprocessed by refining, bleaching, and deodorizing to improve their quality.  This is true whether the laurics are to be used in the base soap or are added for superfatting.

It is feasible to use a refined, bleached, and deodorized bleachable fancy tallow as a feed stock to a ConSap unit, but the economics are less attractive than those of using edible tallow.  If the edible/bleachable fancy tallow   premium differential remains at about the $0.03/lb level, edible tallow will continue to be preferred.

## THE RENDERING PROCESS & BAR SOAP QUALITY

The fat on a living animal is water-white and odorless and contains less than 0.5% free fatty acid.  Appropriate processing can produce fresh tallow of the same high quality.  The deterioration of tallow quality (color, odor, and free fatty acids) during rendering can be attributed to:

- excessive time to process
- improper process controls
- improper treatment or storage of finished tallow

The level of deterioration that has occurred can be easily measured by the free fatty acid level and more importantly by the color, particularly the red color as measured by the Lovibond method. The 2 color measurements used are as-is color and refined and bleached (RB) color.

The objective for the soap manufacturer is to use tallow as close as possible to the water-white, odorless, fresh tallow.  Thus the renderer's operation is an essential part in obtaining good quality soap.

The process may be either wet rendering or dry rendering (Table 2).

Table 2. Tallow Quality and Rendering Methods for Soap

| Specification | Inedible Dry Render Batch (1) | Edible Wet Render Continuous (2) | Continuous |
|---|---|---|---|
| Color (as is) | Basis | Poorer | Better + |
| Color-RB | Basis | Poorer | Better + |
| Odor | Basis | Poorer | Better + |
| Free Fatty Acid | Basis | Poorer | Better + Required Vacuum |
| Moisture %H O Drying Step (3) | Basis | Same | Drying |
| Impurities | Basis | Same | Better |
| Unsaponifiables | Basis | Same | Better |

1) The batch process offers better control of quality and segregation practices as well as the preferred lower cooking temperatures.

2) The continuous dry process offers higher production rates and generally lower operating costs. The disadvantages are higher cook temperatures and difficulty in maintaining uniform cooking times across the mass of material in the cooker.

3) Lower process temperatures($< 212^\circ$ F /$100^\circ$ C ) requires a final in line vacuum drying step to reduce the moisture to a 0.1% H O maximum. Higher moistures can activate enzymatic reactions that can produce higher FFA and sour odors during storage and transit. Difficult to handle foaming problems may also be seen.

Edible wet rendering entails boiling the raw materials in a vat of water, softening the cell wall tissue, and releasing the fat for subsequent separation. Operational temperatures range from 180 to 205°F (82 to 96°C). In dry rendering, the water is evaporated away from the fat and solid materials at atmospheric conditions. This process frees the fatty material from the solid bone and protein products (in successive steps) by dehydrating the tissues at operating temperatures ranging from 240 to 280°F (115 to 140°C) (Figure 2).

The wet method is no longer practiced for volume production of inedible tallow. However a continuous variation of it is used to produce nearly all edible grade tallow. The dry rendering method is conventionally done using either small batch cookers or continuous large volume cookers. It is the method of choice for all inedible tallows but is no longer approved for edible grade fat according to US Department of Agriculture protocols.

Since the late 1960s the continuous dry inedible process has been the first choice for most meat packer installations in their production of inedible tallow. The batch method retained popularity in certain quarters of the industry.

# Figure 2.

## *"SCNC-N"*    *CONTINUOUS NEUTRAL FAT SAPONIFICATION PLANT*

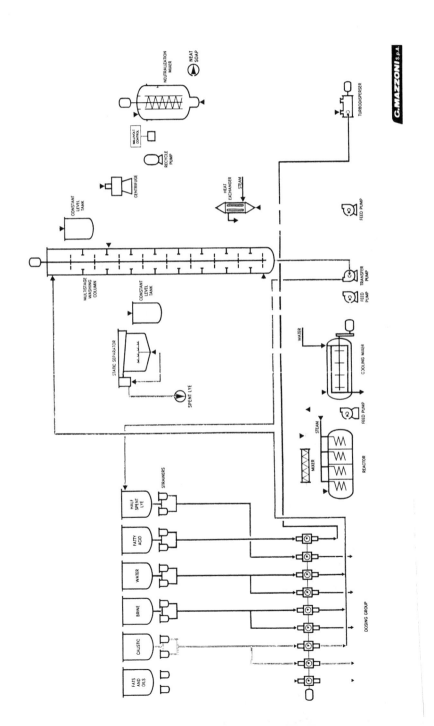

All rendering processes are designed to separate the 3 major components of the feedstocks—fat (or tallow), solids (bone and protein), water. Since the animal fat begins to deteriorate from the moment of slaughter, the tallow should be processed and separated as expeditiously as possible. It is important to remember that the cleanest feedstocks give the best tallow quality. If, for instance, manure and blood are allowed in the process, color and odor levels will be seriously compromised. Furthermore, a small amount of poor quality tallow will spoil a large amount of good tallow: The importance of good separation practices cannot be overemphasized.

The soap manfacturers' move to edible tallow was therefore made on very sound quality issues that directly addressed their needs for the ConSap soap-making process as illustrated in Table 2.

## GLOBAL COMPETITION FOR TALLOW IN BAR SOAP FORMULATIONS

The United States is the world's largest producer of tallow and greases with more than 50% of world production. Of all tallows produced, roughly half is of the better quality that can be used in soap products. In recent years the export market for these higher quality tallows has accounted for the disposition of about half of their total production. Technical grade tallow represents 30% of exports; the balance is edible. Lard and grease exports are also significant but they usually move to markets other than soap. Mutton tallow (sheep) is much less available globally and also suffers quality disadvantages relative to beef tallow for soap. It is used only if the local economics and quality parameters overwhelming favor it.

Worldwide all the animal fats represent only 15% of the total production of all fats and oils, which in 1995 was estimated at 93 million metric tons. By the year 2010 vegetable oil production is expected to rise to 132 million metric tons when animal fats will represent only 12% of total supply. (For more details on this refer to chapter 5 in this text.)

Utilization of tallow in the international markets is determined by a number of factors, including:

- regional or local tariffs
- religious restrictions
- availability of competing fats and oils
- consumer preferences
- formulation preferences (synthetic detergents, liquid or gel bath soaps)
- shipping variables (cost, quality degradation, availability)

In the last decade or so the availability of competitive materials has been significant. Chief among them is palm oil products. To better understand this interchangeability we should look at the chemical composition of the major oils (Table 3).

As the table shows, the animal fats are composed mostly of fatty acids with 16 or 18 carbon atoms in the fatty acid chain (~90%). In the world of oleochemicals, which includes soap, tallow can be used whenever chemical requirements call for a $^{16}C$ or $^{18}C$ chain length. The degree of saturation or unsaturation as measured by the iodine value is equally important to interchangeability. Processing options that can alter chain length distribution and the degree of unsaturation include fractionation, separation, cleavage, and hydrogenation. But, these processing options have a significant price tag, which might make them economically undesireable.

One need only look at the table's major vegetable oils category (85% of the world's supply) to see that that animal fats have $^{16}C$ and $^{18}C$ chain lengths in common with all but the lauric oils (coconut and palm kernel). Comparing just the chain length, tallow appears to face massive competition. But the higher degree of unsaturation of vegetable oils is generally a negative in applications in which tallow has excelled—soaps, emulsifiers, tire compounding, etc. The single exception is palm oil, whose iodine value is similar to that of tallow, which partially explains the interest in palm oil for soap formulations.

Vegetable oils generally contain fewer impurities than tallow; edible tallow, however, is on a par with vegetable oils in terms of "cleanness." In the end, the tallows have cost significantly less than most vegetable oils.

For bar soap applications, tallow has been partially replaced by palm oil and some palm stearine, particularly in the Middle and Far East, where shipping cost differentials mitigate the oil price disparity. Much of this usage is related to religious preferences, although Islamic countries will accept 100% beef tallow if so certified. The improving quality picture for commercial palm products is also a significant draw. Palm oil products are normally traded in refined, bleached, deodorized versions while tallow is not. However, when combined with the increased use of the ConSap process, the improved feedstock quality can have appeal in formulating bar soaps to meet performance standards expected by today's consumers.

Increasing production of palm oil in Malaysia and to a lesser extent in Indonesia, will keep the pressure on these producers to increase their market penetration. They have done this in recent years by continuing to offer high quality and process improvements at little extra cost to the user. There is no reason to believe they will change this approach.

Another global development that started in the early 1980s was the construction of a number of detergent fatty alcohol plants. The majority of these plants were built in Malaysia and elsewhere in the Far East. Detergent range fatty alcohols are based on the $^{12}C$ and $^{14}C$ chain lengths found in the lauric oils. These chain lengths are selected by fractionation of either the fatty alcohols or fatty esters and in some cases the fatty acids. The byproducts from this detergent alcohol processing are the short chains ($^8$C and $^{10}$C) and the longer chains ($^{16}$C and $^{18}$C), called heavy cuts. For palm kernel oil, the heavy cut portion is a nominal 25% of the feedstock to the alcohol process. With 2 billion to 3 billion lb of alcohol feedstock involved at full capacity, 500 million to 700 million lb of these heavy cuts may become available for disposition on the world market. This volume equates roughly to half of the current US technical grade tallow exports. These heavy cut byproducts will be priced to move either as alcohols, esters, or acids or a combination of all 3 chemicals. In some areas such fatty acid byproducts could compete with tallow acids.

## TALLOW USAGE FOR OTHER OLEOCHEMICALS

Tallow is composed of glycerine and fatty acids. Glycerine is the backbone of the molecule and to it are attached 3 fatty acid chains, creating a triglyceride.

Both the glycerine and the fatty acids are valuable commodity chemicals in the world market. The tallow fat is split into the component parts through a hydrolysis process in which water is added at moderately high pressure and temperature. Theoretically 100 lb of tallow yields 10 lb of glycerine and 97 lb of fatty acid. Some of the added water forms the hydroxyl groups on both the fatty acid and glycerine molecules.

In the United States, the overall market for triglyceride-derived fatty acid in 1996 was estimated to be about 1.4 billion lb annually. In addition, there is a market for an additional 400 million to 500 million lb of tall oil-derived fatty acids. These tall oil acids are the unsaturated versions of the $^{18}$C chain length and are recovered from crude tall oil. The crude tall oil is a byproduct from processing pine trees in the kraft paper pulp industry. The tall oil fatty acids by their very chemical make-up (refer to Table 3) find some usage in oleochemicals similar to those of the triglyceride-derived tallow fatty acid. Because tall oil fatty acids are 98% unsaturated acids, many of their uses differ from those of tallow.

In 1996, of the 1.4 billion lb of triglyceride acids, tallow will account for about 1 billion lb. European production and usage is about the same as in the United States. Worldwide, annual fatty acid consumption has been ranging between 4.5 billion and 5 billion lb, excluding tallow that goes directly into soap production. The potential for major increases in fatty acid consumption are present when one considers that Eastern Europe, Russia, and China could soon become major players.

## TALLOW FATTY ACID CONSUMPTION CATEGORIES

Several hundred categories of chemical processes and formulations use tallow fatty acids. Annual volumes consumed range from less than

1 million lb to more than 100 million lb annually, depending on the purpose.

- **Emulsion Polymerization—Rubber and Plastics**
  The polymerization of styrene and butadiene into SBR rubber is usually accomplished in an emulsion polymerization operation. A soluble soap made from a partially hydrogenated tallow acid is used to solubilize the reaction mass. The soap then remains as a part of the SBR. Approximately 80 million lb of tallow acid is consumed annually for SBR and in a similar emulsion process to manufacture acrylonitrile/butadiene/styrene (ABS) plastics. With the trends to longer tread life for both auto and truck tires this category may have limited growth potential although ABS plastic could have substantial growth in the transportation field.

- **Rubber Compounding**
  Approximately 75 million lb of a fully hydrogenated tallow fatty acid, also called rubber grade stearic acid, is used in rubber compounding annually. It is used in the form of zinc stearate made in situ with zinc oxide and is an accelerator for the vulcanization process. It remains in the compounded rubber where it can also act as a rubber lubricant.

- **Heavy Metal Salts**
  Metal stearates, principally as calcium and zinc, are used in 2 major applications. They are used as lubricants in the molding of plastics and for the manufacture of coated papers. The majority of these are hydrogenated tallow acids with the volume estimated at 150 million lb of acid per year.

- **Fabric Softeners**
  Quaternary ammonia salts are broadly used as fabric softeners in the United States and abroad. A major portion of the 140 million lb of fatty acid is tallow derived. The dimethyl dihydrogenated tallow ammonium chloride (or methyl sulfate) is a major player in this category. On a global basis there have been major shifts in this softener formula and thus it is difficult to make any firm trend predictions for the future, but shrinkage is probable.

- **Lubricants & Plasticizers**
  A limited capacity for the ozonolysis of oleic acid is available. Some of this oleic acid is derived by separation from tallow acid. The products from this process are the mono and dibasic $^9C$ acids which are then used in plasticizers and synthetic lubricants. The synthetic lubricants were developed for the high performance required in jet airplanes.

These lubricants have to be fluid at low temperatures (−50°C) and not decompose under engine-operating conditions. The backbone of the formulations manufactured according to precise military specifications, are called "hindered esters." They are made by reacting a blend of $^6$C to $^9$C fatty acids with a polyol, such as pentaerythritol, to form a polyester. Oleic acid consumption is in the 50 million lb range annually. Specific volumes for tallow have not been specified.

- **Other Categories**
  Tallow fatty acid appears in many other chemical categories, including candles, crayons, waxes cleaners, animal feeds, personal care products, buffing compounds, lubricants, greases, various amine derivatives, mining chemicals, and amides. These all fall into the total 1 billion lb of tallow fatty acid consumed annually in the United States.

## OLEOCHEMICALS—FUTURE OUTLOOK FOR TALLOW

Tallow has been a key material for many decades in the production of a broad spectrum of soap products. After the severe volume dislocation caused by the global introduction of synthetic laundry products after World War II there has been a general increase in tallow-based soaps because of worldwide population increases and because of increased global penetration by multinational companies.

However, situations have arisen in recent years that are depressing tallow consumption in bar soaps, and they will continue into the next century. There is every reason to believe that the availability of palm oil products will continue to grow. Another signicant factor is a major shift in consumer habits for personal care, particularly noteworthy in the pan-European markets. Shower gels have broadly displaced bath bar soap. The gels are based on synthetic detergent technology and contain no tallow derivatives. Bar soap markets are consequently shrinking at a fast pace. The one positive is that for the bar volume, tallow will remain predominate globally since palm oil is not broadly economically attractive at this time.

Based on the success in Europe, shower gels are now appearing in the United States, with the multinationals leading the charge. We fully expect that these companies have already started evaluating global applications for the gels as well.

In the United States, liquid hand soaps, again based on synthetic formulations, have settled into a comfortable niche at a 5 to 7% share of the bar soap category. Their usage predominates among consumers in the bathroom sink and kitchen sink washing practices.

**Table 3.** Chemical Composition of Selected Fats and Oils

| Carbon Chain Length & Unsaturation - % | ANIMAL FATS | | | VEGETABLE OILS | | | | | | | |
|---|---|---|---|---|---|---|---|---|---|---|---|
| | Tallow Beef | Lard Hog | Poultry | Soybean | Cotton Seed | Coconut | Palm Kernel | Palm | Palm Stearine | Tall Oil |
| 6C Hexanoic | | | | | | 0.5 | | | | |
| 8C Octanoic | | | | | | 7 | 3 | | | |
| 10C Decanoic | | | | | | 6 | 3 | | | |
| 12C Lauric | | | | | | 50 | 50 | | | |
| 14C Myristic | 3 | 1.5 | 0.5 | 0.5 | 0.7 | 18 | 18 | 1 | 2 | |
| 15C Pentadecanoic | 0.5 | | 1.5 | 0.5 | | | | | | |
| 16C Palmitic | 24 | 27 | 22.5 | 12 | 24 | 8.5 | 8 | 45 | 56 | |
| 16C 1=Palmitoleic | 2.5 | 3 | 8.5 | | 1 | | | | | |
| 17C Margaric | 1.5 | 0.5 | | | | | | | | |
| 18C Stearic | 20 | 13.5 | 5.5 | 4 | 2 | 3 | 2 | 4 | 38 | 2 |
| 18C 1=Oleic | 43 | 43.5 | 40 | 25 | 17 | 6 | 14 | 40 | 2 | 59 |
| 18C 2=Linoleic | 4 | 10.5 | 19 | 52 | 55 | 1 | 2 | 10 | | 37 |
| 18C 3=Linolenic | 0.3 | 0.5 | 1 | 6 | 0.3 | 0.5 | | 0.2 | | |
| 20C Arachadic | 0.5 | | | | | | | | | 1 |
| Iodine Value | 48 | 65 | 90 | 130 | 106 | 10 | 18 | 50 | 5 | 167 |
| Saponification Value | 200 | 200 | 196 | 192 | 192 | 255 | 250 | 200 | 210 | 180 |
| Titer | | | | | | | | | | |
| C—fatty acid basis | 43 | 36 | 32 | 34 | 34 | 22 | 24 | 44 | 55 | 5 |

Data from fatty acid calculator—Procter and Gamble

While the personal care bar soap category utilizing tallow is expected to decline further in the decade ahead, the good news is that the future should look brighter in the broader oleochemicals markets. This optimism stems from a review of global chemical markets in which tallow participates.

Tallow acid consumption in the United States has nearly doubled in the last 15 years from about 500 million lb to the 1995 level of 1 billion lb, and European usage has shown a similar pattern. While consumption has doubled, the growth has been a steady straight line . Over the last 30 years, acid consumption has followed a cyclical pattern substantially correlating to industrial or economic activity. In recessionary periods consumption declines but has rebounded when the economy recovers. The central uptrend line cuts through several peaks and valleys with the most recent valleys being the recessionary periods in the early 1980s and again in the early 1990s.

The situation in Europe, while we do not have firm data, should have followed a similar pattern; hence when their economy improves, additional good news for fatty acids may follow.

Another cause for optimism is the volume of tallow acids compared with the much broader markets enjoyed by the competition (Figure 3).

Increasing population trends in the Western developed countries has been an important trend setter for growth of cyclical industries in which tallow acids participate. Therefore the impact of world population increases from the current 5.7 billion people to the 7.1 billion expected in 2010 (chapter 5) will create more growth opportunities, even if the predominate growth occurs principally in developing countries. Not to be forgotten are potential growth positions that may occur in Eastern Europe, Russia and its former USSR satellites, China, and India as free market opportunities expand there.

There is ample justification to be optimistic about oleochemical growth on a global basis well into the 21st century. However, a wait-and-see, reactive posture will not be sufficient—proactive tallow programs will be essential to deliver results to meet this optimistic assessment.

**Figure 3.**

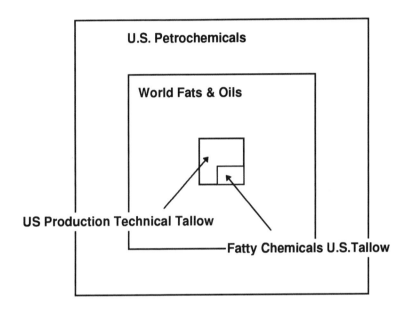

**Ratio of Blocks:**

| | |
|---|---|
| US petrochemicals | 200 |
| world fats & oils | 90 |
| US production technical tallow | 3.2 |
| fatty chemicals US tallow | 0.5 |

In 1995, at 1 billion lb, tallow acid use in the United States is just:

- 1/4 % of the US petrochemical market
- 1/2 % of the total world fats and oils production
- 15% of the US production of tallows and greases

These figures are based on the numbers as presented in chapter 5 in this text. With favorable economics, adapting tallow acids to address just 2 or 3 existing chemical technology areas out of the massive petrochemical complex seems a reasonable expectation for growth.

## Bibliography

*Bailey's Industrial Oil and Fat Products,* 4th edition. John Wiley & Sons, New York, 1979.

*Chemical Economic Handbook Reports (CEH): Detergent Alcohols—1995.* SRI International, Menlo Park, California.

*Chemical Economic Handbook Reports (CEH): Fats and Oils Industry Overview—1993.* SRI International, Menlo Park, California.

*Chemical Economic Handbook Reports (CEH): Natural Fatty Acids—1995.* SRI International, Menlo Park, California.

*Economic and Technical Assessment of the Worlds Oleochemical Industry.* Hewin International, Amsterdam, 1985.

*Fatty Acids & Derivatives—1986 to 1991: Western Europe.* Hull & Co, Greenwich, Connecticut.

*Fatty Acids and Derivatives—1985 to 1991,* Vol 1–3. Hull & Co, Greenwich, Connecticut.

*Fatty Acids and Their Industrial Applications—1968.* Marcel Dekker, Inc, New York.

*Oleochemical Developments—Their Influence in Petrochemical Markets to 1995.* Colin A Houston & Assoc, Mamaroneck, New York.

*Proceedings of the World Conference on Lauric Oils, 1994—Sources, Processing, and Applications, Manila, Philippines.* AOCS Press, Champaign, Illinois.

*Proceedings on Oleochemicals into the 21st Century—1990—Kuala Lumpur, Malaysia.* AOCS Press, Champaign, Illinois.

# 7

# Utilizing Rendered Products:  Poultry

## Henry L Fuller

Much has been written about the phenomenal growth of the poultry industry.  The story of its emergence from a backyard enterprise, a source of "butter and egg money"for the housewife, into an industrial giant makes for exciting reading and also reveals the basis for a unique relationship and interdependence with the rendering industry.

Before the 1930s chickens were bred primarily for egg production traits. On the Pacific coast a demand for white eggs was developed and an aggressive and imaginative marketing program soon led to penetration of the New York markets.  Thus breeding and selection concentrated on the White Leghorn breed.  In New England and much of the Midwest where brown eggs were preferred, the breeds being developed were the New Hampshires, Barred Plymouth Rocks, and Rhode Island Reds.

In the 1930s the practice of sexing chicks at the hatchery led to large supplies of cockerels which could be purchased at low cost.  These would be grown as fryers and sold to restaurants either directly or through local feed stores.  There they would be accumulated, oftentimes held in crates, and fattened before being "New York dressed" for sale to the local restaurants.

The growing of fryers began to expand first in the Delmarva area and soon spread to other parts of the country, notably north Georgia.  On the small farms in the rolling hill country it was no longer profitable to grow cotton. Feed dealers in need of a market for their feed began contracting with the farmers to grow chicks which the dealers supplied along with feed and medication. The dealers would then pick up the finished "broilers," as they began to be called (still called "fryers" in the western United States) and haul them to processing plants according to a pre-arranged schedule.

Jesse Jewell, whose likeness stands in the Georgia Poultry Hall of Fame in Gainesville, Georgia, pioneered the practice of contract growing in this area. The need for a steady market for the broilers led to cooperation with operators of processing plants who, in turn, needed a steady supply of chickens for efficient operation of their plants. Thus a continuing supply of ready-to-cook broilers suitable for handling in supermarkets was developed.

With the supermarket trade came a demand for a more attractive meat type bird and one that could be produced efficiently. The "Chicken of Tomorrow" contest sponsored by the A&P Stores under the direction of Howard "Doc" Pierce created a great deal of interest and competition among poultry breeders and led to the development of the modern broiler breeds.

What began as simple contract growing of broilers soon developed into a completely integrated business with all phases of its operation coming together under one corporate structure. A typical broiler production enterprise today consists of a hatchery, feed mill, and processing plant complete with corporate offices, laboratories, and truck maintenance and storage facilities. In addition, many now include rendering facilities for their byproducts.

The Southeast learned its lessons well from the experience of the growers in the Delmarva area and soon supplanted that area as the leader in broiler production. Subsequently, the leadership began moving west until Arkansas is now number 1 in broiler production. The largest producer in the United States, Tyson Foods with headquarters in Arkansas, produces more than 80 million lb or 25 million birds/week (some 1.25 billion birds/year). Most of the largest companies are divided into several smaller units integrated horizontally throughout large areas of the region and operating as partially independent complexes each with its own hatcheries, feed mills, and processing facilities.

About 35 companies in the United States produce 1 million birds (or more) per week. Most operations of this capacity have their own specialists in such areas as nutrition, genetics, pathology, processing, and marketing or have access via consultants to the latest developments in science and technology. Along with the specialists most have some laboratory facilities for quality control of feed ingredients, finished feeds, and their own products, and conduct continuing performance testing of feed formulas. With access to all phases of production and marketing, the company can consider all costs and returns to determine overall profitability of any feeding program or specific formulas. The remarkable growth of the broiler industry (Table 1) reflects changes in the per capita consumption of poultry (Table 2).

Table 1. Poultry Production, US (1940 - 1993)

| Year | Number of Birds | | | Live Weight (lbs) | | |
|------|------|------|------|------|------|------|
| | Broilers | Chickens* | Turkeys | Broilers | Chickens* | Turkeys |
| 1940 | 143 | 571 | 34 | 413 | 2,220 | 524 |
| 1950 | 631 | 561 | 44 | 1,945 | 2,424 | 820 |
| 1960 | 1,795 | 273 | 84 | 6,017 | 1,164 | 1,471 |
| 1970 | 2,987 | 264 | 116 | 10,819 | 1,190 | 2,198 |
| 1980 | 3,964 | 241 | 165 | 15,541 | 1,180 | 3,032 |
| 1990 | 5,864 | 208 | 282 | 25,631 | 972 | 6,030 |
| 1993** | 6,889 | 197 | 287 | 30,592 | 944 | 6,419 |

Source: 1989 and 1990 Fact Book of Agriculture, Misc. Publ. 1063, USDA, Washington, DC.
*Commercial egg producing hens.
**Estimated.

Table 2. US Per Capita Meat Consumption (lb)

| Year | Beef & Veal | Pork | Chicken | All Poultry |
|------|------|------|------|------|
| 1940 | 43 | 69 | 2 | - |
| 1950 | 50 | 64 | 9 | - |
| 1960 | 64 | 60 | 30 | 37 |
| 1970 | 84 | 62 | 40 | 48 |
| 1980 | 78 | 68 | 50 | 61 |
| 1990 | 80 | 60 | 60 | 73 |
| 1993* | 65 | 52 | 68 | 87 |

Source: 1989 and 1990 Fact Book of Agriculture, Misc. Publ. 1063, USDA, Washington, DC.
*1993 figures derived from various sources.

The commercial egg industry began in the 1920s and maintained its pattern of independent producers and traditional marketing channels until the 1960s and 1970s. Learning its lessons from the broiler industry, it is now largely integrated with large companies having their own hatcheries, feed mills, and egg processing and marketing facilities. Whereas, broiler production is concentrated in the Sunbelt, commercial egg production is widely dispersed throughout the United States. The top 20 egg-producing firms average more than 5 million laying hen capacity, the largest, Cal-Maine Foods in Mississippi, having nearly 16 million. Many of the million-hen layer operations own their production facilities; somewhat fewer producers grow them under contract, then is the case with broiler production.

The growth of the poultry industry would not have occurred were it not for the continued improvement in efficiency of production of both poultry (including turkeys) and eggs (Table 3). Of more interest to consumers is that chicken and eggs have remained more affordable than other common food items since 1950 (Table 4).

**Table 3.** Efficiency in Production of Broilers and Eggs (US)

| | Broilers | | Eggs | | Poultry |
|---|---|---|---|---|---|
| Year | Feed Conversion[1] | Days to Market | Annual Egg Production (Per Hen) | Feed/Doz Eggs (lbs) | Output/hr Labor (Index)[2] |
| 1950 | 3.0 | 84 | 190 | 5.5 | 30 |
| 1970 | 2.1 | 56 | 218 | 4.5 | 195 |
| 1990 | <2.0 | 42 | 252 | 4.0 | >200 |

*Source*: 1989 and 1990 Fact Book of Agriculture, Misc Publ 1063, USDA, Washington, DC.
[1] Wt. feed/live wt. of broiler.
[2] 1965 = 100.

**Table 4.**
What the U.S. Factory Worker Could Buy with One Hour's Pay

| Food Item | 1950 | 1990 | % Increase or (Decrease) |
|---|---|---|---|
| White bread, lbs. | 10.1 | 14.4 | 42.5 |
| Frying chicken, lbs. | 2.5 | 11.1 | 344.0 |
| Milk, qts. | 8.0 | 15.8 | 97.5 |
| Potatoes, fresh, lbs. | 29.0 | 27.0 | (7.0) |
| Eggs, doz. | 2.4 | 9.9 | 312.5 |
| Ground beef, lbs. (1970) | 5.0 | 6.3 | 26.0 |

*Source*: 1989 and 1990 Fact Book of Agriculture, Misc. Publ. 1063, U.S.D.A., Washington, D.C.

## THE POULTRY INDUSTRY MEETS THE RENDERING INDUSTRY

An important step in the building of this industrial giant, one that significantly affected the rendering industry, was the demonstration by poultry scientists that young chickens would respond positively to increased dietary energy and nutrient density. The first evidence of this phenomenon was the publication in 1947 of the Connecticut high energy broiler ration (Scott et al 1947). This was shortly followed by work at the University of Maryland that demonstrated the principle of the calorie:protein ratio in which the need for a balance between energy and protein (and other nutrients as well) was demonstrated (Combs & Romoser 1955). During this time workers at Cornell were also demonstrating the need for a balance between energy and protein (Hill & Dansky 1954). The basis for these "discoveries" was the well-known phenomenon that animals including poultry eat primarily to satisfy their energy needs. Simply stated, this principle tells us that when animals have met their energy needs, they tend to stop eating. If the amount eaten at that time is inadequate in protein or other nutrients, then they suffer from a deficiency of those nutrients and the increased energy is of little or no value.

About this time the rendering industry was seeking new markets for tallow and other animal fats. Thus the need for an inexpensive source of energy was being met by an abundant supply of animal fats seeking a market. It was soon realized that dietary fat provided more than energy. The fats added to broiler rations increased palatability, provided essential fatty acids, reduced losses from dust, in addition to other advantages. It would be nearly 2 decades before the advantages of fat in layer rations became evident and it was largely through the recognition of these physical attributes that the research for such benefits was undertaken. Additional benefits such as the improvement in egg weight would later confirm the unique benefits of added fat in layer rations.

Meat and bone meal has been used as a protein supplement in feed longer than any other protein supplement with the possible exception of skim milk. In nutrition experiments conducted throughout the first half of this century, animal proteins invariably proved to be superior to vegetable proteins in promoting the growth and production of animals. This superiority was thought to be inherent in the protein itself and animal proteins were considered indispensable for all monogastric animals including poultry. Following World War II, as laboratory techniques became more sophisticated, it became possible to evaluate proteins on the basis of their amino acid content. The discovery of vitamin B12 and its identity with the Animal Protein Factor, and the discovery of the essential nature of certain trace elements removed much of the mystery of the various protein concentrates and placed their nutritional attributes on sound qualitative and quantitative bases.

The concentration of the broiler industry in the Southeast made it feasible for the rendering industry to collect and process the offal from the poultry processing plants. This introduced new products, including poultry byproduct meal and feather meal, as well as poultry fat to poultry feed formulators. The phenomenal growth of the poultry industry can be credited largely to the continued improvement in the efficient and economical production of poultry meat and eggs. The price of chicken and eggs to the consumer has remained almost constant during the last 50 years, in contrast to the inflationary cost of most other goods and services. The rendering industry has contributed in no small measure to this improved efficiency of production by providing a constant supply of high energy and high nutrient-density ingredients with a continuing awareness of the exacting demands of an ever more sophisticated poultry industry for quality control in all aspects of their nutritional program.  Renderers have been aided in their effort to supply the highest quality feed ingredients possible by their strong support of the research efforts of the Fats and Proteins Research Foundation. (For the relationship of the Fats and Proteins Research Foundation, the rendering industry, and the poultry and livestock industries, see chapter 11.)

## ADDED FAT IN POULTRY FEEDS

### Energy Value

Dietary fat is a concentrated source of energy containing approximately 2.25 times the energy content of carbohydrates and proteins.  Thus when it is used as a replacement for high carbohydrate ingredients on a calorie-for-calorie basis, it permits a much greater concentration of energy and nutrients in the diet.  It also permits greater flexibility in formulating feeds allowing space in the feed bag for a wider variety of ingredients, some of which may be cost effective.  This is especially important in parts of the world where grain is considered too valuable to be used in animal feeds and is preferentially used for human consumption, leaving the feed manufacturer to rely on low energy and less expensive grain byproducts.

Dietary fat also contributes an energetic effect upon the feed which often exceeds its own inherent caloric value, or its gross energy value.  This effect has been termed the "extra caloric effect" of fat (Forbes & Swift 1944, Horani & Sell 1977, Jensen et al 1970).  A simple explanation is that added fat interacts with other dietary components to increase their absorption which, in turn, increases the metabolizable energy of the diet, and added fat increases utilization of the metabolizable energy by reducing the heat increment, which increases the net energy of the diet.  The extent of this extra caloric effect depends to a great extent upon the level of fat used, the nature of the basal diet, and the use to which the feed is being put, which depends upon the stage of growth or production of the various classes of poultry to which it is fed.

To comprehend the difficulty of assigning an absolute value to the metabolizable energy of fat, consider the fact that the metabolizable energy of a dietary ingredient such as fat is not a direct measurement, but is determined by substitution.  In this procedure the fat is substituted for a small part of the test diet.  Thus it becomes a measure of the effect of the fat on the energy value of the test diet and whatever interaction that takes place between the test fat and the basal diet is interpreted by extrapolation to be the energy value of the test fat.  In such tests the first increment of added fat will always have the greatest influence with declining effects per incremental unit as levels are increased.

IR Sibbald and coworkers (1961), who were then at the University of Guelph, demonstrated the synergism or interaction of fats differing in their absorbability when fed individually or in combination (Table 5). This illustrates the difficulty of placing a value on any fat without defining the conditions under which it is fed.  The scientific literature is filled with similar illustrations where different energy values are derived for the same fat when fed with different types of diets, at different levels or in different combinations.

**Table 5.** Synergistic Effect of Different Fats (Sibbald *et al* 1961)

| Kind of Fat | Avg. ME kcal/g |
|---|---|
| Tallow | 6.94 |
| Crude soy oil | 8.46 |
| Tallow and Soy oil mixed (50:50) | 8.41 |

ME = Metabolizable energy

**Table 6.** TME of Test Fats as Determined with Purified and Practical Diets (kcal/g)  (Dale and Fuller 1982)

| | Corn Oil | Tallow |
|---|---|---|
| **Basal Diet** | | |
| Practical[a] | 10.91 ± .39[c] | 10.51 ± .50 |
| Purified[b] | 8.91 ± .18 | 7.79 ±.29 |

[a]Assayed at 2.5% in corn-soybean meal basal diet
[b]Assayed at 15% in glucose-corn starch basal
[c]Standard error of mean

At the University of Georgia the metabolizable energy of corn oil and tallow were determined when assayed at a practical dietary level of 2.5% in a corn–soybean meal diet versus the traditional method of determination which uses a purified diet and a much higher level of fat (Table 6). At the low level and under practical conditions all values exceeded gross energy of fats with no significant difference between corn oil and tallow. This indicated an interaction of tallow with the residual fat in the test diet and a possible improvement in the absorption of other dietary constituents by both corn oil and tallow.  Many poultry feed formulators simply assign a value at or near the gross energy value (about 9 kcal/g) for all fats when used at practical levels in broiler and layer diets, with adjustments in value depending upon their experience with different sources of fat or different feeding conditions.

## OTHER ADVANTAGES OF SUPPLEMENTAL FAT

We have spoken of fat in poultry feeds primarily as a concentrated source of energy.  While this is sufficient justification for its use, there are other reasons just as valid for the use of fat in poultry feeds.

*Physical Improvement of Feed.*  The first increment of supplemental fat will justify its use at any reasonable price by improving the physical characteristics of the feed.  These improvements include its lubricating value, the reduction of dust, the reduction of particle separation, and its improvement of the palatability of feeds for all species.

*Lubrication Value.*  Feed is abrasive and will cause excessive wear on mixing and milling equipment as well as feed-handling equipment in the chicken house.  A small amount of added fat reduces the abrasiveness of the feed, thereby increasing the life of feed mixing and handling equipment.  Similarly, the power requirement for pelleting feeds has been shown to be reduced markedly by adding even 1 or 2% of fat to the feed.  Several-fold increases in the life of the pelleting dies has also been demonstrated.

*Reduction of Dust.*  Feed is dusty.  Prior to the use of fat in feeds, one could spot feed mills many miles away on country roads by the dust that had settled in the trees and foliage along the roadsides in the vicinity.  Feed millers routinely added 1 or 2% to the cost of feed due to dust loss.  Another problem attributed to the dustiness of feed was the impairment of health of the workers in the feed mill and the high degree of absenteeism among feed mill employees as a result of respiratory problems arising from the dustiness at the mill.  The expense of dust collection by mechanical means was a major item of cost in manufacturing feed.  With the addition of fat to feed, these problems were minimized.

*Reduction of Particle Separation.*  Even the best mixed feeds tend to separate and become stratified according to the density of the particles while being transported long distances over rough country roads and in poultry houses where automatic feeders are used to deliver feed at distances of 100 ft or more.  At the University of Georgia the extent of particle separation in automatic feeders in laying houses was studied.  OW Charles (personal communication, 1970) reported great differences in the mineral content of the feed at the entry point and at various distances along the feeder chain.  The nutritional significance of such particle separation is not difficult to imagine particularly in large broiler and layer houses.  This factor alone became a significant contribution to the use of fat in layer feeds beginning in the early 1970s.

*Palatability.*  While taste is not a great factor in poultry feeds, it is well-known that a small amount of supplemental fat greatly enhances the palatability of feed, not only for poultry but for all livestock.  Before the advent of fat in feeds, birds spent much more time walking between the feed troughs and the water fountains and a great deal of feed was often found in the bottom of the water fountains. This additional loss of feed has been reduced considerably with the use of added fat.

*Essential Fatty Acids.* Another important reason for adding fat to feed is to provide a supplemental source of linoleic acid (18:2) to help meet the requirement of the chicken for essential fatty acids. Diets for all classes of poultry that do not rely on corn as the major source of energy are usually borderline or grossly deficient in essential fatty acids. The use of supplemental fat in such cases is not only desirable, but imperative. Most feed grade fats contain enough linoleic acid to fulfill the requirement for additional essential fatty acids when used at levels of 2 or 3% in the ration. The value of linoleic acid as a source of essential fatty acids should not be confused with its contribution to the energy value of the fat which is similar for all unsaturated fatty acids.

Since the value of fat for its physical attributes is difficult to quantitate, most feed formulators now simply specify a minimum level of 2 or 3% supplemental fat which takes care of the needed improvement in physical quality of feed it also provides a margin of safety for the essential fatty acid requirements. These low levels of fat also make a greater than proportional contribution to the energy value of the feed.

## Reducing Heat Stress with Fat

When food is eaten, there is an increase in heat production over and above that of the fasting or basal heat production (analogous to the basal metabolic rate in human. This is called the heat increment or dynamic effect of eating and arises primarily from the chemical reactions involved in converting food energy to the energy needed for maintenance and production. This is "overhead" and is largely wasted except in extremely cold environments. Heat increment of a diet is less when fat is included in the formula (Dale & Fuller 1978). Thus, added fat increases the energetic efficiency of the ration (ratio of net energy:metabolizable energy is increased).

When the environmental temperature rises to uncomfortable levels, the heat increment of eating adds to the discomfort of the animal. Pigs and chickens are especially sensitive to high temperatures and consequently reduce their feed intake to avoid the discomfort of the heat increment which must be dissipated. Furthermore, energy must be spent in disposing of this heat through panting and increased peripheral circulation. Thus energy needs are actually increasing while energy is being wasted as heat increment and the energy intake is decreasing as a result of reduced feed intake. The value of dietary fat in alleviating heat stress has been demonstrated with broiler chicks at the University of Georgia (Dale

& Fuller 1980).  Thus, one of the major advantages of supplemental fat in rations for poultry is the increase in energy intake in times of stress when there is an increased need for energy.  Several experiments have been conducted in controlled environment chambers and in uninsulated broiler houses to determine whether broiler chicks would reject high fat diets during periods of high temperature.  Contrary to earlier assumptions, chicks demonstrated a highly significant preference for a high fat diet over similar diets containing a low level of fat.  This preference was exhibited at comfortable as well as at high temperatures and regardless of the texture of the feed, whether it was mash or pellets (Jensen 1983).  The increased intake of feed and energy was observed in the chicks subjected to heat stress and was presumed to be a major factor in the alleviation of heat stress.

## SUPPLEMENTAL FAT IN LAYER RATIONS

As young pullets come into production, they begin laying small eggs which become progressively larger throughout the laying cycle.  For commercial layers, it usually requires 20 to 30 weeks after onset of production in a flock before most eggs fall into the profitable "large" category.  The energy intake of young pullets at onset of production is frequently too low to sustain the climb to peak production and maximum egg weight while at the same time supporting the normal increase in body weight.  This can be more pronounced when the pullets are coming into production in hot weather.  Not only is feed and energy intake reduced, but energy requirements are increased due to the energy required for heat dissipation.

The importance of essential fatty acids in achieving maximum egg size has been known for many years.  Nevertheless, researchers continued to report beneficial effects of added fat on egg weight and production even when the diet was presumed to contain adequate linoleic acid.  Eggs contain about 10% fat which means 4 to 5 g of fat must be deposited in the egg daily by hens in 80% production.  A corn–soy diet contains about 3% fat or less so with an average feed intake of 100 g, the ration would  provide at the most only 3 g of fat.  The rest of the fat deposited in the egg would have to be synthesized from carbohydrates and proteins which are relatively inefficient processes.  With added fat the fatty acids could be used directly in the synthesis of egg lipids by way of the liver and ovary which is an energetically efficient process.  At the University of Georgia, Leo Jensen conducted a series of experiments to determine the effect of added fat in the diet of young pullets during the first 16 weeks of production (Table 7).  Results of his experiments demonstrated that supplementary fat during those first 16 weeks of egg production generally results in an accelerated increase in egg weight, even when those diets already contained adequate levels of linoleic acid and equal levels of energy.  It was concluded that the beneficial effect of the fat was due neither to its linoleic acid nor its energy content, but rather to the effect of fat per se.

**Table 7.** Effects of Dietary Animal Fat on Performance of Pullets from 22-38 Weeks of Age (Jensen 1983)

| Added Fat | Egg Production (%) | Body Weight Gain (g) | Egg Weight Category (%) | |
|---|---|---|---|---|
| | | | Small & Medium | Large & Extra Large |
| 0 | 66.4 | 362 | 53.1 | 46.3 |
| 1% | 69.3 | 334 | 45.0 | 54.2 |
| 2% | 70.0 | 358 | 46.8 | 52.5 |

At the University of Arizona (Reid 1983) it was observed that fat has its greatest potential in laying hen diets as a concentrated energy source since energy intake above maintenance limits egg production during periods of high environmental temperature. Limited energy intake is also partially responsible for smaller eggs during hot weather. Their studies showed that added animal fat can increase energy intake about 29 to 30 kcal/day, thereby increasing the amount of energy available for production. Young birds tend to deposit this increased energy as increased egg numbers or egg size, while older hens tend to deposit the additional energy as body tissue.

## Supplemental Fats for Growing Turkeys

The turkey industry has been more reluctant than the broiler industry to take advantage of the beneficial effect of fats in their feeds. This was due, in part, to the perception that fats in turkey feeds would increase carcass fat which was undesirable from a marketing standpoint. Secondly, research had shown that young turkeys until about 6 weeks of age do not utilize fats as efficiently as do chickens. Since the 1970s, however, fat has been routinely used in turkey growing diets. Research conducted at Iowa State University (Sell et al 1985) has emphasized the value of supplemental fats for creating diets of high metabolizable energy content for growing turkeys. This research has also shown that the economical use of supplemental fat to boost dietary metabolizable energy should not be hindered by the notion that certain specific calorie:protein ratios must be maintained in diets of growing turkeys. To the contrary, dietary metabolizable energy and protein levels were reported to exert essentially independent effects on turkey performance and most carcass traits when used within practical limits. Those limits will be determined by the costs of supplemental fats versus the cost of other major energy sources, the economic benefits anticipated from the use of fats, physical limitations related to feed preparation and handling equipment, and concern about fat content of market turkeys.

Despite the fact that fats are poorly utilized in the very young poult, supplemental fats can be used effectively in turkey starter feeds. However, the improvements will not be as large as when they are used in grower and finisher diets. According to JL Sell and colleagues (1986), data show that for each increase of 35 to 40 kcal of metabolizable energy/kg of diet (which can be achieved with a 1% inclusion of feed grade fat in corn–soybean meal base diets) feed efficiency from hatching to 6 weeks of age will be improved from 0.8 to 1.2%. Concurrently, rate of gain often is improved but to a lesser degree depending upon the ingredient composition and metabolizable energy concentration of the diets. From 6 weeks onward, however, improvements of 1.5 to 2.0% in feed efficiency for that same increase in metabolizable energy (1% added fat) are usually obtained together with frequent increases in rate of gain.

## USED COOKING FATS

As the marketing of red meats moved farther west closer to the feed lots, the renderer's source of raw materials has changed, particularly those renderers in the eastern United States.  Much of what is now classified as yellow grease consists of used cooking oil or restaurant grease that has been used for deep frying of potatoes, poultry, fish, and other products.  These fats consist more and more of partially hydrogenated vegetable oils.  The extent to which fats and oils may be damaged by heat and oxidation has been the subject of much research.  These studies have demonstrated that chemical changes in the fats and oils may, depending upon severity and conditions of the heating, result in the appearance of a wide variety of byproducts including certain polymers.  The feeding value of fats containing such polymers for monogastric animals has been studied extensively in The Netherlands. Janssen (1985) reported that the polymer content of feed fats had little influence on the metabolizable energy value of fats for poultry.  He tested fats that contained levels of polymers of 2, 5, or 8% and found no negative effects of increasing polymer content on growth rate or feed efficiency of broilers.

The concern over the polymer content of feed grade fats led workers at the University of Georgia, sponsored by the Fats and Proteins Research Foundation, to conduct feeding trials involving several samples of both used and unused cooking oils.  None of the samples contained more than 3% polymer (or oligomer) content after being used in a normal cooking process.  When these fats were fed to broiler chicks there was no significant difference in body weight gain, feed efficiency, fat retention, or metabolizable energy of the diet between the new and used fats within each sample. The researchers concluded that used cooking oil or restaurant grease is safe for feeding to poultry (Jensen 1990).

## Characterization of Fats

In 1953 the American Meat Institute Foundation established grades of inedible animal fats according to their physical properties (Table 8). These grades were suitable for the soap industry which was still the primary market for inedible animal fats, but bore little relationship to nutritional values. Feed grade fat or more properly, "fat product, feed grade," as officially defined by the Association of American Feed Control Officials (1992) is "any fat product which does not meet the definitions for animal fat, vegetable fat, or oil, hydrolyzed fat or fat ester." It must be sold on its individual specifications which will include the minimum percentage of total fatty acids, the maximum percentage of unsaponifiable matter, maximum percentage of insoluble impurities, maximum percentage of free fatty acids, and moisture. The specifications must be guaranteed on the label. If an antioxidant(s) is used, the common name(s) must be indicated followed by the words "used as a preservative." The industry often uses the terms "yellow grease" and "feed grade fat" interchangeably, leading to some confusion; most feed grade fat falls into the original classification of yellow grease. If it is sold on its individual specifications as defined above, there should be no difficulty.

In the poultry industry, poultry fat is usually considered to be the standard for quality when fatty acid profile alone is considered as the quality criterion. This is only natural since it has been demonstrated that poultry fat can be converted to carcass fat in broilers with a maximum metabolic efficiency (Fuller & Rendon 1977). On the other hand, it can be mistreated in handling and processing just as with any other fat. Furthermore, it has been well-established by numerous workers that when used at practical feeding levels, little difference if any can be found among the various classifications of fat, whether animal, vegetable, or blends, when measured by the performance of the class of poultry involved. The important factor is that they meet the standards demanded by the buyer in terms of stabilization and specifications for moisture insoluble impurities and unsaponifiables (MIU).

## ANIMAL PROTEIN SUPPLEMENTS IN POULTRY FEEDS

Meat and bone meal and poultry byproduct meal have long been favorites of feed formulators because they consist of concentrated sources of essential nutrients. Consider that a 100-lb bag of meat and bone meal contains roughly 50 lb of high quality protein, 8 to 9 lb of calcium, 4 to 4.5 lb of phosphorus, and 10 lb of fat. A similar 100-lb bag of dehulled soybean meal, the standard of comparison, contains about 48 lb of protein and little else in the way of critical nutrients. As noted with fat, meat and bone meal can be used to advantage to increase the energy and nutrient density of a poultry ration and permit greater flexibility of formulation by occupying less space per unit of energy and nutrients than can be found in virtually any other practical ingredient.

**Table 8.** Characteristics of Inedible Grades of Animal Fat

| Fat Grade | Titer* (0C min) | FFA** (% max) | MIU*** (% max) |
|---|---|---|---|
| **Tallow** | | | |
| Fancy | 41.5 | 4 | 1 |
| Choice | 41.0 | 5 | 1 |
| Prime | 46.5 | 6 | 1 |
| Special | 40.5 | 10 | 1 |
| No. 1 | 40.5 | 15 | 2 |
| No. 2 | 40.5 | 20 | 2 |
| No. 3 | 40.0 | 35 | 2 |
| **Grease** | | | |
| Choice White | 37.0 | 4 | 1 |
| A White | 37.0 | 8 | 1 |
| B White | 36.0 | 10 | 2 |
| Yellow | 36.0 | 15 | 2 |
| House | 37.0 | 20 | 2 |
| Brown | 38.0 | 50 | 2 |

*Solidification point
**Free fatty acid level
***Moisture, insoluble and unsaponifiable matter

## Meat and Bone Meal

Dr OHM Wilder at the American Meat Institute Foundation (1956) was among the first to demonstrate the extent to which meat and bone meal could be used in broiler rations using constraints of modern feed formulation. He fed levels of meat and bone meal from 0 to 20% of the ration replacing soybean meal and the phosphorus supplement to maintain constant protein, calcium, and phosphorus in all rations. In one test, 8% meat and bone meal gave optimal results with only a slight reduction in performance when levels were increased to 17%. All levels of meat and bone meal below 20% gave significantly better growth and feed efficiency than the soybean meal control. In another trial optimal results were obtained at the 14% level of inclusion.

These results are typical of the results obtained in subsequent years, and meat and bone meal continues to be a staple ingredient of feed formulators, but standing on its own nutritional attributes devoid of the magic that once made it an "indispensable" ingredient. More recently at the University of Georgia, Martisiswoyo & Jensen (1988) tested levels of meat and bone meal from 5 to 40% in a corn–soybean meal ration maintaining constant levels of energy and all major nutrients. Results demonstrated that the performance of broilers fed 10% meat and bone meal were at least equal to those receiving corn–soybean meal.

A part of the limitations in the use of meat and bone meal in the past has been the relatively low energy value ascribed to it in the various tables of composition. For instance, in the tables of composition published by the National Research Council (1984), meat and bone meal was listed as having a metabolizable energy value of 1960 kcal/kg. The value listed by Scott and coworkers (1982) at Cornell University in their widely used textbook, *Nutrition of the Chicken,* was 1980 kcal/kg. Because classic metabolizable energy determinations are made by substitution, it is customary to use levels as high as 40% of the test ingredient in the determination in order to reduce the errors obtained when extrapolating from small levels of substitution. Yet such a level of substitution is not applicable to practical feeding conditions and would lead to an underestimation of its actual energy value. This underestimation would result in actual calorie:protein ratios in feed formulas wider than calculated and would contribute to the deposition of excess carcass fat in broilers which presented a worldwide problem in broiler production. Furthermore, underestimation of the metabolizable energy value would greatly reduce the opportunity price of meat and bone meal in least cost feed formulation. In 1985 Lessire and colleagues showed that the metabolizable energy value of 2 different meat meal samples declined markedly as the level of substitution increased in the test diets. In the experiments from Jensen's laboratory (1990) it was found that when the level of substitution was reduced from 40 to 20%, the metabolizable energy value increased from an average of 2130 to about 2560 kcal/kg. When meat and bone meal was incorporated into practical broiler rations using this new value, it was found that carcass fat was reduced significantly indicating that the calorie:protein ratio had been corrected. They concluded that the actual energy value of 50% protein meat and bone meal was closer to 2500 kcal/kg. Most poultry nutritionists in the broiler growing areas are now using energy values that reflect these findings which has increased the usage of meat and bone meal in poultry rations.

## Poultry Byproduct Meal

The feeding value of poultry byproduct meal for poultry was established in the beginning of the 1950s. The earliest reports of feeding tests demonstrated that poultry byproduct compared favorably with fish meal and all other sources of presumed, but unidentified growth factors (Fuller 1956, Naber & Morgan 1956, Romoser 1955, Wisman et al 1958). When the composition of poultry byproduct meal is compared with the nutrient requirements of broilers, layers, or turkeys as recommended by the National Research Council, it is apparent that its incorporation into such rations enriches energy and all essential nutrients. This makes the marketing of poultry byproduct meal relatively simple. Originally poultry byproduct meal and poultry fat were returned by the renderer to the supplier of raw materials to be recycled by way of feed to the next generation of poultry. This is still true to a great extent, however, an increasing percentage of poultry byproduct meal is finding its way into pet foods with premium prices being paid for the poultry byproduct meal of the highest quality.

The scarcity of research into the nutritional values of poultry byproduct meal since those early reports attests to its acceptability by the poultry and pet food industries. Recently, GM Pesti and colleagues (1986) at the University of Georgia undertook extensive research into the nutritional value of poultry byproduct meal. As in the case of meat and bone meal, it was suspected that the metabolizable energy value of poultry byproduct meal was underestimated as reported in the various tables of composition in use by the feed industry. Scott and others (1982) list the metabolizable energy value of poultry byproduct meal as 2.91 kcal/g and the National Research Council (1984) as 2.67 kcal/g. The first report issuing from the research of Pesti et al (1986) demonstrated that MEn (corrected metabolizable energy) values determined by the method of Matterson et al (1965) were 12% higher when substituted into the test ration at 20% than the more traditional 40% substitution. Values were found to be 3.33 kcal/g and 2.97 kcal/g, respectively. Obviously the 20% level of substitution more nearly approached practical levels of use. When Sibbald's true metabolizable energy (TMEn) method was used, the TMEn value was found to be 3.55 kcal/g (1976). Projections from relationships found between metabolizable energy and the nutrient compositions of their samples and the average sample used by the poultry industry in the southeast indicated an average of 3.39 kcal/g on an "as fed" basis. Using carcass fat deposition as a basis for estimating energy value just as they had done with meat and bone meal, Mendonca and Jensen (1988) suggest that metabolizable energy should be assigned a value of at least 3.30 kcal/g, a value that corresponds remarkably closely to the values determined by Pesti et al (1986). Furthermore, they demonstrated that the performance of older broilers fed diets containing poultry byproduct meal was better than that expected from the determined metabolizable energy of the diets. This suggests that older broilers obtain a higher yield of energy from metabolizable energy than do younger broilers.

The quality of protein in poultry byproduct meal has the poultry industry competing with the pet food industry for available supplies of this material. Not only is the amino acid profile quite compatible with the amino acid requirements of the broiler chick, but the availability of the amino acids is perhaps as high as any other common feed ingredient. Dr Stevenson's laboratory at the University of Arkansas reported that the availability of 17 amino acids in poultry byproduct meal ranged from 94 to 98% using a chick bioassay method. Workers at the University of Georgia (Escalona & Pesti 1987) found that lysine availability determined by the fluorodinitrobenzene method of Carpenter (1960) averaged 87% for the 3 samples of poultry byproduct meal having the highest digestibility (86 to 89%).

## Feather Meal (Hydrolyzed Poultry Feathers)

Feathers are almost pure protein. Most of this is keratin protein which in the raw or natural state is not readily digested by animals. As a matter of fact, in 1952 I was proclaiming to students and practitioners alike that ground up feathers were a good example of a material that was very high in protein, but almost totally useless as a feed ingredient since it was undigestible particularly by monogastric animals. At about this time a few farsighted pioneers, including Jesse Jewell of Gainesville and his byproducts plant manager, Clarence Cumming along with Ed Meyer on the Eastern Shore, were experimenting with cooking methods to make feathers digestible. They developed modern processing methods that cook the feathers under pressure with live steam and partially hydrolyze the protein, denaturing it (breaking apart some of the chemical bonds that account for the unique structure of the feather fibers). The resulting feather meal is a free-flowing palatable product, easily digested by all classes of livestock and poultry.

Feather meal is a concentrated source of protein which can be used to increase the nutrient and energy density of poultry feeds, improving feed efficiency and reducing the amount of feed that must be mixed, handled, and consumed for each pound of poultry meat or dozen eggs produced. In the early days producers of feather meal encountered a great deal of resistance from poultrymen because of its low or inconsistent digestibility and its low level of certain essential amino acids, particularly methionine and lysine. The extent of the shortcomings is arguable and certainly not sufficient to justify the penalty suffered. A great deal of research had to be carried out and given wide publicity in order to overcome this resistance.

In the meantime, the value of feather meal was being demonstrated by reports from the University of Georgia (Romoser 1955), Clemson University (Fuller 1956), University of Guelph (Summers 1976), Iowa State University (Morris & Balloun 1971), and at the University of Maryland (Thomas et al 1971).

Unsupplemented poultry rations based primarily on corn and soybean meal are almost equally deficient in the amino acids, methionine and cystine. Methionine can be converted to cystine in the body of the animal, but the reverse reaction does not take place to any appreciable extent. Since feed-grade methionine is available to the industry, supplemental methionine must be provided to meet the requirement of young chicks for total sulfur amino acids. Feather meal is very rich in cystine which can provide the needed cystine in practical rations and thus spare expensive methionine which otherwise would be required to supply both the methionine and cystine requirements. In order to determine how much of the total sulfur amino acids requirements could be supplied by the cystine in the feather meal, experiments were conducted at the University of Georgia under practical conditions with each ration being fed to 1600 mixed sex broilers (Fuller 1967). The results of that work showed that the feather meal ration actually required less added methionine than did the corn–soybean meal ration and it contained considerably less total methionine, but this was compensated or spared by the higher level of cystine in the feather meal. It was concluded that at least half of the total sulfur amino acid requirements can be met with cystine and that feather meal is a good source of this amino acid.

The extent to which feather meal can be used in practical broiler rations was tested at the University of Guelph (Summers 1969). Summers substituted feather meal protein for soybean meal protein keeping the diets equal in total protein and energy. Their results demonstrated that soybean meal could be replaced by feather meal up to a level of 6% in the starting diet and 4% in the finishing diet without having to add additional amino acids. They concluded that feather meal is a good source of protein if used properly in a broiler ration.

The influence of processing conditions on the nutritional value of feather meal in broiler diets was studied at Iowa State University (Morris & Balloun 1971). The different feather meals were used to supply either 5% or 7.5% of the protein in the diet replacing soybean meal protein. The diets varied in total protein from 16 to 22%, thus at the lower level protein was clearly the limiting factor and would then reflect the quality of any protein used. They added lysine and methionine to bring all diets up to the National Research Council standards calculated on tabular values. All 5 of the feather meals tested produced excellent results when used to supply 5% protein at all protein levels, clearly indicating that the protein and amino acids in the feather meals were equally as available to the chick as were those in the soybean meal.

In similar experiments conducted at the University of Maryland (Thomas et al 1972), it was demonstrated that feather meal can be added up to 7% of the diet without adversely affecting performance of broiler chicks. This corroborated the experiments of Summers (1976) since 7% of feather meal would contribute between 5 and 6% of protein.

At the University of Arkansas Dr Stevenson's laboratory (Mendonca & Jensen 1988) reported amino acid content and availability data on feather meal, poultry byproduct meal, a combined feather and poultry meal cooked together, and a blend of the 2 cooked separately. Average availability of all amino acids exceeded 95% with individual values ranging from 92 to 98% in the products cooked separately. Greater variation occurred both within and between samples when the feathers and offal were processed together. Chick bioassays with feather meal (Baker et al 1981) demonstrated that at least 10% of the dietary protein could be supplied with feather meal supplemented with methionine. With both lysine and methionine supplementation, up to 40% of the crude protein (corresponding to 8% protein in a 20% protein diet) could be supplied by feather meal without affecting growth or feed efficiency.

## Energy Value of Feather Meal

Early reports of the metabolizable energy values of feather meal were apparently based on samples having very low digestibility, some were actually as low as 1.0 kcal/ME/g. Dr John Summers at the University of Guelph challenged this value and reasoned that if the protein in feather meal was 90% available, the meal should have a metabolizable energy content of 3.08 kcal/g. Based on metabolizable energy determinations conducted in his laboratory, Summers (1969) assigned a metabolizable energy value of 3.01 kcal/g for feather meal.

Using the true metabolizable energy (TME) assay, Fuller and Dale (1986) found an average value of 3.07 kcal/g for 4 samples of feather meal being marketed in the Southeast. In later research at the University of Georgia in Dr Pesti's laboratory, the average of TMEn and AMEn assays of feather meal was found to be 3.36 kcal/g of dry matter which is equivalent to 3.12 on an "as is" basis (Wisman et al 1958). Dr Ian Sibbald (1987) of Agriculture Canada, who was the originator of the TME method of assay and has produced an extensive table of TME values, lists feather meal as 3.42 kcal/g of dry matter (3.18 as is).

## Product Evaluation

Several years and a great deal of money have been invested by the Fats and Protein Research Foundation in an effort to develop an in vitro procedure that would predict actual protein digestibility more accurately than does the current official Association of Official Analytical Chemists pepsin digestibility method. Hopefully, the method also could be accomplished more rapidly. Han and Parsons (1990) at the University of Illinois compared in vitro pepsin digestibility with biological assays. Their work corroborates that of Dr Craig Coon at the University of Minnesota and others to the effect that pepsin digestibility values for feather meal and meat and bone meal were much lower when determined with 0.002% pepsin than with 0.2% pepsin which is the current official method, and the 0.002% pepsin values were more highly correlated with bioassays. The results of extensive digestibility trials showed excellent utilization of the protein and fat in meat and bone meal, poultry byproduct meal and feather meal.

## Feather Meal for Turkeys

Feather meal has also been found to be a useful feed ingredient in turkey feeds. Dr Paul Waibel at the University of Minnesota and his co-workers have conducted a series of experiments testing feather meal, meat and bone meal, and blood meal fed separately, or in various combinations, in practical turkey rations (Liu et al 1987). When diets were equalized in nutrient composition according to the 1984 National Research Council requirements, there were no differences in body weight gains among treatments and all treatments resulted in body weights greater than the standard published in *Turkey World* (Sell 1986). The combination of feather meal, meat and bone meal, and blood meal resulted in significantly greater feed efficiency than the controls. Dr Waibel suggested using blood meal at 2%, feather meal at 2 to 4%, and meat and bone meal at 7 to 8% of rations for growing turkeys.

## REFERENCES

Association of the American Feed Control Officials. 1992. *Official Publication,* p 334.

Baker DH, Blitenthal RC, Boebel KP, Czarnecki GL, Southern LL, & Willis GM. 1981. *Poultry Science* 60:1865.

Carpenter KJ. 1960. *Biochemical Journal* 77:604.

Combs GF & Romoser GL. 1955. Maryland Agricultural Experiment Station Miscellaneous Publcation no 126.

Dale NM & Fuller HL. 1978. *Poultry Science* 57:1635.

Dale NM & Fuller HL. 1980. *Poultry Science* 59:1434.

Escalona RR & Pesti GM. 1987. *Poultry Science* 66:1067.

Forbes EB & Swift RW. 1944. *Journal of Nutrition* 27:453.

Fuller HL. 1956. *Poultry Science* 35:1143 (abstr).

Fuller HL. 1967. *Proceedings of the Georgia Nutrition Conference, Atlanta,* p 24.

Fuller HL & Dale NM. 1986. *Proceedings of the Georgia Nutrition Conference, Atlanta,* p 98.

Fuller HL & Rendon M. 1977. *Poultry Science* 56:549.

Fuller HL & Wilder OHM. 1987. *The Science of Meat and Meat Products,* 3rd edition, p 531. Food and Nutrition Press, Westport, CT.

Han Y & Parsons CM. 1990. *Poultry Science* 69:1544.

Hill FW & Dansky LM. 1954. *Poultry Science* 33:112.

Horani F & Sell JL. 1977. *Poultry Science* 56:1972.
Janssen WMA. 1985. *Voendervetten,* p 65.

Jensen LS. 1983. *Feedstuffs* 55(25):15.

Jensen LS. 1990. *Fats and Proteins Research Foundation Directors Digest,* p 44.

Jensen LS, Schumaier GW, & Latshaw JD. 1970. *Poultry Science* 49:1697.

Lessire M, Leclercq B, Conan L, & Hallonis JM. 1985. *Poultry Science* 64:1721.

Liu JK, Waibel PE, & Noll SL. 1987. *Proceedings of the Minnesota Conference on Turkey Research,* p 101.

Martisiswoyo A & Jensen LS. 1988. *Poultry Science* 67:280.

Matterson LD, Potter LM, Stutz MW, & Singsen EP. 1965. Connecticut Agricultural Experiment Station Report #7.

Mendonca CX & Jensen LS. 1988. *Poultry Science* 67 (suppl):117.

Morris WC & Balloun SL. 1971. *Poultry Science* 50:1609.

Naber EC & Morgan CL. 1956. *Poultry Science* 35:888.

National Research Council. 1984. *Nutrient Requirements of Poultry.* National Academy Press, Washington, DC.

Pesti GM, Faust LO, Fuller HL, & Dale NM. 1986. *Poultry Science* 65:2258.

Reid BL. 1983. *Proceedings of the National Renderers Asociation Symposium for the Feed Industry,* Atlanta, GA.

Romoser GL. 1955. *Proceedings of the Maryland Nutrition Conference, Washington, DC,* p 41.

Scott HM, Singsen EP, & Matterson LD. 1947. Mimeograph series. University of Connecticut, Storrs.

Scott ML, Nesheim MC, & Young RJ. 1982. *Nutrition of the Chicken.* ML Scott Associates Publishers, WF Humphrey Press Inc, Geneva, NY.

Sell JL. 1986. *Turkey World.* Watt Publishing Co, Mount Morris, IL.

Sell JL, Hasiak RJ, & Owwings WJ. 1985. *Poultry Science* 64:1957.

Sell JL, Krogdahl A, & Hanyu N. 1986. *Poultry Science* 65:546.

Sibbald IR. 1976. *Poultry Science* 55:303.

Sibbald IR. 1987. *Canadian Journal of Animal Science* 67:221.

Sibbald IR, Slinger SJ, & Ashton GC. 1961. *Poultry Science* 40:303.

Summers JD. 1969. *Feedstuffs* 16Mar, p 36.

Summers JD. 1976. *Proceedings of the National Renderers Symposium, Atlanta, GA.*

Thomas OP, Bossard EH, Nicholson JL, & Twining PV Jr. 1972. *Proceedings of the Maryland Nutrition Converence, Washington, DC,* p 86.

Wilder OHM. 1956. American Meat Institute Foundation Circular #23.

Wisman EL, Holmes CE, & Engel RW. 1958. *Poultry Science* 37:834.

# 8

# Utilizing Rendered Products: Ruminants

## Ric R Grummer & Terry Klopfenstein

## Fats and Greases
### Ric R Grummer

The major use for rendered fats and greases in feeding ruminants is to increase the energy density of their diet. Fat contains approximately 3 times more utilizable energy per unit mass than corn and 3.5 to 5 times more energy than forage. Traditional feedstuffs for ruminants usually contain about 3% fat and 97% protein and carbohydrate. Energy density of the diet can be increased by increasing the concentrate:forage ratio. If forage concentration in the diet becomes too low, rumen fermentation becomes too active, acid production becomes excessive, and health of the animal is jeopardized. Long-chain fatty acids, the major component of fats, are not fermented in the rumen. Therefore, they can be used to increase the energy density of the diet and minimize the risk of the animals' developing acidosis.

Fat can be toxic to rumen microorganisms and result in partial inhibition of rumen fermentation. Fermentation of fibrous feeds, eg, forages, is most markedly affected. The ramifications of this depends on the animal being fed. For example, this would be of little consequence when feeding a finishing beef steer a diet that is almost all concentrate. In contrast, a dairy cow consumes a diet containing 40 to 60% forage and is very dependent on the energy derived from fiber digestion for milk production. Much of the past research on fat supplementation of ruminant diets has investigated means by which fat can be used in the diet to maximize energy delivery to the animal without interfering with rumen fermentation. Today, producers are successfully feeding 2 to 4% supplemental fat in ruminant diets. Tallow, grease, and animal–vegetable fat blends are economical sources of fat that are very important to the feed industry.

Of the many uses for rendered fats and greases, the largest market is animal feeds Their use as a feed ingredient increases the market value of livestock animals and represents an ecologically sound cycle.

## FAT DIGESTION AND ABSORPTION IN RUMINANTS

Before reviewing the applied aspects of feeding rendered fats and greases to ruminants, it is important to understand how the ruminant digests and absorbs fats. Dietary sources of fat are usually long-chain fatty acids in free or esterified form. Triglycerides and galactolipids are the primary forms of esterified fatty acids, the former being most abundant in cereal grains, the latter, in forage plants. Triglycerides consist of 3 fatty acids esterified to the 3 carbon atoms of glycerol. Galactolipids are similar to triglycerides except that 1 of the esterified fatty acids is replaced by a sugar, specifically a galactose monomer or dimer. Supplemental fats may be free fatty acids, esterified fatty acids, or mineral salts of fatty acids. Fats and greases are predominantly triglycerides.

Esterified fatty acids are rapidly hydrolyzed to free form by lipolytic microorganisms within the rumen. Following hydrolysis, unsaturated fatty acids are hydrogenated by ruminal microorganisms. Unsaurated fatty acids are those that have 1 or more double bonds between carbons atoms. Hydrogenation refers to the conversion of a double bond to a single bond. Extent of hydrogenation is dependent on the degree of unsaturation of fatty acids, level and frequency of feeding, and pH of the rumen. Excessive amounts of polyunsaturated fatty acids (PUFA) fed to the animal, may exceed the capacity of the ruminal microorganisms to hydrogenate (saturate) fatty acids. If pH of the rumen is lowered by feeding too much concentrate or finely chopped forage, hydrogenation is less complete. This is undesirable because unsaturated fatty acids are toxic to ruminal microorganisms. Estimates for ruminal hydrogenation of PUFA range from 60 to 90% . Most of the fatty acids entering the rumen are linoleic acid (also referred to as C18:2, a fatty acid with 18 carbons and 2 double bonds) or linoleic acid (C18:3). Because of hydrogenation in the rumen, stearic acid (C18:0) and oleic or vaccenic acid (both C18:1 fatty acids) are the major fatty acids leaving the rumen. Long-chain fatty acids are not degraded in the rumen. Digestion coefficients for total fatty acids within the rumen are negative, which reflects microbial synthesis of fatty acids. The majority of fatty acids synthesized by rumen microbes are incorporated into phospholipids. Approximately 85 to 90% of the fatty acids leaving the rumen are free fatty acids, and approximately 10 to 15% microbial phospholipids. Since fatty acids are hydrophobic, they associate with particulate matter and pass to the lower gut.

Although little triglyceride reaches the small intestine of ruminants, bile and pancreatic secretions are required for lipid absorption. If triglycerides are fed at moderate levels in a form that protects them from ruminal hydrolysis (eg, formaldehyde-treated casein–fat emulsion), there appears to be sufficient pancreatic lipase activity in the small intestine for triglyceride hydrolysis (Noble 1981). However, pancreatic lipase does not appear to be inducible (Johnson et al 1974) and may become limiting if large quantities of triglyceride are presented to the small intestine. In the absence of substantial amounts of monoglyceride reaching the small intestine, ruminants are dependent on lysolecithin and C18:1 for fatty acid emulsification. Lysolecithin is formed by pancreatic phospholipase activity on lecithin which may be of microbial or hepatic origin. Mono-unsaturated fatty acid comes predominantly from digesta leaving the rumen. Even though C18:1 is inhibitory to rumen microorganisms, it is critical that a portion of the unsaturated fatty acids avoid complete hydrogenation in the rumen and pass to the small intestine to serve as an emulsification agent. Fatty acid emulsification and micelle formation in the small intestine is essential for efficient fat digestion and absorption.

## EFFECTS OF FAT ON RUMEN FERMENTATION

Fats that are rich in polyunsaturated fatty acids are more likely to interfere with ruminal fermentation. They are more soluble in an aqueous medium than saturated fatty acids and, therefore, more likely to adversely affect rumen microorganisms. For years, many people avoided feeding their animals animal fats thinking the fats would interfere with ruminal fermentation. There was very little research to support or refute this notion. However, based on the fatty acid profile of tallow and grease (Table 1), we might actually suspect the opposite. Animal fats have a relatively low unsaturated:saturated fatty acid ratio relative to vegetable oils.

Animal fats have a high titre value. Titre is a test that measures the temperature at which melted fatty acids, obtained by hydrolysis of a fat source, congeal upon cooling. It measures the hardness of a fat. The harder the fat is, the less likely it will interfere with rumen fermentation. Another common measure for hardness of fat is iodine value. Iodine value (IV) measures the amount of double bonds in fatty acids and indicates the degree of saturation. The higher the IV, the more unsaturated a fat is and the lower the melting point. In other words, values for titre and IV are inversely related. Once again, data would imply that the effects of animal fats in the rumen might be quite subtle.

California research (DePeters et al 1987) indicates that moderate amounts of yellow grease can be added to diets containing whole cottonseed without interfering with rumen fermentation. Tallow was added at 1, 2, or 3% of diet dry matter to a totally mixed diet already containing 2.8% supplemental fat from whole soybeans (Grummer et al 1993). There were no adverse effects of tallow on feed intake, rumen fiber digestion, and milk fat percentage (Table 2). Note that the basal diets used in both studies contained whole oilseeds, cottonseeds, or soybeans. Oilseeds are typically the first source of supplemental fat in dairy diets because they are an inexpensive source of fat, they provide other nutrients in addition to fat, and the oil within oilseeds is essentially encapsulated and will not adversely affect rumen fermentation.

Very few studies have been conducted to compare various fat sources as a second increment of fat in dairy diets. Wu et al(1993) added 2.5% tallow, calcium salts of long chain fatty acids, or prilled hydrogenated tallow fatty acids to diets containing 7.2% whole cottonseed. The latter 2 fat sources are often referred to as specialty fats and are manufactured to have low solubility and to be inert in the rumen. Fat supplementation did not affect fiber digestion and resulted in greater milk and FCM yield, and decreased milk protein. There were no significant differences between fat sources indicating that tallow can be inert in the rumen even if the diet contains oilseeds.

The data from these studies indicate that tallow and grease are essentially inert in the rumen when fed as part of a totally mixed ration at 2 to 3% of diet dry matter. A note of caution: diets fed in these studies were alfalfa based. Evidence indicates that fat may be more likely to interfere with rumen fermentation when the forage source is corn silage. Smith and Harris (1993) compiled data from lactation trials in which various fat sources were fed with either corn silage, alfalfa, or corn silage/alfalfa-based diets. They concluded that decreased milk and (or) milk fat percentage were more likely when extruded soybeans, whole cottonseeds, and rendered animal fats were fed with corn silage-based diets than with alfalfa-based diets. Mechanisms by which fat may be more detrimental to fermentation on corn silage-based diets have not been identified. Replacement of 25% of the corn silage with alfalfa may alleviate the adverse effects fats have when feeding corn silage as the sole forage source (Smith et al 1993).

**Figure 1.** Energy utilization from fatty acids

Gross Energy ➔ Digestible Energy ➔ Metabolizable Energy ➔ Net Energy
of Lactation

| ↓ | ↓ | ↓ |
|---|---|---|
| Feces | Gas and Urine | Heat |
| Variable, 20-60% of GE | 0% of DE | 20% of ME |

**Table 1.** Fatty Acid Composition of Fat Supplements

| Source | Fatty Acid Content, g/100g Fatty Acid | | | | | | | |
|---|---|---|---|---|---|---|---|---|
| | C14:0 | C16:0 | C16:1 | C18:0 | C18:1 | C18:2 | C18:3 | U/S[a] |
| Soybean oil | -- | 10 | -- | 4 | 23 | 51 | 7 | 5.64 |
| Tallow | 3 | 27 | 5 | 21 | 41 | 2 | 1 | 0.96 |
| Poultry | 1 | 24 | 10 | 5 | 43 | 17 | 1 | 2.44 |
| Choice white grease | 2 | 24 | 4 | 12 | 45 | 11 | 3 | 1.70 |
| Yellow grease | 1 | 18 | 2 | 10 | 46 | 21 | 1 | 2.33 |
| Animal-vegetable | 2 | 26 | 2 | 18 | 34 | 16 | 2 | 1.17 |
| PHT[b] | 4 | 26 | 3 | 35 | 32 | -- | -- | 0.54 |
| SLFA[c] | 2 | 47 | -- | 36 | 14 | 1 | -- | 0.18 |

[a]U/S = Ratio of saturated to unsaturated fatty acids.
[b]PHT; partially hydrogenated tallow; Alifet; Alifet U.S.A., Inc.(Cincinnati, Ohio).
[c]SLFA: relatively saturated long chain fatty acids; Energy Booster 100; Milk Specialties, Inc. (Dundee, Illinois).

**Table 2.** Indications that Tallow Is Not Detrimental to Rumen Fermentation when Added to Alfalfa/Corn Silage Based Diets Containing Roasted Soybeans and Fed as a Totally Mixed Ration

| | Tallow in Diet (dry matter basis) | | | |
|---|---|---|---|---|
| | 0 | 1 | 2 | 3 |
| Dry matter intake, ib/d | 58.4 | 59.7 | 57.76 | 57.9 |
| Milk fat, %[a] | 3.08 | 3.01 | 3.13 | 3.07 |
| Ruminal pH | 6.2 | 6.1 | 6.0 | 6.0 |
| Ruminal acetate:propionate | 2.7 | 2.6 | 2.7 | 2.5 |

[a]Milk fat percentages were low because cows averaged 99.6 lb milk/day
Source: Grummer et al ,1993

## POSTRUMINAL DIGESTION OF FATS

In addition to being ruminally inert, fats must be highly digestible in the small intestine. The 2 major factors influencing the energy content of a fat source is the proportion comprised by fatty acid (vs other components such as glycerol, calcium, carriers) and postruminal digestibility of the fatty acid. The net energy of lactation ($NE_l$) value of fat (ie triglyceride) is approximately 2.60 Mcal/ lb or about 2.9 times more than that of ground corn (NRC 1989). Energy utilization from fatty acids is depicted in Figure 1. Conversion of DE to ME is assumed to be 100% because there is no loss of energy as gas or urine during the metabolism of fatty acids. The efficiency of conversion of ME to $NE_l$ is assumed to be 80% (NRC 1989) and constant among long-chain fatty acids. Consequently, fecal energy loss is the primary factor affecting the $NE_l$ value of a fat. To obtain a $NE_l$ of 2.60 Mcal NEl/ lb fat, the digestibility coefficient must be approximately 80%. Reductions in fatty acid digestibility below 80% will reduce the energy value of a fat supplement and erode the advantage that feeding fat has over carbohydrates and protein.

Fat composition of the basal diet, animal characteristics (eg, bile salt secretion, intestine pH), and characteristics of the supplemental fat are the major factors influencing postruminal digestibility of fat. Very little research is available with ruminants to quantitate the importance of basal diet and animal characteristics; characteristics of the supplemental fat that influence digestibility are well documented. Degree of saturation of the fatty acids is probably the characteristic of fat that has the greatest influence on postruminal digestion. Although unsaturated fatty acids are subject to hydrogenation in the rumen, the process is not complete. Therefore, degree of saturation of fatty acids reaching the duodenumis affected by fat sources. Degree of saturation influences the melting point of the fatty acid and probably affects the solubility of the fatty acid in an aqueous medium. This may influence the ease with which fatty acids are transferred from particulate matter to a micelle prior to absorption. Unsaturated fatty acids are more hydrophilic, interact better with bile salts to form micelles, and pass more easily from the unstirred water layer adjacent to the microvilli of the small intestine. If triglycerides escape hydrolysis in the rumen, they must be hydrolyzed before micelle formation and absorption. The degree of saturation of constituent fatty acids also may influence the extent of triglyceride hydrolysis by pancreatic lipase.

Firkins and Eastridge (1994) summarized 11 studies and examined the relationship between IV and fatty acid digestibility. In general, fats with a low IV (high degree of saturation) were poorly digested in the small intestine. Fatty acid digestibility was reduced when IV fell below 45. However, almost all of the data pertained to fats with IV below 25 and above 45, therefore, they (Pantoja et al 1995) conducted a trial to determine the digestibility of fats with intermediate IV. Tallow and partially hydrogenated tallow were mixed to obtain blends with IV of 45, 35, 26, or 16. Total fatty acid digestibilities of the control diet and diets with the fat blends were 75.1, 73.1, 64.6, 59.8, and 57.1. These data support the notion that fat should have an IV of 45 or greater to be well digested.

Not all fats with low IV have low postruminal digestibility. Another characteristic of fat that can influence digestion is chain length of fatty acids. Melting point and solubility of fatty acids increase as chain length decreases. Therefore, decreasing chain length may facilitate micelle formation. Steele and Moore (1968) fed sheep purified sources of myristic (C14:0), palmitic (C16:0), and stearic (C18:0) acid and observed almost a 2-fold increase in fatty acid digestibility when feeding myristic compared to stearic acid (Table 3). True intestinal digestibility of C16:0 (66%) was greater than that of C18:0 (54%) in lactating dairy cows fed calcium salts of palm oil fatty acids or animal–vegetable blends (Wu et al 1991). Feeding lactating cows tallow, a C16:0-rich fat or a C18:0-rich fat also resulted in greater intestinal digestibility of C16:0 compared to C18:0 (Weisbjerg et al 1992b).

**Table 3.** Apparent Digestibility Coefficients and Melting Points of Supplemental Fatty Acids in Sheep

|  | Myristic | Palmitic | Stearic |
|---|---|---|---|
| Melting point, 0C | 58 | 64 | 70 |
| Fatty acid digestibility, % | 99.8 | 81.6 | 52.7 |

Source: Steele & Moore, 1968

Particle size is another factor that may influence the digestibility of low IV fat sources (eg, as hydrogenated tallow) that are solid at rumen temperature. MacLeod and Buchanan-Smith (1972) fed hydrogenated tallow to sheep as a flake or after melting and blending with feeds. Digestibility of total fat (ether extractable material) was 34.8 and 42.2%, respectively. Total fatty acid digestibility was greater when feeding prilled vs flaked hydrogenated tallow to dairy cows but the difference was not statistically significant (36.7 vs 45.6%; Eastridge & Firkins 1992). The extent that flaking influences digestibility may depend on how brittle the flake is and how much particle size is reduced during feed mixing, mastication, and rumination.

Concentration of fat in the diet may also affect postruminal fat digestion. Increasing supplemental fat (yellow grease or animal–vegetable blend) from 1 to 2.5 g/kg body weight in beef diets decreased digestibility of the added fat from 80 to 60% (Zinn 1994). Similar results have been observed in dairy cows. True fatty acid digestibility of tallow was curvilinear with diminishing digestibility as fat intakes increased between 200 and 900 g fatty intake per day (Weisbjerg et al 1992a). Chandler (1993) indicated that digestibility of tallow was only 45 to 65% when added to diets that contained supplemental fat from vegetable sources. Weisbjerg et al (1992a) indicated that the depression in fatty acid digestibility with increasing intake was greater for saturated fatty acids (particularly C18:0) than unsaturated fatty acids. Fats that are inherently low in digestibility may be most susceptible to digestion depression as intake is increased.

Fatty acids are typically fed in 1 of 3 forms: free (nonesterified), esterified (usually, triglyceride), or calcium salt. Esterified fatty acids are usually assumed to be rapidly hydrolyzed in the rumen. However, that assumption may be incorrect for fats such as hydrogenated tallow that have a high melting point and remain solid in rumen fluid. Normally, very little triglyceride reaches the small intestine of ruminants, therefore, some think (eg Firkins & Eastridge 1994) that fat digestion may be limited if substantial amounts of triglyceride avoid hydrolysis in the rumen and reach the small intestine.

## FEEDING OF RENDERED FATS AND GREASES

Much of the information below relates to feeding fat to ruminants in general. When available, data specific to rendered fats and greases is discussed.

### Dairy Cattle

Immediately after calving, dairy cattle are in negative energy balance. Feed intake is insufficient and energy intake does not meet the cow's requirement for maintenance and copious milk secretion. Dairy cows may lose 2 to 3 lb of body weight per day during early lactation to support milk production. If rate of body weight loss is excessive or if body fat stores are depleted, milk production, health, and reproduction will be compromised. Consequently, maximizing energy intake during early lactation becomes critical  To increase energy density of the diet, supplemental fat can be fed or the proportion of the diet comprised of grain can be increased. The latter option is often practiced following calving, however, there are upper limits of grain that can be fed to dairy cattle. Excessive grain feeding results in depressed fiber digestion, decreased ruminal pH, and a low ratio of acetate:propionate, the 2 major volatile (short-chain) fatty acids formed during fermentation of feedstuffs. Long-term depression of ruminal pH and acetate:propionate will lead to acidosis, founder, and milk fat depression. Supplementing fat is a means by which energy density of the diet can be increased without reducing fiber levels below that required for optimal rumen fermentation.

An extensive review of the literature on fat supplementation of dairy cattle diets was presented by Shaver (1990); Table 4 summarizes his findings regarding lactation performance when cows are fed a single source of supplemental fat. In general, milk yield increases 3 to 4 lb/day when supplementing fat at 2 to 4% of ration dry matter; greater responses have been observed. Milk yield response tends to be lower when supplementing cottonseeds, but fat percentage responses are usually greater. Milk protein percentage almost always is decreased when feeding fat, but total protein synthesized by the mammary gland usually remains constant. In other words, the decrease in milk protein percentage reflects a dilution of protein because of enhanced milk yield.

**Table 4.** Performance of Cattle Fed Various Fat Sources

| Source (n) | Suppl. fat, % of DM | Change From Control | | | | |
| | | DMI ib/d | Milk ib/d | FCM ib/d | Fat % | Protein % |
|---|---|---|---|---|---|---|
| Roasted SB (5) | 2.5-3 | .2 | 4.2 | 4.1 | .06 | -.08 |
| Cottonseeds (4) | 3-3.5 | -.7 | .5 | 2.9 | .28 | -.09 |
| Megalac (10) | 2-3 | -1.1 | 3.1 | 4.0 | .11 | -.08 |
| Tallow (5) | 4-5 | 1.0 | 3.8 | 4.3 | .11 | -.15 |

*Source:* Adapted from Shaver, 1990

Because protein content influences cheese yield from milk, considerable efforts have been made to identify ways to maintain milk protein percentage during fat supplementation. Milk protein premiums have been increasing and probably will continue to increase in the future. Numerous investigators have hypothesized that supplemental fat reduces milk protein by reducing the amount of microbial protein synthesized in the rumen and absorbed in the small intestine. This could occur if fat reduces the amount of organic matter fermented in the rumen. Fermentation of organic matter provides energy for microbial growth. A reduction in fermentable organic matter can result if fat (nonfermentable) is incorporated into the diet at the expense of a readily fermented feed such as corn, if fat adversely affects rumen microbes so that fermentation is reduced, or both. Feeding additional protein or amino acids that are not degraded in the rumen is a way to compensate for potential reductions in microbial flow to the intestine. Although research results have been mostly disappointing, in some instances this strategy has partially reversed milk protein depression (Grummer 1993). Feeding supplemental niacin may also improve milk protein percentage when feeding supplemental fat (Grummer 1993).

Numerous trials have indicated that there is little benefit to milk production from feeding fat during the first 5 to 7 weeks postpartum (Grummer 1994). In essence, there seems to be a lag time prior to obtaining a milk response (Figure 2). Surprisingly, cows seem to best respond to fat near the time they reach positive energy balance. Similarly, body weight loss may not be reduced by feeding additional fat. However, gain usually is accelerated once the cow reaches positive energy balance. The lack of an early lactation response seems to be related to a depression in feed intake which offsets any advantage that may be gained by increasing the energy density of the diet. The early lactation cow that is rapidly mobilizing body fat seems to be "metabolically programmed" to consume a given amount of energy.  Fat should probably be left out of the diet immediately postpartum, but management factors may preclude doing so.

**Figure 2.** Milk response to fat is often delayed when supplementation is initiated at or shortly after calving.

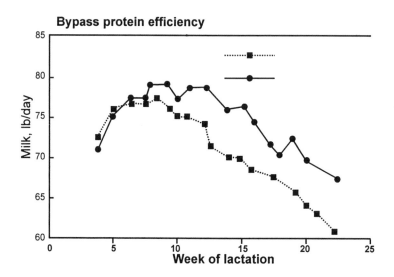

*Source:* Hoffman et al 1991

Field trials conducted in Pennsylvania (Chalupa & Ferguson 1990) and university trials conducted at South Dakota State University (Schingoethe & Casper 1991) indicated that milk yield advantages from feeding fat during the first half of lactation are maintained even when fat is withdrawn at mid lactation (Figure 3).  This probably should be expected if cows are in positive energy balance at the time fat is removed from the diet.  Neither the Pennsylvania nor the South Dakota research addressed whether cows could have produced additional milk if fat had been left in the diet for the remainder of the lactation.  Once again, logic says that cows would not respond to fat supplementation if they were in positive energy balance.  However, numerous trials have indicated that low producing cows (<60 lb/day), presumably in positive energy balance, respond to fat supplementation (Shaver 1990).  The reason for the milk response is not known, however, fat supplementation may increase availability of glucose to milk producing cells.  Glucose is a precursor for lactose synthesis and the amount of lactose synthesized is a major determinant of milk volume produced by the mammary gland.

**Figure 3.** The "carry over" effect when fat is withdrawn from the diet of mid-lactation cows.

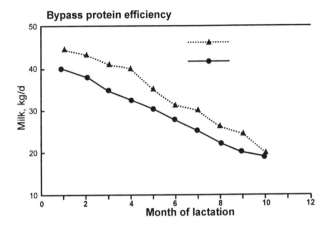

*Source:* Chalupa & Ferguson 1990.

It is clear from the literature that heifers respond differently to fat supplementation than mature cows (Grummer 1994). Increases in milk and fat-corrected milk yields were 4.9 and 6.1 lb/day for multiparous cows and 1.8 and 2.9 lb/day for heifers when fat was fed in 5 research and field trials. Little difference was observed in the milk fat percentage responses between heifers and mature cows. Energy supplied to heifers is used for growth in addition to maintenance and lactation. Therefore, a lower proportion of the energy supplied by fat may be available for milk production in heifers. The lower milk response by heifers relative to mature cows may be economically important because heifers may constitute 35 to 40% of the herd. However, one should be cautioned against basing the decision of whether to feed fat to heifers solely on predicted milk responses. Fat supplementation may enable heifers to better withstand the stress of the first lactation, maintain better body condition, and consequently perform better during the second lactation.

The decision of whether to feed supplemental fat to mature cows as well as heifers should not depend solely on milk response. Other potential benefits from feeding fat to lactating cows may be improvement in body condition, reproductive performance, and metabolic status and alleviation of heat stress. Documentation of these effects is limited. Improvement in reproductive performance due to fat supplementation may be the consequence of improved energy status, provision of essential fatty acids, or stimulation of progesterone production by the corpus luteum (Grummer & Carroll 1991). The majority of studies have not shown an improvement in reproductive performance of cattle fed supplemental fat, however, this is probably the consequence of too few animals on trial to detect a response. Ferguson et al (1990) observed an improvement in first service conception rate and a decrease in services per conception, while Sklan et al (1991) noted a decrease in days open and an increase in pregnancy rate when feeding supplemental fat.

Supplemental fat is primarily metabolized by extrahepatic tissues, but fatty acids mobilized during negative energy balance may be utilized by the liver. Consequently, a potential benefit from feeding fat to dairy cattle may be to reduce fatty acid mobilization and decrease the amount of fatty acids taken up by the liver, which could result in less fat deposition in the liver and lower ketone production. Feeding a specialty fat beginning at 17 days prepartum and lasting through early lactation did not reduce liver fat content, and the positive influence on blood ketone levels was relatively small (Grummer & Carroll 1991). In contrast, Drackley et al (personal communication) fed tallow to cows during the entire dry period and prevented development of fatty liver at calving.

Fat supplementation may be particularly beneficial when environmental temperature and humidity are high and cows are heat stressed. Digestion and metabolism of feed nutrients produces heat. If an animal is heat stressed, it eats less to reduce the heat load and energy expenditures associated with dissipating heat. Numerous species of animals have been shown to generate less heat during digestion and metabolism of fat than of proteins and carbohydrates. Therefore, fat feeding during heat stress may serve a dual function. It may lessen the heat load and it will increase the energy density of the diet during periods when feed intake is likely to be depressed.

## Beef Cattle

Very little research is available on fat supplementation to beef animals relative to swine, poultry, and dairy. Fat supplementation of diets fed to finishing beef in commercial feedlots is common, particularly in the Southwest and Southeast. Feeding strategies to incorporate fat into beef diets differs somewhat than for dairy diets. Correct use of fat in dairy diets allows producers to increase energy density in the diet without overfeeding grain, thereby avoiding depression in fiber digestion, acidosis, and low-fat milk. In contrast to feeding fat to lactating dairy cows, avoiding depression in fiber digestion is of lesser concern when feeding high concentrate (>80% of ration dry matter) diets to finishing beef cattle. To a large extent, the cost of fat supplementation must be competitive with the cost of feeding cereal grains. Consequently, most of the fats used in beef rations can be purchased locally and are low cost, typically yellow grease or acidulated soapstocks.

The major use of fat in beef cattle diets is to increase average daily gain and efficiency of feed utilization (gain/feed). For example, supplementing 4% fat in diets containing 80% flaked milo increased daily gain and feed efficiency and improved the carcass characteristics of finishing beef cattle (Brandt & Anderson 1990; Table 5). Similarly, Gramlich et al

(1990) observed an increase in gain/feed when 4% tallow was added to diets consisting primarily of dry-rolled corn. Finishing cattle fed barley-based diets supplemented with 0, 4, or 8% yellow grease or animal–vegetable fat blends showed linear improvements in weight gain, feed conversion, and carcass characteristics (Zinn 1989). There were no interactions between the level of fat supplementation and fat type. These data indicate that high levels of fats with varying fatty acid composition can be used in finishing beef diets. Not all studies have demonstrated enhanced performance due to fat supplementation, but more data are needed to identify the critical factors that mediate response. Most of the negative responses have occurred when fat was supplemented at 5% of diet dry matter or higher.

**Table 5.** Effects of 4% Supplemental Fat on Finishing Yearling Steers

| | | Supplemental Fat Source | | |
| --- | --- | --- | --- | --- |
| | Control | Soybean Oil | Tallow | Yellow Grease |
| Initial wt., lb. | 811 | 799 | 799 | 815 |
| Final wt., lb. | 1191 | 1207 | 1199 | 1235 |
| Daily gain, lb. | $3.13^e$ | $3.39^{cd}$ | $3.30^d$ | $3.50^c$ |
| Daily feed, lb. | $19.6^{cd}$ | $19.6^{cd}$ | $19.1^c$ | $20.1^d$ |
| Gain/feed | $.160^b$ | $.173^a$ | $.174^a$ | $.175^a$ |
| Dressing percentage | $63.42^d$ | $64.57^c$ | $64.15^c$ | $64.13^c$ |

[a,b] Means in a row with different superscripts differ (P<0.01).
[c,d,e] Means in a row with different superscripts differ (P<0.05).
*Source:* Brandt & Anderson 1990

It is typically recommended that fat be added to high concentrate finishing rations at the level of 2 to 4% of ration dry matter. Above this concentration, fat digestibility will probably be reduced and feed intake make be adversely affected (Zinn 1994). Optimal level of fat feeding may depend on the type of cereal grains comprising the concentrate. Hale (1986) speculated that less supplemental fat may be desired in diets containing corn, which contains 4% fat, than in diets containing other cereal grains such as barley, wheat, and sorghum which have relatively little fat. In general, results have been more positive when adding fat to barley- or sorghum-based finishing diets than corn-based diets. However, results from an experiment specifically designed to evaluate the feeding value of yellow grease in steam-flaked corn or wheat diets indicated no interactions between grain type and supplemental fat on steer growth (Zinn 1992).

Subacute acidosis is a common problem in finishing beef cattle. Feeding a small amount of forage instead of an all-concentrate diet often improves performance of finishing beef cattle, presumably due to increased salivation and fewer cases of acidosis and liver abscesses. Nebraska researchers (Huffman et al 1992, Krehbiel et al 1995) speculated that feeding fat may prevent subacute acidosis. They hypothesized that fat might bind to grain and alter the rate or extent of acid production from starch fermentation in the rumen. If true, this could explain why favorable responses to fat supplementation have been most consistent when feeding grains that are highly fermentable (eg, barley and wheat; Krehbiel et al 1995). Feeding 4% supplemental fat did not affect rumen fermentation and starch digestion when finishing cattle were fed diets with 0 or 7.5% forage (Huffman et al 1992). Unexpectedly, acid concentration in the rumen was often increased when 2 to 8% tallow or yellow grease was fed and corn–wheat grain mixes were placed directly into the rumen as an acidosis challenge to steers not accustomed to a high grain diet (Krehbiel et al 1995).

Ionophores are commonly included in finishing diets. Fat and ionophores may influence rumen fermentation in similar ways. Specifically, both additives may decrease methanogenesis and increase the molar proportion of propionate found in the rumen fluid. Zinn (1988) observed no interaction between 4% yellow grease and monensin on performance of feedlot steers. Both monensin and fat decreased estimated methane production and acetate to propionate ratios in the rumen, but the effects were not additive. In 1 trial monensin had no effect on animal performance, but in a second trial monensin reduced feed intake and feed required per unit of gain. However, neither trial demonstrated fat by monensin interactions on animal performance. In contrast, recent reports indicate that monensin did not influence animal performance when fat was in the diet (Clary et al 1991). It was speculated that monensin may be rendered inactive when fed with fat because it is fat soluble.

The net energy values for fat published by the National Research Council (NRC 1994) for beef may be low when fat is incorporated into high concentrate finishing diets. The $NE_m$ and $NE_g$ value for fat reported by the NRC is 4.75 and 3.51 Mcal/kg. Most estimates derived from the literature are higher, typically being 5.0 to 6.4 Mcal $NE_m$/kg and 4.0 to 4.7 Mcal $NE_g$/kg (Brandt & Anderson 1990; Zinn 1988, 1989). Energy values for tallow tended to be higher than those for vegetable sources, such as soybean oil and soybean soapstocks. The energy content of soybean soapstocks was estimated to be below NRC values, which may be due to the unsaturated fatty acid profile or the high free fatty acid content. Energy values for yellow grease have varied greatly which may reflect the variable make-up of this fat source. The $NE_g$ value cited by the NRC assumes fat digestibility to be 80% and efficiency of conversion of ME to $NE_g$ to be 55%. It is likely that the efficiency of ME usage for tissue gain is greater than 55% (Zinn 1988).

Another potential role of fat in beef production is in feeding the postpartum beef cow. Reproduction of the cow–calf herd is a major factor affecting production in beef cattle. Postpartum cows, particularly those in poor body condition may fail to become pregnant when inadequately nourished. Inadequate nutrition may result from insufficient feed supplies or poor quality feeds. Supplemental fat may enhance reproductive efficiency by improving energy balance of the postpartum cow or through mechanisms independent of energy status. Feeding fat to cattle almost always increases plasma cholesterol. Consequently, it has been postulated that feeding fat may improve reproductive performance by increasing conversion of cholesterol to progesterone. Improved fertility in cattle has been associated with high circulating concentrations of progesterone during the luteal phase before and after insemination (Grummer & Carroll 1991). Feeding fat to postpartum beef cows significantly increased plasma cholesterol and progesterone concentrations (Hightshoe et al 1991, Williams 1989) and increased average life span of the corpus luteum (Williams 1989). Recent data from Texas A&M indicate that 4% supplemental fat increases serum concentrations of insulin, growth hormone, follicular fluid IGF-I concentrations, and medium-sized follicle populations in beef cows after 20 days of feeding (Thomas et al 1993, 1994). Effects on plasma insulin, follicular fluid IGF-I, and medium-sized follicles were greatest for cows fed soybean oil vs those fed fish oil or tallow. Consequently, they postulated that C18:2-rich fats alter rumen fermentation toward greater rumen propionate production which in turn influences endocrine status of the cow.

# Protein
## Terry Klopfenstein

The value of renderers' byproducts as protein sources depends primarily upon the escape (or bypass) value of the protein in these sources. Escape protein is protein that escapes degradation in the rumen and is then digested in the intestinal tract of the ruminant. The animal has 2 sources of protein to meet its productive functions: escape protein and microbial protein. The net absorbed protein from these sources is called metabolizable protein. Microbial protein is important to the economical production of ruminants. However, for animals in productive situations such as growth or lactation, some escape protein is required. Most protein sources at least partially escape rumen degradation. Many plant proteins have escape values from 20 to 40% of the crude protein, whereas renderers' byproducts have escape values ranging from 45 to 85%.

Blood meal, meat and bone meal, and feather meal are higher in escape protein than oil meals and forages, and increase performance when included in forage-based diets sufficient in rumen degradable protein. Both processing conditions and raw materials influence the nutritive value of animal byproduct meals.

Renderers apply heat to drive off moisture, extract fat, and eliminate bacterial contamination from animal tissues. This cooking also denatures proteins, creating cross-links and insoluble bonds within and between protein chains, and enhancing resistance to microbial degradation in the rumen. However, processing at very high temperatures can limit extent of enzymatic breakdown of proteins, reducing digestibility and absorption in the small intestine. Feathers are a keratinous protein source of low digestibility in their native state. With hydrolysis under heat and pressure, the protein in feathers is highly digested.

Variable inputs (deadstock, tankage, meat trimmings, and bones) contribute to the great diversity of commercial meat and bone meals. Concentration of meat and bone meal components, specifically bone, hair, and lean tissues, influence protein quantity and quality. High bone content, exhibited through ash, reduces crude protein, whereas hair is high in protein but poorly digested. Animal performance with meat and bone meal supplementation has been inconsistent, perhaps a result of inadequate escape protein or poor protein digestibility arising from raw materials or processing conditions. Meat and bone meals and feather meals are known to be high in escape protein but total tract digestibility of the protein is questionable. Research with meat and bone meal and other renderers' products sheds some light on the digestibility issue.

Meat and bone meal from various species (n = 36), feather meal (n = 9), and blood meal (n = 2) samples were obtained from renderers throughout the United States; the samples represent the variety of processing conditions and raw material that generate commercially available meals.  All samples were incubated in situ and in vitro to estimate escape protein, ashed at 1,112°F to determine mineral content, and fed to lambs to determine ruminant protein digestibility in vivo.  The results of several trials were compiled to generate a large data set.  Soybean meal and corn gluten meal were included to serve as standards of comparison for crude protein digestibility.

Metabolizable protein and escape protein digestibility were determined for individual animal byproducts using computed values for escape protein and true nitrogen digestibility.  Metabolizable protein was calculated as escape protein − (100−true nitrogen digestibility), and is the portion of crude protein that escapes microbial degradation and is digested in the small intestine.  Escape protein digestibility was determined by dividing metabolizable protein by escape protein.

Processing temperatures were known for 15 of the meat and bone meals; 14 of these products stemmed from 7 individual batches obtained from different producers.  These batches were divided, and the same raw materials were processed at a low (249°) and high (286°F) temperature.  Temperature did not influence true nitrogen digestibility, escape protein, escape protein digestibility, or metabilizable protein, and no significant correlations were exhibited ($P > .05$).  Processing temperatures of materials in this study were not extreme enough to substantially decrease protein digestibility, but are within the range routinely used in the rendering industry.

In vitro ammonia release and in situ incubation were highly correlated as measures of escape protein.  However, calculations of escape protein based on ammonia release exhibited higher values than those determined in situ, especially in products with higher degradability (Figure 4).  This may have been the result of DM loss from the polyester bags during in situ washing and indicate an underestimation of escape protein content of meat and bone and poultry byproduct meals.  Correlations were conducted using escape values obtained through ammonia release, as these were considered to be more accurate estimates.  Table 6 summarizes values for measured variables and product components, and illustrates the disparity in values between in vitro ammonia release and in situ procedures.

The digestibility of the escape protein in meat and bone and poultry byproduct meals ranged from 61 to 96%.  Only 4 of the 36 samples were below 70%. The average escape protein digestibility of the meat and bone and poultry byproduct meals equaled that of soybean meal (Table 7).

**Table 6.** Analysis of Animal Byproducts

| Item (n) | Ash[a] | Crude Protein[a] | Escape Protein[b] |
|---|---|---|---|
| MBM+PBM[c] (36) | | | In Situ |
| Range | 12.3 - 50.6 | 39.5 - 69.5 | 32.0 - 56.1 |
| Mean | 27.2 | 54.6 | 43.5 |
| SD | 9.3 | 7.2 | 6.7 |
| | | | NH₃ Release |
| Range | | | 43.8 - 74.1 |
| Mean | | | 59.5 |
| SD | | | 6.4 |
| Feather Meal (9) | | | |
| Range | 1.2 - 3.1 | 81.7 - 92.1 | 50.0 - 82.8 |
| Mean | 2.4 | 86.8 | 67.1 |
| SD | .7 | 3.7 | 10.0 |
| Blood Meal (2) | | | |
| Range | 1.9 - 3.6 | 82.1 - 93.5 | 89.6 - 97.3 |
| Mean | 2.7 | 87.8 | 93.5 |
| SD | 1.2 | 8.1 | 5.4 |
| Soybean Meal (2) | | | |
| Range | 7.3 - 7.8 | 42.8 - 49.3 | 30.0 - 31.6 |
| Mean | 7.5 | 46.1 | 30.8 |
| SD | .3 | 4.6 | 1.1 |
| Corn Gluten Meal (1) | 1.7 | 63.9 | 64.9 |

[a]Expressed as a percentage of dry matter.
[b]Percentage of crude protein.
[c]Meat and bone meal (MBM), poultry byproduct meal (PBM).

**Figure 4.** Correlation of protein escape value, obtained through ammonia release, and in situ escape protein for meat and bone, and poultry byproduct meals.

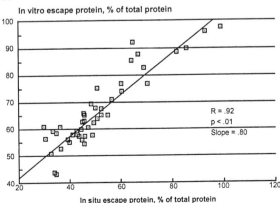

In vitro escape protein, % of total protein

R = .92
p < .01
Slope = .80

In situ escape protein, % of total protein

**Figure 5.** Correlation of in vitro escape protein and ash content in meat and bone meals.

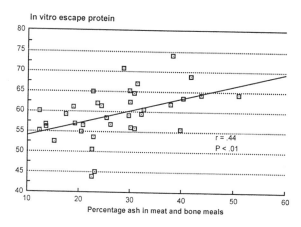

Ash content of meat and bone meal exhibited a positive relationship with escape protein ($r$ = .44, $P$ <.01; Figure 5). Protein identified with bone is comprised predominantly of collagen, and may be more resistant to degradation by ruminal microorganisms than protein in lean tissues. Although ash concentration was related to microbial protein degradation, it had no significant negative relationship to true nitrogen digestibility ($r$ = −.26, $P$ = .13; Figure 6). This suggests that protein associated with bone is adequately digested in the ruminant small intestine. Although ash content was positively related to escape protein, a relationship was not observed between ash and metabolizable protein ($r$ = .20, $P$ = .22). True nitrogen digestibility of meat and bone meal did not exhibit a strong negative correlation with escape protein ($r$ = −.28, $P$ = .09), but the accompanying probability level suggests that a negative relationship may exist. High escape protein content in meat and bone meal may stem either from processing technique or raw materials.

**Figure 6.** Correlation of in vivo true nitrogen digestibility and ash content in meat and bone meals.

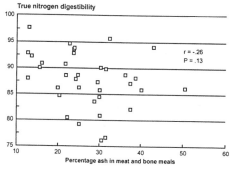

Hydrolyzed feather meal samples ranged from 68 to 93% digestibility of the escape protein. Escape values ranged from 50 to 83%.

Metabolizable protein is the protein calculated to be absorbed as amino acids from the small intestine. These metabolizable protein values ranged from 31 to 59% for meat and bone and poultry byproduct meals. Feather meals ranged from 34 to 75%. This suggests an opportunity to select sources of these products with higher feeding values.

This study indicates that meat and bone meal, feather meal, and blood meal possess adequate protein digestibilities, when properly processed, which are comparable to soybean meal and corn gluten meal. Raw materials (based on ash contents) were related with measures of feed value of animal byproducts in our evaluation more than processing temperature; in situ incubation may not be the appropriate means to determine escape protein content of meat and bone meals.

**Table 7.** Digestibility and Metabolizable Protein of Animal Byproducts

| Item (n) | True Nitrogen Digestibility | Metabolizable Protein[a] | Escape Protein Digestibility[b] |
|---|---|---|---|
| MBM+PBM[c] (36) | | | |
| Range[d] | 76.4 - 97.8 | 18.6 - 46.5 | 52.1 - 95.2 |
| Mean | 87.8 | 31.3 | 72.0 |
| SD | 5.2 | 7.0 | 10.9 |
| Range[e] | | 31.1 - 58.7 | 61.1 - 96.4 |
| Mean | | 47.4 | 79.6 |
| SD | | 7.0 | 8.4 |
| Feather Meal (9) | | | |
| Range | 80.8 - 94.9 | 34.1 - 74.8 | 68.2 - 93.0 |
| Mean | 87.8 | 54.9 | 80.7 |
| SD | 5.2 | 14.1 | 9.9 |
| Blood Meal (2) | | | |
| Range | 84.9 - 86.0 | 75.6 - 82.2 | 84.4 - 84.5 |
| Mean | 85.5 | 78.9 | 84.4 |
| SD | .8 | 4.7 | .1 |
| Soybean Meal (2) | | | |
| Range | 91.4 - 91.7 | 21.7 - 23.0 | 72.3 - 72.7 |
| Mean | 91.6 | 22.4 | 72.5 |
| SD | .2 | .9 | .3 |
| Corn Gluten Meal (1) | 96.7 | 61.6 | 94.9 |

[a]Calculated as: escape protein − (100 − true nitrogen digestibility).
[b]Calculated as: (metabolizable protein/escape protein) x 100.
[c]Meat and bone meal (MBM), poultry byproduct meal (PBM).
[d]Calculated using in situ protein escape values.
[e]Calculated using in vitro protein escape values.

Studies evaluating protein sources should be designed to meet 1 of 2 objectives:   accurately assess the bypass content of protein sources, or confirm the bypass value in production feeding systems.   Accurate evaluation of protein is absolutely necessary before systems of meeting ruminant protein requirements can be used with confidence.  Estimates of the bypass values for protein sources can be made from laboratory analyses or by directly measuring bypass of a protein source with intestinally fistulated animals.   While these values are useful as supporting evidence, animal growth or production is the best way to obtain these bypass values.

## GROWTH STUDIES DETERMINING BYPASS VALUE

In growth trials, it is absolutely essential that proteins be compared below the animal's protein requirement.  Otherwise, protein is not the first limiting nutrient, and valid comparisons cannot be made.  For example, blood meal compared with soybean meal meets the animal's protein requirement (maximum gain) with about 40% as much supplemental protein (Figure 7).  Therefore, blood meal is worth 2.5 times as much, per unit of protein, as soybean meal.  Intestinally fistulated cattle studies and lab analyses support this value.  Blood meal just does not degrade in the rumen, whereas soybean meal protein is about 70% degraded.  These growth response data are supported by estimates of bypass made with intestinally fistulated cattle (Loerch et al 1983, Stock et al 1986).

A growth trial (Figure 8) indicates that calves consuming blood meal, feather meal, and the combination of feather meal and blood meal gained faster than steers fed soybean meal.  The improved protein efficiency for the combination of blood meal and feather meal compared with either fed alone may be due to sulfur amino acids supplied by the feather meal and lysine or other amino acids, supplied by blood meal.  These data indicate that feather meal protein is highly bypassed, is digestible, and can be utilized in growing ruminant diets.  The utilization of the protein may be increased when fed in combination with blood meal possibly due to a complementary effect of amino acids.

Pure feather meal normally contains 90% crude protein and 3 to 5% fat.  Processing methods affect quality of feather meal, and raw feathers may contain blood, heads, and offal.   Blood contamination alters crude protein level insignificantly as both have similar protein contents. The blood may be added before or after feathers are hydrolyzed.  While hydrolysis is necessary to make feathers nutritionally available to animals, hydrolyzing blood may damage the protein and reduce the nutritional value.

A dacron bag trial was conducted to determine the bypass value of feather meal with blood added before or after hydrolysis.   Protein sources included soybean meal, feather meal without blood, ring dried poultry blood meal, and 2 mixtures of 45% feathers and 55% raw poultry blood. Feathers and blood were either combined before or after steam hydrolysis of feathers. Dry, the mixtures contained about 33% blood.

**Figure 7.** Natural protein fed/day vs daily gain above urea control (Stock et al 1983).

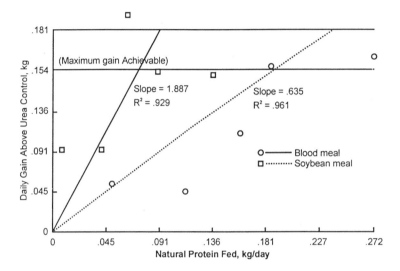

**Figure 8.** Regression of gain protein intake for growth study. The resulting slopes (numbers on graph) are the protein efficiencies from the growth study. Standard errors of treatment means were 0.228 for soybean meal, 0.374 for blood meal, 0.227 for feather meal and 0.296 for blood meal + feather meal (Goedeken et al 1990a).

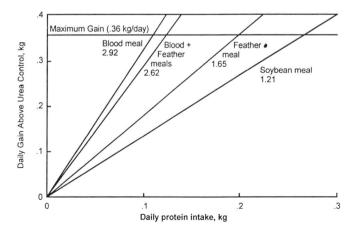

Bypass protein of feather meal was greater than soybean meal but less than blood meal (Table 8).   Adding raw blood to feathers and hydrolyzing together did not increase bypass above that of feather meal without blood.   Adding blood after hydrolysis increased bypass compared to feather meal   Total tract protein digestibility was similar for soybean meal, blood meal, feather meal, and the mixture of blood and feathers when blood was not hydrolyzed.   When the blood was hydrolyzed with the feathers, protein digestibility of the blood and feather mixture was lower than that of the other treatments.   The reduced digestibility probably is a result of damage to blood protein during the hydrolysis.   Net bypass is an estimate of digestible protein presented to the small intestine.   Hydrolyzing blood with feathers resulted in a 15% reduction in net bypass compared to blood added after hydrolysis.

Since blood meal is more than twice the cost of feather meal, it would be advantageous to know the minimum amount of blood meal required to maintain economical and biological efficiency when using feather meal. A growth trial was conducted to determine whether small additions of blood meal to feather meal would result in protein efficiencies greater than those obtained when feather meal is used as the sole escape protein source.

The urea control calves gained 0.38 kg/day while maximum gain due to protein supplementation was 0.71 kg/day.   The most efficiently used protein supplement was 100% blood meal (Figure 9).   No differences in protein efficiency were observed among the supplements containing the various combinations of blood and feather meals.   Relative to the supplement containing only feather meal, all combinations yielded significantly higher protein efficiencies.   A complementary relationship between blood meal and feather meal (Figure 10) existed.   A 59%, 23%, and 4% improvement in protein efficiency relative to the 100% feather meal and 100% blood meal supplements were obtained when 12.5%, 25%, and 50% blood meal were added, respectively.

If all the blood from poultry slaughter is available, it will amount to about 10% of the dry weight of the feathers.   Based on this, use of feather meal with that amount of blood would be an advantageous option. However, as shown previously, it is important that blood be added after feathers are hydrolyzed to prevent a reduction in blood meal protein digestibility and net bypass due to the hydrolyzing process.   It is important for the producer and nutritionist to be aware of the processing method used when formulating supplements containing feather meal.

Protein efficiency was maintained when amounts equal to 12.5% and 25% blood meal were added to feather meal compared with 50% addition.   Formulation of protein supplements containing feather meal can be made more economical without compromising biological efficiency by using relatively small amounts of blood meal.

**Table 8.** Effect of Hydrolyzing Blood with Feathers on Protein Bypass and Digestibility

| Protein Source | Bypass[a] | Digestibility[b] | Net bypass[c] |
|---|---|---|---|
| Soybean meal | 26[d] | 100[e] | 26 |
| Blood + raw feathers hydrolyzed, ring dried | 76[e] | 87[d] | 63 |
| Blood + hydrolyzed feathers then ring dried | 82[f] | 96[e] | 78 |
| Blood meal | 90[g] | 100[e] | 90 |
| Feather meal | 73[e] | 96[e] | 69 |

[a]Bypass determined as percentage of protein remaining after 12 hours of ruminal incubation in dacron bags.
[b]Total tract digestibility determined in lambs.
[c]Net bypass=Bypass minus indigestibility.
[d,e,f,g]Means within columns with unlike superscripts differ (P<.07).
*Source:* Goedeken et al 1990b

**Figure 9.** Protein efficiency of calves fed feather meal (FTH) and blood meal (BM) combinations (Blasi et al 1991).

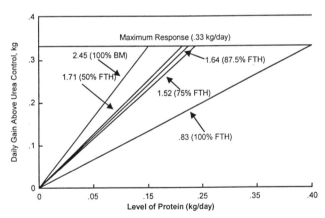

Feather meal is a good source of bypass protein for ruminants. The complementary effects of blood meal when added to feather meal indicate that blood meal supplies an amino acid(s) that is lacking in the feather meal Meat and bone meal and blood meal contain similar levels of many of the essential amino acids. Because meat and bone meal is cheaper per unit of protein and has a high level of phosphorus, it would be economically favorable if it had the same complementary effect as blood meal when combined with feather meal.

In a growth trial, a combination of feather meal and meat and bone meal, fed as 50% of the supplemental protein resulted in the highest numerical daily gains, indicating that protein was limiting in the other treatments (Table 9). Other than the 75% meat and bone meal, 25%

feather meal combination, all escape protein supplements resulted in better daily gain than the urea control calves. Inclusions of meat and bone meal to feather meal linearly decreased daily gains indicating no complementary effect between the 2. Apparently an amino acid(s) limited growth of the calves.

**Figure 10.** Complementary effect of feather meal–blood meal combinations (Blasi et al 1991).

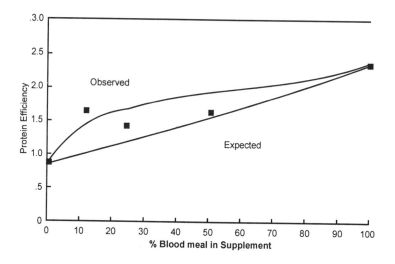

In another growth trial, feather meal was utilized more efficiently than soybean meal, meat and bone meal being intermediate (Table 10). There was no complementary effect of meat and bone meal when added to the feather meal  Apparently an amino acid(s) limits the efficiency of utilization of feather meal and meat and bone meal combinations.

Growth responses to meat and bone meal have been variable and may reflect the wide variety of tissues. The protein content of meat and bone meal can be a reflection of the different tissues making up the meal Generally, increasing bone content of meat and bone meal decreases protein which is quite low in essential amino acids, and depending on the tissues used, can make up a high percentage of meat and bone meal protein. Adding a high-quality protein, such as blood meal with meat and bone meal, may enhance protein quality by supplying amino acids that limit growth in meat and bone meal and may allow for a complementary response when fed with feather meal.

A 3 way combination of blood meal, meat and bone meal, and feather meal was tested in a growth trial. The objective was to determine the minimum levels of blood meal necessary to feed with meat and bone meal and feather meal mixtures (1/3:2/3 and 2/3:1/3) in order to obtain an optimum complementary effect.

**Table 9.** Performance of Calves Fed Feather Meal and Meat and Bone Meal Combinations (Gibb et al, 1992)

| Supplement[a] | Daily Gain, kg | Daily Feed, kg | Feed/ Gain |
|---|---|---|---|
| Urea | .55 | 6.35 | 11.6 |
| 100% Feather Meal[b] | .65 | 6.35 | 9.8 |
| 75% Feather Meal, 25% Meat and Bone Meal | .63 | 6.35 | 10.1 |
| 50% Feather Meal, 50% Meat and Bone Meal | .63 | 6.35 | 10.2 |
| 25% Feather Meal, 75% Meat and Bone Meal | .58 | 6.35 | 11.0 |
| 100% Meat and Bone Meal | .60 | 6.35 | 10.6 |
| Soybean Meal | .59 | 6.35 | 10.7 |
| High Level 50/50[c] | .67 | 6.35 | 9.5 |

[a]Fed to supply 35% of the supplemental protein, remainder from urea.
[b]Dacron bag bypass: meat and bone meal 75%, feather meal 56%. Protein digestibility: meat and bone meal 87%, feather meal 91%.
[c]50% feather meal and 50% meat and bone meal fed at 50% of supplement protein.
*Source:* Gibb et al 1992

**Table 10.** Protein Efficiency Values of Feather Meal and Meat and Bone Meal

| Protein Source | Protein Efficiency[a] |
|---|---|
| Feather Meal | $1.38^b \pm 0.12$ |
| Meat and Bone Meal | $.82^c \pm .20$ |
| Combination | $1.17^{bc} \pm .39$ |
| Soybean MEal | $.47^c \pm .26$ |

[a]Additional gain above the urea controls per unit (kg) of protein supplied above the urea controls.
[b,c]Values with different superscripts differ ($P<.05$).
*Source:* Gibb et al 1992

BM = meat and bone meal

Urea control calves gained 0.45 kg/day, while the greatest daily gain due to protein supplementation was 0.65 kg/day for the 100% blood meal treatment. Blood meal promoted the greatest protein efficiency (1.88); the 2/3 meat and bone meal, 1/3 feather meal mixture, the lowest 0.68. An increase in protein efficiency was observed by adding 10% and 20% blood meal to the 1/3 meat and bone meal, 2/3 feather meal.

Laboratory analysis indicated that protein bypass levels were 86, 43 and 71% for blood meal, meat and bone meal, and feather meal, respectively. The greater growth response to blood meal was due to a larger concentration of high quality protein able to escape rumen degradation. The efficiency of bypass protein use was determined by the units of bypass protein needed for each additional unit of gain. This analysis eliminates response differences due to the bypass protein concentrations of the supplements (Figure 11). Both combinations of 2/3 meat and bone meal, 1/3 feather meal and 1/3 meat and bone meal, 2/3 feather meal reached a bypass protein efficiency nearly equal to that of 100% blood meal when each fas fed with 20% blood meal.

**Figure 11.** Protein efficiency of supplemental bypass protein use versus level of protein from blood meal Slopes do not differ ($P <.05$). Standard errors for treatment means were 0.33 for 100% blood meal; 0.52 for 2/3 meat and bone meal, 1/3 feather meal; 0.63 for 2/3 meat and bone meal, 1/3 feather meal, 10% blood meal; 0.23 for 2/3 meat and bone meal, 1/3 feather meal, 20% blood meal, 0.49 for 1/3 meat and bone meal, 2/3 feather meal; 0.36 for 1/3 meat and bone meal, 2/3 feather meal, 10% blood meal; 0.30 for 1/3 meat and bone meal, 2/3 feather meal, 20% blood meal (Herold et al 1993).

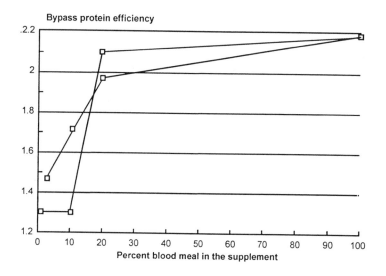

These data suggest that 20% of the supplemental natural protein from blood meal enhances the protein efficiency of meat and bone meal, feather meal combinations, although the protein efficiencies were not statistically different. Furthermore, if the bypass fraction of meat and bone meal could be increased through improved methods of processing, the performance response in growing calves would likely be higher when fed in combination with feather meal and small amounts of blood meal.

Studies have shown a lower protein efficiency for meat and bone meal relative to blood meal in calf growth studies. This has been attributed to the escape protein or to amino acid composition of meat and bone meal being inadequate to meet the specific needs of the growing calf. Collagen, which can comprise a fraction of meat and bone meal protein, contains negligible amounts of the essential amino acids methionine and tryptophan.

Recent research has identified methionine as the first limiting amino acid in meat and bone meal (Klemesrud et al 1994). Efficiency of protein utilization was greater in steers consuming meat and bone meal plus rumen protected methionine than for meat and bone meal alone. Rumen protected methionine, and lysine did not improve protein efficiency over methionine alone, suggesting that meat and bone meal contains adequate lysine.

Two methods for increasing the flow of methionine to the small intestine are supplementation with a rumen-protected form of methionine, or increasing the amount of methionine from meat and bone meal that escapes ruminal degradation.   While non—enzymatic browning of soybean meal with sulfite liquor has been successful in increasing the escape protein value from 30 to 75%, the value of this procedure in increasing the escape protein of meat and bone meal remains undetermined.

Two calf growth trials were conducted using meat and bone meal and meat and bone meal treated with sulfite liquor.  Treatments consisted of: urea (control); meat and bone meal; treated meat and bone meal; meat and bone meal plus rumen-protected methionine; and treated meat and bone meal plus rumen-protected methionine.  Rumen-protected methionine was included by feeding 3.5 g/day of Smartamine M[TM] (Rhône—Poulenc Animal Nutrition, Atlanta, GA), which supplied 2.2 g/day metabolizable methionine.

In trial 2, treatments consisted of:  urea (control); meat and bone meal; and treated meat and bone meal.  Rumen-protected methionine and tryptophan were included in both meat and bone meal treatments so that protein efficiency could be evaluated without being limited by methionine or tryptophan content.  The 2.8 g/day of Smartamine M[TM] supplied 1.8 g/day metabolizable methionine, and 4.0 g/day of Promate T (Showa Denko, Tokyo, Japan) supplied 1.0 g/day metabolizable tryptophan.

For each trial, material for the treated meat and bone meal was collected from the same run of rendered material as the untreated meat and bone meal to keep the composition of the products as homogeneous as possible.  The meat and bone meal products differed between trials, with the treated meat and bone meal used in trial 2 being processed more extensively for a greater escape protein value.  The escape protein values of the meat and bone meal products were determined by 24—hour in vitro ammonia release.  A lamb digestion trial was conducted to determine the true protein digestibility of the meat and bone meal products relative to a urea control.

*Trial 1.*  Averaged across level of protein fed, differences in daily gain and feed efficiency approached significance ($P$ = .12 and .15, respectively; Table 11). The urea control steers gained 1.57 lb/day, while maximum gain due to protein supplementation, determined by nonlinear regression, was 0.78 lb/day above that of the urea controls (2.35 lb/day).

There was no meat and bone meal source methionine supplement interaction so results were pooled for analysis of protein efficiency. Sulfite liquor-treated meat and bone meal tended ($P = .15$) to be used with greater efficiency of protein utilization than untreated meat and bone meal (1.35 vs 1.19), suggesting that treated meat and bone meal was higher in escape protein than untreated meat and bone meal. This is consistent with laboratory ammonia-release values in which untreated meat and bone meal had an escape value of 51.9% while treated meat and bone meal had an escape value of 66.0%.

True protein digestibility of untreated meat and bone meal in lambs was 93.9%, while treated meat and bone meal was 94.8%. Overheating during processing, which has been blamed for reduced nitrogen digestibility, did not appear to be a problem for either treated or untreated meat and bone meal. This indicates that while nonenzymatic browning with sulfite liquor increased escape protein value of meat and bone meal, it did not affect protein digestion.

Methionine supplementation increased ($P < .10$) protein efficiency in steers consuming meat and bone meal (1.62 vs 0.86 ), indicating that methionine is the first limiting amino acid inmeat and bone meal. Based on protein and amino acid composition of live weight gain, the 2.2 g of metabolizable methionine supplied at the highest level of protein supplementation is adequate for 0.50 lb of gain, while the difference in gain was only 0.23 lb. This would suggest that once the requirement for methionine was met, another amino acid likely limited the potential for growth. Tryptophan, because of its reported low concentration inmeat and bone meal, may have become limiting.

**Table 11.** Performance of Steers Fed Meat and Bone Meal[a], Trial 1.

| Supplement[b] | Daily Gain, lb[c] | Daily DMI % Body Weight | Gain/ Feed[d] |
|---|---|---|---|
| Urea | 1.57 | 2.08 | .130 |
| MBM | 1.62 | 2.08 | .133 |
| Treated MBM | 1.59 | 2.08 | .130 |
| MBM + Met | 1.79 | 2.08 | .145 |
| | 1.72 | 2.08 | .139 |
| Treated MBM + Met | | | |

[a]Averaged across protein levels.
[b]Meat and bone meal, treated meat and bone meal, meat and bone meal plus protected methionine, and treated meat and bone meal plu protected methionine.
[c]P=.12.
[d]P=.15.

**Table 12.** Performance of Steers Fed Meat and Bone Meal[a], Trial 2

| Supplement[b] | Daily Gain, lb | Daily DMI % Body Weight | Gain/ Feed |
|---|---|---|---|
| Urea | .39[c] | 1.84 | .034[c] |
| MBM | .85[d] | 1.84 | .073[d] |
| Treated MBM | .98[d] | 1.84 | .084[d] |

[a]Averaged across protein levels.
[b]Meat and bone meal, and treated meat and bone meal
[c,d] Values in the same column with different superscripts differ ($P$<.05).

*Trial 2.* Steers that received the untreated and treated meat and bone meal supplements gained 0.85 and 0.98 lb/day, respectively, which were greater ($P$ < .05) than the 0.39 lb/day gained by the urea control steers (Table 12). The increase was due to additional metabolizable protein supplied by these meat and bone meal supplements. Feed efficiency was also greater ($P$ <.05) for these treatments (Table 8) due to the increase, since daily feed intake was equal for all treatments.

Protein efficiency was numerically greater for treated meat and bone meal than for untreated meat and bone meal (2.55 vs 1.58, respectively), however this difference was not statistically significant because the standard error was large. The trend, however, would suggest a greater escape protein value for treated meat and bone meal which is consistent with measured escape protein values, determined by ammonia release, of 49.5% and 71.4% for untreated meat and bone meal and treated meat and bone meal, respectively.

The greater protein efficiency and escape protein values for the treated meat and bone meal used in Trial 2 relative to Trial 1 suggest that the more extensive processing was beneficial. Likewise, the greater protein efficiency of the untreated meat and bone meal used in trial 2 relative to trial 1, despite its lower escape protein value, could be attributed to the addition of both rumen-protected methionine and tryptophan.

Results of this research indicate that treatment of meat and bone meal by nonenzymatic browning with sulfite liquor is a feasible means of increasing escape protein value and protein efficiency in growing calves. The added response to protected methionine suggests that methionine is the first limiting amino acid in meat and bone meal. Whether tryptophan is the second limiting amino acid cannot be determined from this research.

To make the best use of treated meat and bone meal, adequate supplies of methionine or sulfur-containing amino acids should be assured. Corn protein is a good source of methionine, so corn gluten meal or distillers' grains would complement treated meat and bone meal. Obviously more corn in the diet would also supply more methionine. Feather meal is a good source of sulfur-containing amino acids but much of the amino acids is in the form of cystine rather than methionine. Feather meal should complement treated meat and bone meal but just how effectively cystine can replace the methionine is not clear. Finally, protected methionine is an effective means of supplementing treated meat and bone meal to assure adequate methionine supplies.

## FEATHER MEAL
## Growth Studies

Calves weaned in the fall are often pastured on protein-deficient, dormant native range or cornstalk fields, or fed grass hay throughout the winter. Supplemental rumen-degradable and escape protein are essential for microbial activity and cattle growth during this time. Feather meal is an excellent source of escape protein for growing calves. However, palatability, feeding level, possible combinations with rumen-degradable sources, and method of supplementation are issues of concern. Therefore, a trial was conducted to determine the maximum level of feather meal that can be used in a supplement for growing calves; and whether urea or a rumen-degradable plant protein is more desirable to mix with the feather meal. Range cubes are a popular method of supplementing pasture cattle, therefore the pelleting characteristics of feather meal were studied to determine whether it could be incorporated at high levels into cube supplements.

Although this trial (Hollingsworth et al 1991) was conducted in a feedlot, a protein-deficient roughage diet consisting of 20% prairie hay, 30% corncobs, and 35% sorghum silage was fed to animals in all pens ad libitum to simulate winter range grazing. The cube supplements were formulated to comprise about 15% of the diet supplying .36 kg of protein/hd/day. Sunflower meal was used as an economical source of rumen-degradable protein and carrier for other ingredients. It could then be compared with urea using soyhulls as a carrier. The cubes were fed at .9 kg/hd/day except for the 100% sunflower supplement which was fed at 1.0 kg/hd/day to supply the same amount of crude protein as the other supplements. Cubes were fed in one end of the bunk while the roughage was always maintained ad libitum at the opposite end. Sufficient bunk space was available so all calves had access to both cubes and roughage at the same time.

No consumption problems associated with the addition of feather meal were observed. Observations of cattle being supplemented revealed that cattle on sunflower meal combinations cleaned the bunks immediately. Those on urea combinations took 3 or 4 hours to finish the cubes, and the urea control cattle took all day.

After some experimentation with the amount of pellet binder, cubing proved to be a convenient method of supplementing. With feather meal, more binder was needed to maintain cube quality. Winter range is deficient in trace minerals, phosphorus, and vitamin A as well as protein. The range cube provides a means of delivering these nutrients in small quantities in addition to the protein. Supplementing with an escape protein source such as feather meal in addition to urea or a rumen-degradable protein source on winter pasture can support microbial activity and cattle growth before spring grazing or feedlot finishing. Feather meal appears to be an acceptable protein source for use in calf cubes. Cube quality could be maintained, acceptance by the cattle was not a problem, and feather meal reduced the total feed cost per kilogram of gain.

Current estimates of escape protein in the animal protein sources are presented in Table 13. The values are based on reports of intestinally fistulated animals and growth studies where protein was demonstrated to be limiting. Generalized values relative to soybean meal have been developed.

Table 14 shows 3 computer-formulated rations. The all natural 40% protein supplement using soybean meal had ingredient costs of $191/ton. A comparable supplement using blood meal and feather meal cost $121/ton. If our assumptions are correct, the 2 supplements are equal in feeding value (Klopfenstein et al 1985). A supplement using bypass sources, meat meal, blood meal, and feather meal cost $119/ ton. The meat and bone meal is an excellent source of phosphorus which reduces the supplement cost.

Receiving calves offer an excellent opportunity to use feather meal. When young calves enter the feedlot, protein supplementation is vital not only for growth but for health care as well. Many calves entering the feedlot have not been weaned. The stresses of removal from their dam and weaning, adjusting to a new and different environment, immunization against viruses, and challenges from bacterial invasions combine to create a situation in which many calves become sick; the death rate is at least twice as high as it is among yearlings.

Stressed calves may eat less, which exacerbates health problems, as reduced feed intake reduces the amount of microbial protein that is normally synthesized. In addition, most of the forages fed during the receiving period (alfalfa hay, corn silage) are low in bypass protein. Thus, diets fed to receiving calves may be deficient in metabolizable protein. Feather meal may be used in receiving diets to improve animal gain and efficiency and to reduce sickness.

In the fall in 2 consecutive years 816 Continental English steers (243 kg) were received (McCoy et al 1994, Stock et al 1993), vaccinated, and randomly allotted to a supplemental protein treatments of urea, soybean meal, or feather meal. Receiving diets consisted of (dry matter basis) 48% alfalfa hay, 6% molasses, and 46% dry-rolled corn and supplement. Calves were fed for approximately 28 days. No significant differences in animal performance or health were observed among the treatments (Table 15). The combination of microbial protein and bypass protein from the corn and alfalfa hay were sufficient to meet the calve's protein requirement.

**Table 13.** Bypass Estimates of Protein Sources

| Protein Source | % Protein Escape (Bypass)[a] | | |
| | Duodenal Collection | Animal Growth | Soybean Meal Equivalent Value[b] |
| --- | --- | --- | --- |
| Soybean Meal | 24.6 | 30 | 1.0 |
| Blood Meal, Ring Dried | 82.4 | 84.6 | 2.5 |
| Blood Meal[c], Old Process | | | 2.0 |
| Meat Meal | 63.9 | 61.8 | 2.0 |
| Feather Meal | | 68.0 | 2.0 |
| Fish Meal | 68.0 | | |

[a]From Poos-Floyd et al, 1985.
[b]Value relative to SBM
[c]Value based on reduced protein digestibility in nonruminants.

In another receiving trial (McCoy et al 1995), a combination of 80% feather meal:20% blood meal was supplemented to diets containing (dry matter basis) either 45% alfalfa hay, 45% dry-rolled corn, 6% molasses, and 4% supplement or 45% alfalfa hay, 52% wet corn gluten feed, and 3% supplement (Table 16). Wet corn gluten feed is a byproduct of the wet corn milling industry that produces either fuel ethanol or high fructose, corn sweetener. Wet corn gluten feed contains 16 to 20% crude protein, but only 20% escape protein.

For treatment, 398 Continental English calves (257 kg) were received, vaccinated, and randomly allotted. Supplementation of feather meal, blood meal (Table 17) did not affect the performance of calves fed dry-rolled corn, but did improve daily gain and feed conversion ($P < .10$) of calves fed wet corn gluten feed. Metabolizable protein intake of the dry-rolled corn diet was higher than the wet corn gluten feed diets; and feather meal, blood meal supplementation further increased metabolizable protein intake. Statistically, the number of calves requiring treatment for respiratory disease did not differ ($P > .10$) among treatments. However, metabolizable protein intake and the number of calves treated for respiratory disease were negatively correlated ($r = -.95$; $P < .05$), indicating that feather meal, blood meal supplementation probably reduced sickness in these calves.

## Finishing Calves

Yearling finishing cattle typically do not respond to escape protein supplementation because most of their gain is fat. In addition, microbial protein synthesis from the digestion of grain is high, and the escape protein content of corn is also quite high (65%; Sindt et al 1993a). However, large-frame, Continental English calves, weaned at 7 to 8 months of age and fed high-grain finishing diets may require escape protein supplementation. These large–framed calves are lighter (250 kg) when they enter the feedlot than yearlings, but gain rapidly. Calves typically are fed 180 to 200 days in the feedlot. These calves are more efficient than yearlings (Lewis et al 1990) and more of their weight gain is muscle. Therefore, these calves may need more escape protein than yearlings.

**Table 14.** Soybean Meal Equivalent Supplements

| Ingredient | Soybean Meal | Blood Meal/ Feather Meal | Blood Meal/ Feather Meal/ Meat Meal |
|---|---|---|---|
| Soybean Meal | 88.8 | | |
| Blood Meal | | 1.8 | 1.4 |
| Feather Meal | | 10.1 | 8.2 |
| Sunflower Meal | | 83.4 | 83.6 |
| Meat Meal | | | 3.5 |
| Midds | 8.8 | | |
| Urea | | 2.7 | 2.7 |
| Dical | 2.4 | .9 | |
| Limestone | | 1.1 | .6 |
| Price/ton | 191 | 121 | 119 |

Price ($/ ton): soybean meal, $200; blood meal, $440; feather meal, $261; sunflower, $94; meat meal, $209; midds, $78; urea, $204.

**Table 15.** Effect of Protein Source on Receiving Performance and Health

| Item | Supplemental Protein Treatment | | |
|---|---|---|---|
| | Urea | Soybean Meal | Feather Meal |
| Dry Matter Intake, kg/day | 5.91 | 5.90 | 5.80 |
| Daily Gain, kg | 1.09 | 1.07 | 1.07 |
| Feed/Gain | 5.58 | 5.79 | 5.78 |
| Number of Cattle Treated[a] | 46 | 50 | 47 |

[a] Treated for bovine respiratory disease (shipping fever).

Six finishing studies have been conducted using 1,440 large-frame calves. Calves were adapted to high-grain finishing diets in 21 days. The final finishing diet consisted (dry matter basis) of 80% dry rolled corn, 5% molasses, 5% corn silage, 5% alfalfa hay, and 5% supplement. Calves were fed various protein supplements. Calves fed a feather meal–urea supplement (50:50 combination, protein basis) were similar in efficiency compared with calves fed soybean meal (100% of supplemental protein) (Table 17). Feeding a combination of urea and feather meal or urea and feather meal, blood meal combinations improved efficiency 2.3 and 2.5%, respectively, compared with urea alone.

**Table 16.** Effect of Energy and Protein Source on Receiving Performance and Health

| Item | Treatment[a] | | | |
| | DRC-Urea | DRC-EP | WCGF | WCGF-EP |
|---|---|---|---|---|
| Total Head/ Treatment | 101 | 100 | 99 | 98 |
| DM Intake[b], kg/day | 5.71 | 5.65 | 5.20 | 5.03 |
| Daily Gain[c], kg | 1.11 | 1.13 | .91 | 1.03 |
| Feed/Gain[d] | 5.12 | 5.02 | 5.67 | 4.84 |
| Number of Treated Cattle[e] | 20 | 17 | 25 | 21 |
| MP Intake[b,f,g], kg/day | .56 | .60 | .47 | .50 |

[a]DRC = dry-rolled corn ; EP=escape protein (80% feather meal, 20% blood meal); WCGF = wet corn gluten feed. All diets contained 45% alfalfa hay.
[b]DRC vs WCGF ($P < .01$).
[c]DRC vs WCGF ($P < .05$).
[d]No escape protein supplement vs escape protein supplement ($P < .10$).
[e]Treated with antibiotic injection to control respiratory disease.
[f]No escape protein supplement vs escape protein supplement ($P < .01$).
[g]MP = metabolizable protein. MP requirement of a 272 kg steer gaining 1.13 kg/day = 0.55 kg/day (Ainslie et al 1993).

Among these 6 trials, the greatest response to escape protein occurred when the calves were exhibiting compensatory growth (Table 18), or when the diet contained high-moisture corn (Table 19) or 45% wet corn gluten feed (Table 20). Calves exhibiting compensatory growth may require more metabolizable protein than noncompensating calves.  High-moisture corn and wet corn gluten feed contain less escape protein than dry-rolled corn, thus increasing the need for escape protein supplementation.

**Figure 12.** Deposition of lean tissue and fat of calves and yearlings in the feedlot.

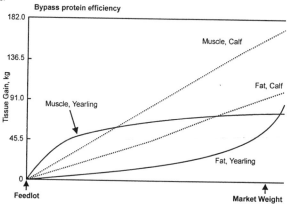

Nutritionists must carefully consider the protein needs of the cattle as well as the degradable and escape protein content of the basal ingredients in the diet. The amount of supplemental escape protein required will vary depending on cattle type and basal ingredients. Nutritionists need to formulate diets to meet the degradable protein requirement of the cattle. If metabolizable protein is still deficient, escape protein should be used to supplement the animal's diet. Feather meal or a combination of feather meal and blood meal can economically be used to meet these escape protein needs.

## RENDERERS BYPRODUCTS FOR DAIRY CATTLE

Lactating dairy cows have high requirements for metabolizable protein. The concept of supplementing escape protein to complement microbial protein is not new (Clark 1975). The dairy cow is similar to the beef animal in how it ferments and utilizes feedstuffs. Diets may have somewhat different proportions but often contain similar ingredients to those of beef cattle. Dairy cows consume more feed relative to body weight and therefore rate of passage of feed particles from the rumen may be more rapid. With shorter residence time in the rumen, protein may not be as completely degraded. On the other hand, rumen pH in lactating cows may be higher than in finishing beef cattle. Certainly rumen pH in beef cows and growing beef calves would be higher than in dairy cows and finishing cattle. While these factors influence protein degradation and microbial protein synthesis, the overall similarities between beef and dairy cattle are much greater than the differences.

Therefore, the above discussion about beef cattle should apply in general to dairy cattle as well.

Waltz et al (1989) showed that feather meal had a higher escape value than soybean meal in dairy cows. They further suggested that a combination of blood meal and feather meal could increase the intestinal supply of amino acids better than soybean meal.

Florida researchers (Harris et al 1992) supplemented diets containing 14 or 18% CP with 0, 3, or 6% feather meal (dry matter basis). The feather meal replaced soybean meal. Milk protein percentage was decreased as the amount of feather meal in both the 14% and the 18% CP diets was increased. Milk production was not altered by adding feather meal except for an increase in milk production for cows receiving the 14% CP diet containing 3% feather meal. The disappointing results may have reflected a poor metabolizable amino acid balance due to supplementing the majority of undegradable protein from a single protein. Moss et al (1990) replaced soybean meal with feather meal at either 4.2 or 8.3% of ration dry matter. They observed decreases in dry matter intake, milk production, and milk protein percentage as feather meal in the diet was increased. This provides additional evidence that feather meal should not be fed as the sole supplemental source of undegradable protein.

Wattiaux et al (1993) fed a blend of animal proteins and noted a significant increase in body condition score.

Meat and bone meal is rich in protein and undegradable protein. It, like blood meal, is an excellent source of lysine but a poor source of methionine (Figure 4). Meat and bone meal has become a more popular protein supplement in dairy diets, but because of the low methionine content, its value in alfalfa-based diets may be limited.  Very few lactation trials have been conducted to evaluate the dietary value of meat and bone meal. In most trials (Lu et al 1990, Mansfield et al 1990, Sandrucci et al 1992), milk yield was not influenced by supplementation with meat and bone meal or blood meal. The absence of response may have been due to a limiting amino acid, such as methionine, that was not provided by the animal proteins.  In the single study on feeding meat and bone meal, feather meal combinations to dairy cattle, Utah researchers (Kellems et al 1989) replaced 50 or 100% of the meat and bone meal in dairy diets with feather meal and found no changes in lactation performance. However, meat and bone meal, feather meal, or the meat and bone meal, feather meal blend contributed only 45% of the supplemental protein and the feeds that provided the remaining 55% of the supplemental protein were not described in the abstract.

The data base is larger for the feeding value of blood meal, feather meal blends. Blood meal is similar to meat and bone meal in being deficient in methionine.  The effect between blood meal and feather meal is synergistic when fed to growing beef cattle, and the complementary effect may be due to the sulfur-containing amino acids in feather meal (Goedeken et al 1990b).  Feeding a blend of blood meal and feather meal to dairy cattle did not enhance milk yield, however, the control diet was fed to provide 100% of undegradable protein requirements (Palmquist & Weiss 1994).  Therefore, metabolizable amino acids may not have been limiting.  Increasing undegradable protein by feeding a blood meal, feather meal blend (15:85, dry matter basis) at 5% of ration dry matter did not enhance performance of early lactation cows (Grant et al 1993; forage was 63% alfalfa silage, 37% corn silage). Increasing the contribution of a blood meal, feather meal blend from 0 to 100% of supplemental protein increased nonammonia, nonmicrobial nitrogen flow to the intestine of dairy cows, but total amino nitrogen flow was not increased because microbial nitrogen flow was reduced (Cunningham et al 1994). This may have been due to insufficient degradable protein and ruminal ammonia to support maximal microbial protein synthesis.  A subsequent lactation study indicated that there was no milk production response when adding urea to diets containing a blood meal, feather meal blend (Johnson et al 1994).  Ruminal ammonia concentrations were not measured in that study; therefore, it is difficult to estimate whether ammonia was limiting.  Experiments designed to access the feeding value of animal proteins must incorporate precautions to avoid limiting microbial protein synthesis.

**Table 17.** Performance of Large-framed Calves Fed Dry Rolled Corn Finishing Diets Supplemented with Feather Meal

| Finishing Study | Treatment | | | |
|---|---|---|---|---|
| | Urea | Soybean Meal | Urea-FTH[a] | Urea-FTH/BM[a] |
| | ---------- Dry Matter Intake, kg/day ---------- | | | |
| Sindt et al, 1993a | 9.05 | | | 9.04 |
| Sindt et al, 1993b | 9.24 | 9.52 | 9.19 | 9.02 |
| Sindt et al, 1994 | 9.33 | 9.25 | 9.33 | 9.19 |
| Stock et al, 1993 | 8.70 | 8.71 | 8.55 | |
| McCoy et al, 1994 | 9.19 | 8.98 | 9.01 | |
| McCoy et al, 1995 | 10.33 | | | 10.23 |
| | ------------------ Daily Gain, kg ------------------ | | | |
| Sindt et al, 1993a | 1.54 | | | 1.58 |
| Sindt et al, 1993b | 1.41 | 1.45 | 1.42 | 1.41 |
| Sindt et al, 1994 | 1.47 | 1.48 | 1.45 | 1.46 |
| Stock et al, 1993 | 1.37 | 1.43 | 1.38 | |
| McCoy et al, 1994 | 1.24 | 1.27 | 1.32 | |
| McCoy et al, 1995 | 1.73 | | | 1.74 |
| | ------------------ Feed/Gain, kg ------------------ | | | |
| Sindt et al, 1993a | 5.88 | | | 5.68 |
| Sindt et al, 1993b | 6.54 | 6.62 | 6.42 | 6.39 |
| Sindt et al, 1994 | 6.33 | 6.21 | 6.45 | 6.29 |
| Stock et al, 1993 | 6.33 | 6.10 | 6.17 | |
| McCoy et al, 1994 | 7.41 | 7.04 | 6.85 | |
| McCoy et al, 1995 | 5.95 | | | 5.88 |

[a]Urea supplied 50% and feather meal or feather meal/blood meal supplied 50% of supplemental protein.

**Table 18.** Effect of Compensatory Growth on Response to Escape Protein Supplementation with Large-frame Finishing Calves[a]

| Item | Noncompensating Calves | | | Compensating Calves | | |
|---|---|---|---|---|---|---|
| | Urea | Soybean Meal | Escape Protein[b] | Urea | Soybean Meal | Escape Protein[b] |
| Dry Matter Intake, kg/day | 8.63 | 8.89 | 8.47 | 9.84 | 10.14 | 9.68 |
| Daily Gain, kg | 1.39 | 1.36 | 1.34 | 1.42 | 1.53 | 1.49 |
| Feed/Gain | 6.21 | 6.66 | 6.30 | 6.94 | 6.62 | 6.52 |

[a] Sindt et al, 1993b.
[b] Urea supplied 50% and feather meal or feather meal/blood meal supplied 50% of supplemental protein.

**Table 19.** Effect of High-moisture Corn on Response to Escape Protein Supplementation with Large-frame Finishing Calves[a]

| Item | Dry Rolled Corn | | High Moisture Corn | |
|---|---|---|---|---|
| | Urea | Urea-FTH/BM[b] | Urea | Urea-FTH/BM[b] |
| Dry Matter Intake, kg/day | 9.24 | 9.03 | 9.21 | 8.77 |
| Daily Gain, kg | 1.41 | 1.41 | 1.37 | 1.39 |
| Feed/Gain | 6.56 | 6.43 | 6.71 | 6.31 |

[a] Sindt et al, 1993b.
[b] Urea supplied 50%, feather meal supplied 25%, and blood meal supplied 25% of supplemental protein.

**Table 20.** Effect of Wet Corn Gluten on Response to Escape Protein Supplementation with Large-frame Finishing Calves[a]

| Item | Treatment[b] | | | |
| | DRC/ Urea | DRC/ EP+Urea | WCGF | WCGF/ EP |
|---|---|---|---|---|
| DM Intake[c], kg/day | 10.31 | 10.22 | 9.83 | 9.97 |
| Daily Gain, kg | 1.73 | 1.74 | 1.69 | 1.72 |
| Feed/Gaind | 5.96 | 5.88 | 5.83 | 5.78 |
| MP Intake[c,e,f], kg/day | .90 | .96 | .80 | .88 |
| DIP[g], % | 7.4 | 7.9 | 8.3 | 8.8 |

[a]McCoy et al 1995.
[b]DRC =dry rolled corn; EP=escape protein (80% feather meal, 20% blood meal fed at 50% of supplemental protein); WCGF=45% wet corn gluten feed and 40% dry rolled corn.
[c]DRC vs WCGF ($P<.05$).
[d]DRC vs WCGF ($P=.13$).
[e]No escape protein supplement vs escape protein supplement ($P < .01$).
[f]MP=metabolizable protein. MP requirement of a 449 kg steer gaining 1.74 kg/day=.83 kg/day (Ainslie et al 1993).
[g]DIP=Degradable intake protein. DIP requirement=6.8%.

# REFERENCES

Ainslie SJ, Fox DG, Perry TC, Ketchen DJ, & Barry MC. 1993. Predicting amino acid adequacy of diets fed to Holstein steers. *J Anim Sci* 71:1312.

Blasi DA, Klopfenstein TJ, Drouillard JS, & Sindt MH. 1991. Hydrolysis time as a factor affecting the nutritive value of feather meal and feather meal–blood meal combinations for growing calves. *J Anim Sci* 69:1272.

Brandt RT & Anderson SJ. 1990. Supplemental fat source affects feedlot performance and carcass traits of finishing yearling steers and estimated diet net energy value. *J Anim Sci* 68:2208.

Chalupa W & Ferguson JD. 1990. Immediate and residual responses of lactating cows on commercial dairies to calcium salts of long chain fatty acids. *J Dairy Sci* 73 (suppl 1):244 abstr.

Chandler P. 1993. Research examines the role of tallow as a rumen inert fat for dairy cows. *Feedstuffs* 65(33):12.

Clark JH. 1975. Lactation responses to postruminal administration of proteins and amino acids. *J Dairy Sci* 58:1178.

Clary E.M, Brandt RT, Anderson SJ, Pope RV, & Elliot JK. 1991. Effect of fat and ionophores on performance of finishing cattle fed 90% concentrate diets. *Abstracts, Midwestern Section of the American Society of Animal Science,* p 156. Des Moines, IA.

Cunningham KD, Cecava MJ, & Johnson TR. 1994. Flows of nitrogen and amino acids in dairy cows fed diets containing supplemental feather meal and blood meal *J Dairy Sci* 77:3666.

DePeters EJ, Taylor SJ, Finley CM, & Famula TR. 1987. Dietary fat and nitrogen composition of milk from lactating cows. *J Dairy Sci* 70:1192.

Eastridge ML & Firkins JL. 1992. Feeding tallow triglycerides of different saturation and particle size to lactating dairy cows. *J Dairy Sci* 75 (suppl 1):172.

Ferguson JD, Sklan D, Chalupa WV, & Kronfeld DS. 1990. Effects of hard fats on in vitro and in vivo rumen fermentation, milk production, and reproduction in dairy cows. *J Dairy Sci* 73:2864.

Firkins JL & Eastridge ML. 1994. Assessment of the effects of iodine value on fatty acid digestibility, feed intake, and milk production. *J Dairy Sci* 77:2357.

Gibb D, Karges K, Klopfenstein T, & Sindt M. 1992. Combinations of rendered protein meals for growing calves. *J Anim Sci* 70:2581.

Goedeken F K, Klopfenstein TJ, Stock RA, & Britton RA. 1990a. Evaluation of hydrolyzed feather meal as a protein source for growing calves. *J Anim Sci* 68:2945.

Goedeken FK, Klopfenstein TJ, Stock RA, Britton RA, & Sindt MH. 1990b. Protein value of feather meal for ruminants as affected by blood additions. *J Anim Sci* 68:2936.

Gramlich SM, Brandt RT Jr, & Pope RV. 1990. *Dose Response to Supplemental Fat by Finishing Steers,* p 4. Kansas Agricultural Experiment Station Report of Program 592. Manhattan.

Grant RJ, Larson LL, & Son J. 1993. Tallow and escape protein supplementation of alfalfa–based diets for early lactation dairy cows. *J Dairy Sci* 76 (suppl 1):215 (abstr.).

Grummer RR. 1993. Factors affecting production responses of dairy cattle to supplemental fat. *Proceedings of the Cornell Nutrition Conference for Feed Manufacturers,* p 186. Cornell University, Ithaca, NY.

Grummer RR. 1994. Fat sources and levels for high milk production. *Proceedings of the Southwest Nutrition Management Conference,* p 130. University of Arizona, Tucson.

Grummer RR & Carroll DJ. 1991. Effects of dietary fat on metabolic disorders and reproductive performance of dairy cattle. *J Anim Sci* 69:3838.

Grummer RR, Luck ML, & Barmore JA. 1993. Rumen fermentation and lactation performance of cows fed roasted soybeans and tallow. *J Dairy Sci* 76:2674.

Hale WH. 1986. Fat in the diets of growing finishing cattle. *Proceedings of the Southwest Nutrition Conference,* p 46. University of Arizona, Tucson.

Harris B, Dorminey DE, Smith WA, Van Horn HH, & Wilcox CJ. 1992. Effects of feather meal at two protein concentrations and yeast culture on production parameters in lactating dairy cows. *J Dairy Sci* 75:3524.

Herold D, Klopfenstein T, & Huffman R. 1993. Blood meal, meat and bone meal and feather meal combinations for growing calves. *Nebraska Beef Cattle Report* MP 59–A:32.

Hightshoe, RB, Cochran RC, Corah LR, Kirocofe GH, Harmon DL, & Perry RC. 1991. Effects of calcium soaps of fatty acid on postpartum reproductive function in beef cows. *J Anim Sci* 69:4097.

Hoffman PC, Grummer RR, Shaver RD, Broderick GA, & Drendel TR. 1991. Feeding supplemental fat and undegraded intake protein to early lactation dairy cows. *J Dairy Sci* 74:3468.

Hollingsworth K, Klopfenstein T, & Sindt M. 1991. Supplementing growing calves with feather meal cubes. *Nebraska Beef Cattle Report* MP 56:25.

Huffman RP, Stock RA, Sindt MH, & Shain DH. 1992. Effect of fat type and forage level on performance of finishing cattle. *J Anim Sci* 70:3889.

Johnson TR, Cecava MJ, Sheiss EB, & Cunningham KD. 1994. Addition of ruminally degradable crude protein and branched–chain volatile fatty acids to diets containing hydrolyzed feather meal and blood meal for lactating cows. *J Dairy Sci* 77:3676.

Johnson, TO, Mitchell GE, Tucker RE, & Schelling GT. 1974. Pancreatic lipase secretion by sheep. *J Anim Sci* 39:947.

Kellems RO, Powell KL, Romo GA, Wallentine MV, Andrus D, & Jones R. 1989. Effect of replacing 50% and 100% of the supplemental crude protein derived from meat and bone meal with feather meal on performance of high producing dairy cows. *J Dairy Sci* 72 (suppl 1):531.

Klemesrud MJ, & Klopfenstein TJ. 1994. Addition of ruminal escape methionine and lysine to meat and bone meal *J Anim Sci* 72 (suppl 1):94.

Klopfenstein T, Stock R, & Britton R. 1985. Relevance of bypass protein to cattle feeding. *Prof Anim Scientist* 1:27.

Lewis JM, Klopfenstein TJ, Stock RA, & Nielsen MK. 1990. Evaluation of intensive and extensive systems of beef production and the effect of level of beef cow milk production on postweaning performance. *J Anim Sci* 68:2517.

Loerch SC, Berger LL, Plegge SD, & Fahey GC Jr 1983. Digestibility and rumen escape of soybean meal, blood meal, meat and bone meal and dehydrated alfalfa nitrogen. *J Anim Sci* 57:1037.

Lu CD, Potchoiba MJ, Sahlu T, & Kawas JR. 1990. Performance of dairy goats fed soybean meal or meat and bone meal with or without urea during early lactation. *J Dairy Sci* 73:726.

Macleod GK & Buchanan-Smith JG. 1972. Digestibility of hydrogenated tallow, saturated fatty acids and soybean oil-supplemented diets by sheep. *J Anim Sci* 35:890.

Mansfield HR, Stern MD, & Otterby DE. 1990. Effects of beet pulp and animal by-products on milk yield and in vitro fermentation by rumen microorganisms. *J Dairy Sci* 77:205.

McCoy R, Stock R, Klopfenstein T, Shain D, & Huffman R. 1994. Effect of protein source on receiving and finishing performance and health of calves. *Nebraska Beef Cattle Report* MP 61–A:30.

McCoy R, Stock R, Klopfenstein T, Shain D, & White G. 1995. Effect of wet corn gluten feed and escape protein on receiving and finishing performance and health of calves. *Nebraska Beef Cattle Report.* (In press).

Moss BR & Holliman JL. 1990. Evaluation of feather meal as a protein source for lactating cows. *J Dairy Sci* 73 (suppl 1):265.

[NRC] National Research Council. 1984. *Nutrient Requirements of Beef Cattle,* 6th edition, revised. National Academy of Sciiences, Washington, DC.

[NRC] National Research Council. 1989. *Nutrient Requirements of Dairy Cattle,* 6th edition, revised. National Academy of Sciences, Washington, DC.

Noble RC. 1981. Digestion, absorption, and transport of lipids in ruminant animals. WW Christie, editor, *Lipid Metabolism in Ruminants,* p 57. Pergamon Press.

Palmquist DL & Weiss WP. 1994. Blood and Hydrolyzed feather meals as sources of undegradable protein in high fat diets for cows in early lactation. *J Dairy Sci* 77:1630.

Pantoja, J, Firkins JL, & Eastridge ML. 1995. Effects of fat saturation on lactation performance and fatty acid digestibility by dairy cows. *Abstracts,,* p 103. American Dairy Science Association Midwest Branch. Meeting, Des Moines, IA.

Poos–Floyd M, Klopfenstein T, & Britton R. 1985. Evaluation of laboratory techniques for predicting ruminal protein degradation. J. Dairy Sci. 68:829.

Sandrucci A, Crovetto GM, Rapetti L, & Tamburini A. 1992. Effect of blood meal in dairy cow diet on milk yield and composition. *J Dairy Sci* 75 (suppl 1):281.

Schingoethe DJ & Casper DP. 1991. Total lactational response to added fat during early lactation. *J Dairy Sci* 74:2617.

Shaver, RD. 1990. Fat sources for high producing dairy cows. In: *Proceedings of the 51st Minnesota Nutrition Conference,* September 18–19, 1990, Bloomington, IN.

Sindt MH, Stock RA, & Klopfenstein TJ. 1994. Urea versus urea and escape protein for finishing calves and yearlings. *Anim Feed Sci Tech* (In press).

Sindt MH, Stock RA, Klopfenstein TJ, & Shain DH. 1993a. Effect of protein source and grain type on finishing calf performance and ruminal metabolism. *J Anim Sci* 71:1047.

Sindt MH, Stock RA, Klopfenstein TJ, & Vieselmeyer BA. 1993b. Protein sources for finishing calves as affected by management system. *J Anim Sci* 71:740.

Sklan D, Moallem U, & Folman Y. 1991. Effect of feeding calcium soaps of fatty acids in production and reproductive responses in high producing lactating cows. *J Dairy Sci* 74:510.

Smith WA & Harris B Jr. 1993. The influence of forage type on the production response of lactating dairy cows supplemented with different types of dietary fat. *Prof Anim Scientist* 8:7.

Smith WA, Harris B Jr, Van Horn HH, & Wilcox CJ. 1993. Effects of forage type on production of dairy cows supplemented with whole cottonseed, tallow, and yeast. *J Dairy Sci* 76:205.

Steele W & Moore JH. 1968. The digestibility coefficients of myristic, palmitic, and stearic acids in the diet of sheep. *J Dairy Res* 35:371.

Stock R, Huffman R, & Klopfenstein T. 1993 . High lysine corn and protein source on receiving and finishing health and performance of calves. *Nebraska Beef Cattle Report* MP 59–A:54.

Stock R, Klopfenstein T, Brink D, Britton R, & Harmon D. 1986. Whey as a source of rumen–degradable protein. I. Effects on microbial protein production. *J Anim Sci* 63:1561.

Stock R, Klopfenstein T, Brink D, Lowry S, Rock D, & Abrams S. 1983. Impact of weighing procedures and variation in protein degradation rate on measured performance of growing lambs and cattle. *J Anim Sci* 57:1276.

Thomas MG, Bao B, & Williams GL. 1993. Enhanced follicular development in cows fed supplemental fat may be cholesterol-independent. *J Anim Sci* 71 (suppl 1):211.

Thomas MG, Bao B, & Williams GL. 1994. Dietary fatty acids may alter folliculogenesis and luteal function through multiple physiological mechanisms in the bovine. *J Anim Sci* 72 (suppl 2):16.

Waltz DM, Stern MD, & Illlg DJ. 1989. Effect of ruminal protein degradation of blood meal and feather meal on the intestinal amino acid supply to lactating cows. *J Dairy Sci* 72:1509–1518.

Wattiaux MA, Combs DK, & Shaver RD. 1993. Milk yield and intake of cows fed alfalfa silage based diets supplemented with undegradable intake protein. *J Dairy Sci* 76 (suppl 1):201 (abstr).

Weisbjerg M. R., Borsting C, & Hvelplund T. 1992a. Fatty acid metabolism in the digestive tract of lactating cows fed tallow in increasing amounts at two feed levels. *Acta Agric Scand, Sect A, Anim Sci* 42:106.

Weisbjerg MR., Hvelplund T, & Borsting CF. 1992b. Digestibility of fatty acids in the gastrointestinal tract of dairy cows fed with tallow or saturated fats rich in stearic acid or palmitic acid. *Acta Agric Scand, Sect A, Anim Sci* 42:115.

Williams GL. 1989. Modulation of luteal activity in postpartum beef cows through changes in dietary lipid. *J Anim Sci* 67:785.

Wu Z, Huber JT, Sleiman FT, Simas JM, Chen JH, Chan SC, & Fontes C. 1993. Effect of 3 supplmental fat sources on lactation and digestion in dairy cows. *J Dairy Sci* 76:3562.

Wu Z, Ohajuruka OA, & Palmquist DL. 1991. Ruminal synthesis, biohydrogenation, and digestibility of fatty acids by dairy cows. *J Dairy Sci* 74:3025.

Zinn RA. 1988. Comparative feeding value of supplemental fat in finishing diets for feedlot steers supplemented with and without monensin. *J Anim Sci* 66:213.

Zinn RA. 1989. Influence of level and source of dietary fat on its comparative feeding value in finishing diets for steers: feedlot performance. *J.Anim Sci* 67:1029.

Zinn RA. 1992. Comparative feeding value of supplemental fat in steam-flaked corn- and steam-flaked wheat-based finishing diets for feedlot steer. *J Anim Sci* 70:2959.

Zinn RA. 1994. Effects of excessive supplemental fat on feedlot cattle growth and performance and digestive function. *Professional Animal Scientist* 10:66.

# 9

# Utilizing Rendered Products: Swine

## Darrell A Knabe

The protein-rich feeds and energy-dense fats produced by the rendering industry have been, and will continue to be, an integral part of profitable swine feeding programs. Tankage and meat meal were once thought to be essential dietary ingredients for maximum performance of pigs not raised on pasture. This "animal protein factor" was later determined to be vitamin B-12. Nutritionally adequate swine diets can now be made without feeds from the rendering industry because vitamin B-12 and mineral supplements are commercially available. However, their nutrient profile in relation to cost will ensure that rendered feeds and fats will continue to be used in swine diets.

The criteria for selecting a feedstuff for use in swine diets include: nutrient content in relation to nutrient needs; biological availability of the nutrients; variability in content of nutrients and physical traits among samples of the same feedstuff; growth promotion not explained by nutrient content; palatability; physical traits that affect milling and mixing (such as density and viscosity); and presence of toxins or pathogens. This chapter primarily addresses the first 5 points and recommends usages of rendered feeds and fats.

## FUNDAMENTALS OF SWINE NUTRITION AND FEEDING

A brief review of the fundamentals of swine nutrition and feeding will help the novice understand the later discussion of the use of rendered feeds in swine diets.

Pigs need more than 40 individual nutrients in their diet. Fortunately, many nutrients are either present in adequate amounts in the normal feedstuffs or can be easily and economically supplemented from synthetic sources. The nutrients of economic concern in commercial swine diets are energy, protein (amino acids), calcium, and phosphorus. More than 95% of the cost of feeding swine lies in meeting the needs for these nutrients.

## Energy

Energy is measured as either digestible energy, metabolizable energy, or net energy. Each method attempts to quantify the amount of energy a feedstuff can supply by subtracting from the feed's gross (total) energy, the energy that is lost in the waste products resulting from the digestion and utilization of the feedstuff.

- Digestable energy equals gross energy minus fecal energy.
- Metabolizable energy equals digestible energy minus the energy in urine and gases of fermentation
- Net energy equals metabolizable energy minus the heat increment.
- Heat increment is the energy expended by the pig to digest and utilize the feedstuffs. Heat increment varies greatly among feedstuffs, but is lowest for the fats and oils, and highest for the fiber rich grain byproducts.

Swine diets are based on cereal grains because cereal grains are high in energy content. Pigs completely digest the starch in the grain. Fiber-rich feeds have low digestible energy and metabolizable energy because pigs cannot efficiently digest fiber. Bacterial fermentation in the digestive tract, which is required to break down the components of fiber, is limited to the large intestine. Furthermore, the inefficiencies of fermentative digestion and the utilization of energy-yielding metabolites from fermentation require high heat increment. Fats and oils, on the other hand, have the highest digestible energy, metabolizable energy, and net energy due to their high gross energy, high efficiency of digestion and absorption, and low heat increment. Fats and oils provide more than twice the energy as the same amount by weight of cereals.

Energy density affects voluntary feed intake of swine. As energy density of the diet increases, daily intake decreases so that daily energy intake remains about the same. Adding animal fat to diets of growing pigs increases energy density, lowers feed intake, and improves feed efficiency. Because lowering feed intake lowers intake of all nutrients, concentration of nutrients in the diet should increase proportional to dietary energy. Nutrient requirements of pigs are often expressed in relation to energy density, primarily protein/calorie and lysine/calorie ratios.

## Protein

Protein is made up of 22 different amino acids. The pig lacks the metabolic pathways to synthesize 9 amino acids from other precursor molecules. These are the "dietary essential amino acids" and are the real nutrients the pig needs, not protein as such.

Protein is the primary constituent of muscles, enzymes, and some hormones. Because the body synthesizes protein from dietary amino acids, a deficiency of any of the essential amino acids limit protein synthesis and, consequently, growth rate, feed efficiency, and carcass merit of the growing finishing pig and reproductive performance of the sow.

The proportion of the 9 essential amino acids in the average protein synthesized by the pig is called the "ideal protein" pattern (Table 1). By convention, the ratios of the amino acids are expressed in relation to lysine. Examination of the ideal pattern indicates that pigs need relatively large amounts of some amino acids (lysine, leucine, phenylalanine + tyrosine) but small amounts of others (tryptophan).

**Table 1.** Pattern of Amino Acids in the Ideal Protein

| Amino Acid | ARC[a] | NRC[b] | Wang & Fuller[c] | Chung & Baker[d] | Hahn & Baker[e] |
|---|---|---|---|---|---|
| Lysine | 100 | 100 | 100 | 100 | 100 |
| Leucine | 100 | 74 | 110 | 100 | 100 |
| Phe+Tyr | 96 | 81 | 120 | 95 | 95 |
| Valine | 70 | 59 | 75 | 68 | 68 |
| Threonine | 60 | 59 | 72 | 65 | 70 |
| Met+Cys | 50 | 52 | 63 | 60 | 65 |
| Isoleucine | 54 | 56 | 60 | 60 | 60 |
| Arginine | -- | 42 | 42 | 42 | 42 |
| Histidine | 32 | 26 | 32 | 32 | 32 |
| Tryptophan | 14 | 15 | 18 | 18 | 20 |

[a]ARC 1981
[b]NRC 1988
[c]Wang & Fuller 1989
[d]Chung & Baker 1992; profile for 10-kg pig.
[e]Hahn & Baker 1995; profile for finishing pigs.

The proportion of an amino acid in a feed that is absorbed from the digestive tract is called true digestibility. True digestibility is difficult, if not impossible, to determine, because of the endogenous amino acids in feces or ileal digesta from sloughed cells and secretions of the digestive tract. Apparent digestibility does not account for these endogenous losses, and as such is a flawed measure of amino acid absorption. However, because endogenous secretions are difficult to measure, and because the physical and chemical characteristics of a feedstuff affect endogenous losses, apparent digestibility is likely the best measure for practical purposes.

Apparent digestibility of amino acids determined at the end of the small intestine are more accurate than apparent digestibility determined over the total digestive tract. Amino acids are not absorbed from the large intestine, and the microflora in the large intestine degrade and synthesize amino acids. Digestibility determined at the end of the small intestine, in the ileum, is called ileal digestibility.

Protein quality refers to the ability of a feedstuff or diet to provide the dietary essential amino acids the pig needs. Protein quality can be reduced by either a deficiency of one or more dietary essential amino acids, or by an excess of essential amino acids. The protein in cereal grains is low quality because of multiple amino acid deficiencies. Compared with the needs of a 100-lb high-lean genotype pig, for example, corn is deficient in lysine, tryptophan, threonine, isoleucine, and methionine+cystine. Lysine is the first limiting amino acid in corn and all cereal grains because it is most deficient.

High-protein feedstuffs such as rendered meals and oilseed meals are used to balance the amino acid deficiencies of the grains. A good quality protein feedstuff balances the amino acid deficiencies of the cereal grain while minimizing dietary protein. The latter point is important because excess dietary essential amino acids in excess protein may reduce pig performance. Feeding excess protein usually increases cost.

Diets based on corn and using either the rendered high-protein feeds, or common oilseed meals were formulated to meet the digestible amino acid needs of a 100-lb high-lean genotype pig (0.72% digestible lysine, digestible contents of other amino acids based on ratios to lysine in the ideal protein). Protein contents of the diets, and the first-limiting amino acid in each diet are: soybean meal, 17.8% lysine; menhaden fishmeal, 22.2% tryptophan; poultry-byproduct meal, 23.7% tryptophan; peanut meal, 28.2% lysine; cottonseed meal, 29.8% lysine; meat and bone meal 45.1% tryptophan; spray dried blood meal, 48.4% isoleucine; feather meal, 83.7% lysine. The low content of lysine, tryptophan, and isoleucine, makes the rendered high-protein feeds best as a supplement to a diet containing cereals and soybean meal rather than as the sole source of supplemental protein in a cereal-based diet.

The poor protein quality of rendered feeds can be improved by the use of feed-grade lysine and tryptophan to balance the deficiencies of the feeds. By using these 2 amino acids, the protein content of diets formulated as described above are: menhaden fishmeal 16.3%, poultry-byproduct, 17.1%; meat and bone meal, 21.2%; feather meal 20.2%.

## Macrominerals

Of the 6 macrominerals, unsupplemented diets are likely to be deficient in calcium, phosphorus, sodium, and choline. Sodium and choline needs are easily met by adding salt. The cereals are almost devoid of calcium and are low in phosphorus; a dietary deficiency of both minerals will result unless the diet contains supplemental calcium and phosphorus from either the protein feeds or inorganic sources. A deficiency of either calcium or phosphorus or an imbalance of calcium and phosphorus will result in lowered performance (reduced growth, milk production) followed by abnormalities of the bone due to poor mineralization, ricketts in growing pigs, and spontaneous bone fractures in sows. Providing supplemental calcium is inexpensive and easy because ground limestone is abundant and inexpensive. Phosphorus supplementation, on the other hand, is expensive. Because of differences in total content and differences in biological availability of phosphorus, feedstuffs vary greatly in their ability to provide phosphorus to pigs.

"Availability" refers to the proportion of the mineral from a feedstuff that is actually utilized and deposited in the bone. Thus availability includes the effects of both digestion and utilization after absorption. Measurements of bone strength and bone ash are the criteria used to determine availability. Monosodium phosphate, a high-quality inorganic source of phosphorus, serves as a reference point for available phosphorus; it is assigned a relative availability of 100. For example, the availability of phosphorus in corn is estimated to be 15%, compared to a value of 100% for monosodium phosphate.

Phosphorus in the rendered high-protein feeds containing bone is much more available to the pig than phosphorus from cereals and oilseed meals. In the latter case, phosphorus is part of phytin in the seeds and is poorly digested. Availabilities of phosphorus, published by the National Research Council (NRC 1988) are: meat and bone meal, 93%; fishmeal, 100%; soybean meal, 32 to 35%; cottonseed meal, 21%; corn, 15%; sorghum, 22%. Although the availability of phosphorus in poultry-byproduct meal and blood meal have not been reported, their availabilities are likely high. A major nutritional advantage of meat and bone meal, meat meal, fishmeal, and poultry-byproduct meal is their high content of available phosphorus.

## Vitamins and Trace Minerals

The pig has a dietary need for 13 vitamins and 6 trace minerals. The high-protein feeds containing meat are excellent sources of vitamin B-12, niacin, riboflavin, thiamine, iron, manganese, selenium, and zinc. In the early days of swine feeding, blending several high-protein feeds with grains and legume products was necessary to meet the vitamin and trace mineral needs of pigs. Today that is not necessary because of the availability of previously mixed synthetic vitamins and inorganic sources of trace elements. In practical terms, vitamin and trace mineral content of a feedstuff has little bearing on its economic value thanks to low cost of vitamin and trace mineral supplementation.

## HIGH-PROTEIN FEEDSTUFFS
## Content and Availability of Nutrients

An accurate knowledge of the content and biological availability of nutrients to the pig is essential for the proper and economical use of the rendered feedstuffs. Knowing the variability in content of a nutrient among samples of the same feedstuff is also essential for those wishing to ensure a minimum level of a dietary nutrient.

Tables 2 to 11 summarize the protein, calcium, phosphorus, crude fat, and essential amino acid content of the rendered, high-protein feeds. Data are the result of a survey sponsored by the Fats and Proteins Research Foundation to obtain current nutrient content and availability data for the rendered feedstuffs. Data consist of replies from 6 large feed manufacturers or renderers, and 42 university reports published after 1985. Table 12 lists energy contents of the high-protein rendered feeds published by the National Research Council (NRC 1988); energy contents were not found for these feeds in the US and Canadian literature.

## Meat and Bone Meal and Meat Meal

Data from meat and bone meal and meat meal reported by commercial sources were segregated into meat and bone meals that contained at least 4.4% phosphorus, and meat meals that contained less than 4.4% phosphorus (Table 2). Both meals remain excellent sources of calcium, phosphorus, protein, and amino acids. The meat meals were about 3% higher in protein and 0.20% higher in lysine, but 2.3% and 1.2% lower in calcium and phosphorus, respectively. Both types of meals contained 10.7% fat. Meat and bone meal and meat meal would be considered moderate sources of energy (Table 3). Energy from fat helps to balance the lack of energy in the ash content of the meals (26% ash found for 35 samples of meat and bone meal).

As crude protein increases in the meals, amino acid content also increases, but the relationship is not perfect. Table 3 shows the results of regressing amino acid content on protein content of meat and bone meal and meat meal. A perfect correlation of protein and amino acid content would have a correlation coefficient ($r$) of 1.0. The coefficients for the essential amino acids ranged from .57 for threonine to .78 for threonine; lysine had an $r$ value of .69, and tryptophan had an $r$ value of .57 (Figure 1).

**Table 2.** Mean Protein Fat, Calcium, Phosphorus, and Amino Acid Contents of Meat and Bone Meal and Meat Meal[a]

| Nutrient, % | Meat and Bone Meal[b] | | | Meat Meal[c] | | |
|---|---|---|---|---|---|---|
| | n | Mean | SD | n | Mean | SD |
| Crude protein | 255 | 51.4 | 2.64 | 171 | 54.0 | 2.93 |
| Crude fat | 78 | 10.70 | 1.61 | 35 | 10.72 | 1.55 |
| Calcium | 255 | 9.99 | 1.01 | 171 | 7.69 | 1.16 |
| Phosphorus | 255 | 4.98 | .38 | 171 | 3.88 | .41 |
| | | | | | | |
| Arginine | 61 | 3.60 | .35 | 22 | 3.34 | .57 |
| Histidine | 62 | .92 | .19 | 22 | .95 | .28 |
| Isoleucine | 62 | 1.40 | .25 | 22 | 1.58 | .21 |
| Leucine | 62 | 3.10 | .47 | 22 | 3.32 | .49 |
| Lysine | 64 | 2.64 | .36 | 22 | 2.85 | .47 |
| Methionine | 39 | .70 | .14 | 7 | .79 | .18 |
| Cystine | 7 | .46 | .23 | 7 | .45 | .26 |
| Phenylalanine | 62 | 1.67 | .22 | 20 | 1.98 | .58 |
| Threonine | 64 | 1.65 | .23 | 22 | 1.74 | .33 |
| Tryptophan | 29 | .26 | .05 | 2 | .29 | .05 |
| Valine | 62 | 2.11 | .34 | 22 | 2.44 | .43 |

[a]As-fed basis. Data for protein, fat, calcium, and phosphorus from commercial sources. All amino acid values are from data reported by universities. References are: meat and bone meal, 2, 3, 4, 5, 7, 49, 55, 60, 66, 76; meat meal, 4, 27, 28, 30, 40, 41, 46.
[b]Protein, fat, calcium, and phosphorus contents for meals having at least 4.4% phosphorus. The mean protein content of meals analyzed for amino acids was $50.5\pm4.3$.
[c]Protein, fat, calcium, and phosphorus contents for meals having less than 4.4% phosphorus. The mean protein content of meals analyzed for amino acids was $54.9\pm2.1$.

**Table 3.** Regression of Amino Acid Contents and Crude Protein in Meat and Bone Meal and Meat Meal

| Amino Acid | n | Equation | | r |
|---|---|---|---|---|
| Arginine | 70 | y = | .8516 + .0546 x | .70 |
| Histidine | 70 | y = | -.4639 + .0278 x | .57 |
| Isoleucine | 70 | y = | -.4802 + .0373 x | .67 |
| Leucine | 70 | y = | -1.1133 + .0841 x | .78 |
| Lysine | 70 | y = | -.3367 + .0591 x | .69 |
| Methionine | 45 | y = | -.3125 + .0202 x | .66 |
| Phenylalanine | 68 | y = | -.2145 + .0377 x | .63 |
| Threonine | 70 | y = | -.6008 + .0448 x | .78 |
| Tryptophan | 27 | y = | -.0113 + .0055 x | .57 |
| Valine | 70 | y = | -.6981 + .0565 x | .64 |

**Figure 1.**

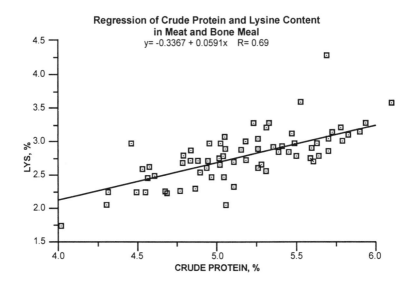

Regression of Crude Protein and Lysine Content
in Meat and Bone Meal
y= -0.3367 + 0.0591x   R= 0.69

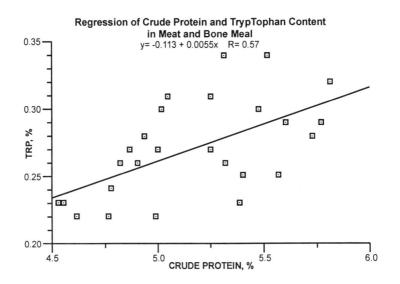

Regression of Crude Protein and TrypTophan Content
in Meat and Bone Meal
y= -0.113 + 0.0055x   R= 0.57

**Table 4.** Mean ± Standard Deviation of Crude Protein, Calcium, and Phosphorus Contents for Meat and Bone Meals from Different Renderers[a]

| Renderer | n | Crude Protein | | | Calcium | | | Phosphorus | | |
|---|---|---|---|---|---|---|---|---|---|---|
| | | Mean | SD | %<50% | Mean | SD | %<8% | Mean | SD | %<4.4% |
| 1 | 24 | 50.6 | 2.1 | 38 | 8.2 | 1.3 | 38 | 4.2 | .6 | 33 |
| 2 | 38 | 50.0 | 1.3 | 47 | 10.8 | .7 | 0 | 5.2 | .3 | 0 |
| 3 | 24 | 54.6 | 2.8 | 8 | 7.5 | 1.3 | 63 | 3.9 | .6 | 50 |
| 4 | 27 | 56.8 | 1.2 | 0 | 6.3 | 1.1 | 93 | 3.6 | .6 | 93 |
| 5 | 29 | 51.5 | .7 | 7 | 8.9 | .5 | 0 | 4.2 | .3 | 83 |
| 6 | 65 | 51.4 | 1.8 | 22 | 10.0 | 1.1 | 6 | 5.1 | .4 | 2 |
| 7 | 23 | 55.8 | 1.7 | 0 | 8.4 | 1.0 | 48 | 4.4 | .4 | 9 |
| 8 | 23 | 56.4 | 2.1 | 0 | 8.1 | 1.0 | 52 | 4.3 | .4 | 13 |
| 9 | 18 | 51.3 | 1.1 | 11 | 10.6 | .4 | 0 | 5.2 | .2 | 0 |

[a] Data provided by a feed manufacturer for a 6 month period in 1994

**Table 5.** Mean Apparent Ileal Digestibility of Protein and Amino Acids in Meat and Bone Meal and Meat Meal[a]

| Nutrient, % | Meat and Bone Meal | | | Meat Meal | | |
|---|---|---|---|---|---|---|
| | n | Mean | SD | n | Mean | SD |
| Crude Protein | 30 | 66 | 5.4 | 2 | 78 | 3.5 |
| Arginine | 30 | 80 | 3.7 | 8 | 73 | 9.4 |
| Histidine | 30 | 68 | 7.2 | 8 | 79 | 3.1 |
| Isoleucine | 30 | 68 | 7.2 | 8 | 63 | 11.0 |
| Leucine | 30 | 74 | 5.1 | 8 | 69 | 8.3 |
| Lysine | 30 | 71 | 6.8 | 8 | 68 | 9.0 |
| Methionine | 2 | 84 | 2.8 | 2 | 84 | 2.8 |
| Cystine | 1 | 63 | - | - | - | - |
| Phenylalanine | 30 | 77 | 5.2 | 8 | 65 | 11.6 |
| Threonine | 30 | 64 | 6.2 | 8 | 56 | 14.8 |
| Tryptophan | 29 | 57 | 9.4 | - | - | - |
| Valine | 30 | 73 | 5.2 | 8 | 66 | 9.2 |

[a] Data reported by universities. References are: meat and bone meal, 2, 7, 49, 60, 55; meat meal, 40, 41, 46.

**Table 6.** Mean Nutrient Content of Apparent Ileal Digestibility for Spray Dried and Ring Dried Blood Meals[a]

| Nutrient, % | Content[bc] | | | Digestibility[d] | | |
|---|---|---|---|---|---|---|
| | n | Mean | SD | n | Mean | SD |
| Crude Protein | 20 | 88.0 | 3.98 | 10 | 87 | 4.1 |
| Arginine | 19 | 3.64 | .35 | 10 | 90 | 5.1 |
| Histidine | 20 | 5.39 | .52 | 10 | 95 | 2.6 |
| Isoleucine | 20 | .93 | .18 | 10 | 67 | 10.2 |
| Leucine | 20 | 11.16 | .67 | 10 | 92 | 2.9 |
| Lysine | 20 | 8.24 | .55 | 10 | 94 | 2.1 |
| Methionine | 17 | 1.15 | .34 | 10 | 84 | 5.4 |
| Cystine | 10 | 1.12 | .11 | -- | -- | -- |
| Phenylalanine | 20 | 6.17 | .44 | 10 | 92 | 2.9 |
| Threonine | 20 | 3.93 | .50 | 10 | 86 | 3.9 |
| Tryptophan | 13 | 1.12 | .30 | 7 | 92 | 5.1 |
| Valine | 20 | 7.76 | .64 | 10 | 92 | 2.7 |

[a] As-fed basis.
[b] References are: 45, 50, 51, 56, 59, and 61 for spray-dried blood meal and 4, 60, and 61 for ring-dried blood meal.
[c] A feed manufacturer reported a protein mean ±SD of 89.3±2.9% for 97 samples of spray dried blood meal and a dry matter content of 89.4±1.7 for 79 samples. An additional feed manufacturer reported a protein content of 89.6±3.2% for 16 samples of ring dried blood meal.
[d] References are 56 and 59 for spray dried blood meal and 60 for ring dried blood meal.

Meat and bone meal and meat meal tend to be variable in nutrient content both among samples produced at the same rendering plant and among different processing plants. The standard deviations (SD) for crude protein content were 3.0 for 426 samples, 4.3 for 71 samples and 1.8 for 676 samples. An example of the variability among processing plants is shown in Table 4. The relatively large processor-to-processor variation suggests that feed formulators may be well-served to modify nutrient contents based on the origin of the meat and bone meal and meat meal.

Meat and bone meal and meat meal have moderate apparent ileal amino acid digestibilities (Table 5) compared with more digestible feeds such as soybean meal or fishmeal. A large variation in amino acid digestibilities also existed among samples of meat and bone meal and meat meal. The mean and standard deviations for lysine, tryptophan, and threonine are 71±7, 57±9, and 64±6. The cause of this variability is undoubtedly linked to method of determining digestibilities, type of beginning material (soft tissue vs bones), and degree of heat treatment during processing. All rendered products must be heated sufficiently to dry and sterilize the material. Any additional heat could lower amino acid digestibility, especially lysine with its free amino group. It should be noted that some meat and bone meals are as digestible as soybean meal (Knabe 1989).

## Dried Blood Products

The dried blood meals, in contrast to the meat and bone meals, were relatively uniform in nutrient content and digestibility (Table 6). Mean protein contents for spray-dried blood meals were 88.3% (n = 11), and 89.3%±2.9% (n = 97 samples); mean protein contents for ring-dried blood meal were 87.6% (n = 7) and 89.6±3.2% (n = 16). Because the number of amino acid analyses for the blood meals was limited (n = 11 or 7 for spray-dried and ring-dried blood meals, respectively), data for spray-dried and ring-dried meals were combined. On average, the blood meals contained 8.24±.55% lysine, 1.22±0.30% tryptophan, and 3.93±0.50% threonine.

Digestibilities of protein and amino acids are uniformly high for both spray-dried (n=6) and ring-dried (n=3) blood meals. Lysine digestibilities were 95±2 and 93±1.5 for spray-dried and ring-dried meals. Of the major protein feeds fed to pigs, only dried skim milk and casein have been found to be as digestible as properly processed blood meals.

The amino acid profile of spray-dried porcine plasma is distinctly different from that of blood meal, as would be expected, and its apparent digestibility is lower than that of spray-dried blood meal (Table 7). Reasons for this lowered digestibility are not evident.

## Poultry-byproduct Meal and Hydrolyzed Feather Meal

Data for the poultry-byproduct meals are derived primarily from university reports (Table 8). Amino acid data were not reported by feed manufacturers. Variability in nutrient content among samples was similar to that found for meat and bone meals. Apparent ileal digestibilities, however, were higher than those found for meat and bone meal, and are similar to those reported for soybean meal and fishmeal. It should be pointed out that samples evaluated for amino acid digestibility were largely free of feathers.

Nutrient contents for feather meals (Table 9) are also derived primarily from university reports, although one feed manufacturer reported 85.7±1.6% as the protein content for 31 feather meal samples. Digestibility data are limited to only one sample; lysine was poorly digested in that sample.

## Menhaden Fishmeal

Data for menhaden fishmeal were divided into "normal" and "select" meals based on the description provided by the feed manufacturer or the fishmeal producer. One set of data for normal fishmeal was provided as the mean±SD for 24 samples, and as such, could not be combined with data for individual samples. Thus Table 10 shows 2 nutrient profiles for normal fishmeal. The select fishmeal data set was from one feed manufacturer. In general, nutrient contents in all 3 columns agree. The simple weighted mean for calcium, phosphorus, protein, lysine, tryptophan, and threonine are: 5.21, 3.04, 62.3, 4.75, 0.53, and 2.63%, respectively.

Apparent ileal digestibilities of protein and amino acids for 7 samples of menhaden fishmeal are shown in Table 11. The limited sample numbers prevented distinction between normal and select meals. Digestibilities were higher than those found for meat and bone meal and similar to those for poultry-byproduct meal. Variability was large also, reflecting possible differences in processing method and storage of fish prior to processing.

## HIGH-PROTEIN RENDERED FEEDS IN SWINE DIETS
## Meat and Bone Meal and Meat Meal

Meat and bone meal and meat meal are the predominant rendered feedstuff fed to swine. As indicated, both are excellent sources of available phosphorus and calcium and are moderate sources of digestible amino acids and digestible energy.

Use of these meals as the only source of supplemental protein in cereal-based swine diets has resulted in inferior performance (Kennedy et al 1974, Stockland et al 1970, Peo & Hudman 1962). Increasing dietary levels of meat and bone meal in diets of growing-finishing pigs (Peo & Hudman 1962) and weaning pigs (Puchal et al 1962, Evans & Leibholz 1979ab) has resulted in linear depression in performance. Results such as these, linked with the variability in nutrient content among meat and bone meals, has resulted in recommendations for low usage rates of the meals in swine diets. With better understanding of amino acid requirements and production of feed grade amino acids, these recommendations are no longer valid.

Low digestible tryptophan content is the primary nutritional factor limiting the use of these meals in diets of growing-finishing pigs, sows, and boars. Collagen protein is devoid of tryptophan and may make up 50 to 65% of all protein in meat and bone meals due to its high content in bone protein, connective tissue, tendons, and cartilage (Eastoe & Long 1960). The reduced digestibility of tryptophan and other amino acids results in part from heat treatment during processing. Increasing heat treatment during processing of meat and bone meals has been shown to lower digestibility of amino acids (Haugen & Pettigrew 1985) and availability of lysine, as determined by the slope-ratio assay (Batterham et al 1986). Evaluating 23 commercially processed meat and bone meals, Knabe (1989) reported that mean ileal amino acid digestibilities for meals processed by the older, higher-temperature batch and Dupps systems had lower digestibilities than meals processed by the newer, lower-temperature, Atlas, Carver-Greenfield, and Stordz-Bards systems. Mean lysine and tryptophan digestibilities for the older and newer systems were 76±5 and 65±6% for lysine, and 63±7 and 52±9% for tryptophan, respectively.

Correcting the low digestible lysine and tryptophan contents of meat and bone meal by additions of feed-grade amino acids allows increased use of meat and bone meal in diets of growing-finishing hogs. Cromwell et al (1991) fed meat meal as the only source of supplemental protein in corn-based diets of finishing pigs with either lysine or lysine plus tryptophan supplementation. Diets contained 10% meat meal. Compared to the control, soybean meal-supplemented treatment, the meat meal diet without tryptophan supplementation reduced daily gains 42%, and worsened feed efficiency 28%; adding 0.05% L-tryptophan to the meat meal diet resulted in performance similar to that found on the control diet. Knabe (1989) also reported equal performance for growing-finishing pigs fed diets based on soybean meal or containing as much as 8% meat and bone meal when digestible lysine and tryptophan were equalized across treatments.

The high mineral content of meat and bone meal was once thought to be responsible for the reduced performance of pigs fed high levels of meat and bone meal (Eastoe & Lacy 1960). Subsequent reports (Evans & Leibholz 1979) show that this not to be true. The reduced performance with increasing bone content of meat and bone meal likely reflects the reduced quality of the protein due to higher collagen content and possible interactions between high calcium content and other dietary ingredients such as phosphorus and zinc.

**Table 7.** Mean Nutrient Content and Apparent Ileal Digestibility of Protein and Amino Acids in Spray-dried Porcine Plasma

| Nutrient, % | Content[a,b] Mean | SD | Digestibility[c] Mean | SD |
|---|---|---|---|---|
| Crude Protein | 70.8 | 5.4 | 78 | 7.1 |
| Arginine | 4.25 | .35 | 86 | 6.3 |
| Histidine | 2.33 | .52 | 89 | 2.8 |
| Isoleucine | 2.75 | .18 | 83 | 3.5 |
| Leucine | 7.03 | .67 | 83 | 1.4 |
| Lysine | 6.33 | .55 | 86 | 2.1 |
| Methionine | .68 | .34 | 63 | 2.1 |
| Cystine | 2.36 | .09 | - | - |
| Phenylalanine | 4.15 | .26 | 85 | 5.0 |
| Threonine | 4.22 | .23 | 80 | 3.5 |
| Tryptophan | 1.29 | .21 | 92 | - |
| Valine | 4.77 | .14 | 84 | 3.5 |

[a]As-fed basis
[b]Based on 4 samples, except cystine which is based on 2 samples. References: 45, 50, 56, and 59.
[c]Based on 2 samples, except tryptophan which is based on 1 sample. Reference: 59.

**Table 8.** Mean Nutrient Content and Apparent Ileal Digestibility of Poultry-byproduct Meal[a]

| Nutrient, % | n | Content[b] Mean | SD | n | Digestibility[c] Mean | SD |
|---|---|---|---|---|---|---|
| Crude Protein | 59 | 64.1 | 2.60 | 6 | 76 | 3.1 |
| Calcium | 28 | 4.46 | .50 | | | |
| Phosporus | 28 | 2.41 | .19 | | | |
| Ash | 31 | 14.4 | 1.44 | | | |
| Dry matter | 27 | 95.1 | 1.79 | | | |
| Crude fat | 45 | 12.6 | 1.47 | | | |
| Arginine | 28 | 4.47 | .52 | 6 | 87 | 2.3 |
| Histidine | 27 | 1.34 | .16 | 6 | 80 | 4.4 |
| Isoleucine | 28 | 2.35 | .27 | 6 | 79 | 2.0 |
| Leucine | 28 | 4.49 | .49 | 6 | 81 | 4.4 |
| Lysine | 29 | 3.73 | .57 | 6 | 84 | 4.6 |
| Methionine | 21 | 1.23 | .12 | - | - | - |
| Cystine | 21 | .99 | .37 | - | - | - |
| Phenylalanine | 28 | 2.47 | .35 | 6 | 83 | 3.5 |
| Threonine | 29 | 2.46 | .22 | 6 | 74 | 3.6 |
| Tryptophan | 13 | .53 | .12 | 6 | 74 | 11.5 |
| Valine | 28 | 2.96 | .51 | 6 | 78 | 2.6 |

[a]As-fed basis.
[b]References: 7, 25, 30, 43, 52, 55, 60, 66, 68.
[c]References: 7, 55, 60.

**Table 9.** Mean Nutrient Content and Apparent Ileal Digestibility of Protein and Amino Acids in Feather Meal

| Nutrient, % | n | Content, %[a] Mean | SD | Digestibility[b] |
|---|---|---|---|---|
| Crude protein | 23 | 82.9 | 5.0 | 63 |
| Ash | 13 | 2.7 | 1.3 | - |
| Dry matter | 20 | 93.3 | 2.9 | - |
| Crude fat | 13 | 5.2 | 1.7 | - |
| | | | | |
| Arginine | 23 | 5.99 | .80 | 79 |
| Histidine | 21 | .81 | .32 | 35 |
| Isoleucine | 22 | 3.99 | .46 | 75 |
| Leucine | 22 | 6.90 | .58 | 75 |
| Lysine | 23 | 1.80 | .30 | 40 |
| Methionine | 20 | .61 | .12 | - |
| Cystine | 20 | 4.61 | .51 | - |
| Phenylalanine | 20 | 4.07 | .30 | 80 |
| Threonine | 22 | 3.79 | .43 | 66 |
| Tryptophan | 3 | .59 | .19 | 60 |
| Valine | 22 | 6.37 | .68 | 77 |

[a]As-fed basis. References: 16, 17, 30, 43, 44, 60, 61, 66, 69. A feed manufacturer submitted data on 31 samples; mean ±SD were, 85.7±1.6% for crude protein, and 6.0±1.5% for crude fat.
[b]References: 60; only 1 sample evaluated.

**Table 10.** Mean Nutrient Content of Menhaden Fishmeals[a]

| Nutrient, % | Normal[b] Mean | SD | n | Normal[c] Mean | SD | Select[d] Mean | SD |
|---|---|---|---|---|---|---|---|
| Crude protein[e] | 62.8 | 1.05 | 8 | 60.8 | 1.18 | 62.2 | 1.53 |
| Calcium | 5.16 | .24 | 4 | 5.10 | .57 | 5.28 | .28 |
| Phosphorus | 3.24 | .15 | 4 | 3.28 | .46 | 2.81 | .14 |
| Ash | 17.2 | .88 | 7 | 18.6 | .73 | - | - |
| Crude fat | 9.9 | .70 | 3 | 7.9 | .74 | 9.5 | .20 |
| | | | | | | | |
| Arginine | 3.68 | .13 | 7 | 3.64 | .20 | 3.61 | .21 |
| Histidine | 1.52 | .15 | 7 | 1.21 | .21 | 1.56 | .10 |
| Isoleucine | 2.35 | .11 | 7 | 2.59 | .05 | 2.26 | .08 |
| Leucine | 4.33 | .11 | 7 | 4.45 | .09 | 4.12 | .15 |
| Lysine | 5.00 | .15 | 8 | 4.78 | .45 | 4.49 | .21 |
| Methionine | 1.98 | .12 | 5 | 1.83 | .11 | 1.72 | .14 |
| Cystine | .62 | .07 | 1 | .60 | - | .45 | .04 |
| Phenylalanine | 2.38 | .12 | 7 | 2.45 | .18 | 2.25 | .11 |
| Threonine | 2.64 | .09 | 7 | 2.53 | .11 | 2.66 | .10 |
| Tryptophan | .54 | .05 | 5 | .49 | .03 | .53 | .07 |
| Valine | 3.00 | .13 | 7 | 3.01 | .10 | 2.66 | .14 |

[a]As-fed basis.
[b]Data for 24 samples provided by 1 fishmeal manufacturer.
[c]References: 56, 57, 60, 83.
[d]Data for 24 samples provided by 1 feed manufacturer. The meals were used in pig starter diets.
[e]An additional feed manufacturer reported 62.6±0.9% as the crude protein content of 20 samples of normal menhaden fishmeal. An additional feed manufacturer reported 63.0±1.3% as the protein content of 39 samples of select Menhaden fishmeal.

Meat and bone meal and meat meal consistently cost more than soybean meal, but are often used in least-cost diet formulations because of their amino acid profile and phosphorus content. Current data indicate that the old recommendations of no more than 3 to 5% meat and bone meal in swine diets are not nutritionally valid, if the formulator has accurate nutrient content for the meals, and formulates to adequate digestible lysine and tryptophan levels. Meat and bone meal and meat meal content will likely never exceed 5 to 7% of the diet, however, because at that level, the need for dietary available phosphorus is usually met and the cost advantage of meat and bone meal diminishes.

The meat and bone and meat meals are usually not included in diets of pigs weighing less than 40 lb. The young-weaned pig requires highly digestible and palatable ingredients for maximum performance.

## Poultry Byproduct Meal

Based on its nutrient profile and high digestibility, poultry-by product meal should be an excellent protein feedstuff for use in swine diets. Research reports on use of the meal in swine diets could not be found. Scarcity and cost of the meal likely prohibits its routine use in swine diets. Most of the meal is either sold to pet food manufacturers at prices that prohibit its economical use in swine diets, or it is retained by the vertically integrated poultry producers for use in broiler and layer diets.

## Hydrolyzed Feather Meal

Low-digestible lysine and histidine content limit the use of feather meal in swine diets. A recent report (Chiba et al 1996) found that as much as 9% feather meal could be used in isolysinic corn—soybean meal diets of the finishing pig without adversely affecting carcass merit, but 3% feather meal was the maximum usage rate without reducing performance. Use of feed-grade lysine and 9% feather meal to replace all of the soybean meal resulted in lowered performance compared to the soybean meal control.

A unique use of feather meal is to provide excess protein in diets of growing-finishing swine (Chiba et al 1995) and broilers (Cabel et al 1988) to reduce fat deposition. Feeding as much as 15% feather meal (24% protein diets) in lysine-adequate corn—soybean meal diets of finishing pigs did not reduce performance but reduced backfat depth and increased leanness; however, the response in carcass leanness was marginal and likely would be uneconomical. The potential for use of feather meal in amino acid-supplemented diets is shown by the work of Chung & Baker (1994) on methionine requirements of the young weaned pig. Pigs fed corn—soybean-meal—dried-whey diets containing 15.5% feather meal and supplemented with lysine, histidine, and methionine performed as well as pigs fed the control diet without feather meal.

**Table 11.** Apparent Ileal Digestibility of Menhaden Fishmeal

|  | n | Digestibility, %<br>Mean | SD |
|---|---|---|---|
| Crude Protein | 7 | 70 | 6.9 |
| Arginine | 7 | 85 | 5.6 |
| Histidine | 7 | 75 | 8.6 |
| Isoleucine | 7 | 80 | 6.6 |
| Leucine | 7 | 81 | 6.2 |
| Lysine | 7 | 81 | 8.0 |
| Methionine | 4 | 81 | 7.7 |
| Cystine | - | - | - |
| Phenylalanine | 7 | 79 | 6.5 |
| Threonine | 7 | 74 | 7.5 |
| Tryptophan | 5 | 77 | 4.3 |
| Valine | 7 | 78 | 6.8 |

References are 56, 57, 60.

In practice, levels of feather meal in swine diets are kept low to obtain maximum performance. As with meat and bone meal, feather meal should not be fed to young-weaned pigs.

## Menhaden Fishmeal

Menhaden fishmeal is a unique rendered product in that the entire fish is rendered instead of just its inedible portions, as with meat and bone meal. This results in a meal with excellent protein quality, high energy content, and high calcium and phosphorus contents. Properly processed menhaden fishmeal can be the only source of supplemental protein in swine diets if adequate digestible lysine and tryptophan contents are maintained in the diet. In practice, however, fishmeal is not fed to growing-finishing pigs because of its high cost. Also, including too much fishmeal (in excess of 1% fish oil) in diets of finishing pigs will result in off-flavored pork as a result of incorporation of fish fatty acids and other lipids directly into the adipose tissue.

Menhaden fishmeal is best suited to the nutrient-dense, highly digestible diets needed by the pig weaned at 21 to 28 days of age. The high cost of menhaden fishmeal can be justified in these diets. Menhaden fishmeal at levels up to 12% of the diets fed during the 8- to 14- or 8- to 21-day periods after weaning (phase II type diets) have been shown to improve pig performance over isolysinic control diets containing soybean meal (Stoner et al 1990). This response cannot be explained by differences in nutrient content. The lower antigenicity of fishmeal than soybean meal for the weaned pig may be partially responsible for this effect. In practice, 3 to 5% menhaden fishmeal is often included in phase

II diets of pigs weaned at 21 days of age due to its ability to stimulate performance.

Quality of menhaden fishmeal is affected by processing conditions and storage conditions of fish during the period between harvesting and processing. Rancid fishmeal or fishmeal with excessive oil or salt content is not uncommon. Processors now market "select" or "premium" fishmeals for use in diets of the young pig to ensure quality. These higher-quality meals are more digestible by the young pig. Three "select" fishmeals had ileal lysine digestibilities of 87, 86, and 86% compared to 65% for a menhaden fishmeal that was noticeably rancid (author's observation).

## Dried Blood Products

Properly processed blood meals are excellent protein feeds for swine, when used in limited quantities to ensure adequacy of dietary isoleucine. Of all the common protein feeds, blood meal has the highest lysine content, as a percentage either of the sample or of protein.

Spray-dried and ring-dried whole blood are vastly superior to the older vat-dried blood meals. Vat-dried blood meals have very low nutritional value because the required heat damages the protein. In a comparison of 2 vat-dried blood meals, spray-dried blood meal and ring-dried blood meal, Knabe (1989) reported ileal lysine digestibilities of 45, 66, 95, and 85%, respectively. Low levels of spray-dried bloodmeal are often used in phase II diets of the weaned pig because improved performance justifies its high cost. Depending upon differences in cost, spray-dried bloodmeal may replace the fishmeal used in phase II diets. Kats et al (1994b) concluded that 2% spray-dried bloodmeal (either porcine, bovine, or avian blood) was the optimum level for phase II diets to improve performance of pigs weaned at 21 days of age. Performance of pigs fed diets containing 2.5% spray-dried bloodmeal was superior to performance of pigs fed diets containing 5% menhaden fishmeal. They also reported no response to bloodmeal in pigs older than 42 days of age.

In sum, spray-dried bloodmeal is an excellent feed for phase II diets of the weaned pig, but its high cost and lack of pigs improvement performance beyond 42 days of age precludes its use in other swine diets.

Spray-dried porcine plasma contains non-nutritive factors that stimulate feed intake in the 14- to 21-day-old weaned pig (Ermer et al 1992, Hansen et al 1993, Kats et al 1994a, Sohn et al 1991). Use of this product at 5 to 7.5% of the phase I diet has essentially eliminated the post-weaning lag in performance common to weaned pigs. This is a short-term response: By 7 days after weaning, pigs are adapted to dry feed intake and the response to spray-dried plasma diminishes.

Its high cost implies that spray-dried porcine plasma is fed at the lowest levels and for the shortest period possible. Goodband et al (1994) concluded that phase I diets, fed for the first 7 days after weaning, should contain 7.5% spray-dried porcine plasma if pigs are 21 days of age or younger at weaning and weigh less than 15 lb. Once pigs achieve 15 lb, they should be fed phase II diets containing spray-dried blood meal with or without fishmeal.

## Rendered Fats—Factors Affecting Energy Content

Fats and oils are the most energy-dense feeds that can be fed to pigs, containing an average of 2.25 times the energy of an equal weight of carbohydrate or protein. They are also a very diverse commodity varying in fatty acid composition and amount of free fatty acids and unsaponifiable material. Fatty acid composition and level of free fatty acids affects digestibility of the fat; unsaponifiable material and other non-lipid material affect the gross energy of the fat.

To be absorbed from the digestive tract, the fat must form micelles with bile salts in the intestinal lumen. The efficiency with which this is done is affected by length of the fatty acid and saturation of the fatty acid.

Short- and medium-chain fatty acids (14 carbons at most) readily form micelles. Apparent digestibility of fat sources high in medium-chain fatty acids in pigs is high (80 to 95%) regardless of the level of saturation (Braude & Newport 1973, Freeman et al 1968, Frobish et al 1970).

In pigs, saturated fatty acids alone have a lower micellar formation potential and thus are less efficiently digested than unsaturated fatty acids (Freeman et al 1968). However, micelle formation and absorption of saturated fatty acids is increased in the presence of unsaturated fatty acids or monoglycerides as reviewed by Freeman (1984). Therefore, the ratio of unsaturated to saturated fatty acids is important in evaluating the potential energy content of a fat.

Powles and coworkers (1993, 1994) reported that for both the growing pig (25 kg) and the young weaned pig (35 days old, 10 kg) apparent fat digestibility increased with increasing unsaturated to saturated ratio. Tallow with an unsaturated to saturated ratio of about 1 was 79.5 and 88.4% digestible in growing and weaned pigs, respectively, compared with 91.2 and 94.2% for soybean oil that had an unsaturated to saturated ratio of about 5.7. The type of response to increasing unsaturated to saturated ratio differed by age; the response was exponential for growing pigs with an unsaturated to saturated ratio of about 2.0 maximizing digestibility but linear for the young pig with consistent improvements up to 5.7 unsaturated to saturated. In a review of 5 experiments, Stahly (1984) reported that an unsaturated to saturated ratio of 1.5 to 2.0 was needed for high digestibility of fats in growing-finishing pigs.

Fat blends incorporated into pig diets may contain high levels of free fatty acids. Increasing free fatty acids with acid hydrolysates of tallow and soybean oil caused linear reductions in fat digestibility of the weanling and growing pig (Powles et al 1993, 1994). On average, each increase in free fatty acid content of 10% reduced digestibility and digestible energy content of the fat by about 1.5%. Reduced digestibility with increasing free fatty acid content suggests that a certain quantity of monoglycerides must be present for the formation of micelles.

Table 13 shows reported energy content for animal fats. The variation among reports likely reflects differences in method and differences in the fats evaluated. As mentioned earlier, fats have a low heat increment, so net energy is high. In the report by Noblet et al (1993), for example, animal fat contained 1.84 times the digestible energy of wheat, but 2.4 times the net energy of wheat.

Powles et al (1995) recently reported regression equations to estimate energy content of fats based on unsaturated to saturated ratio and free fatty acid content. The unsaturated to saturated ratio and free fatty contents suggested by the National Renderers Association (NRA 1990) were used to calculate the digestible energy content of feed-grade animal fats (Table 13).

## USE OF FATS IN SWINE DIETS

The primary reason for adding fat to swine diets is to increase energy content. Adding fat also reduces dust in swine buildings, which benefits both pigs and humans. Chiba et al (1985) reported that adding 5% tallow to ground, meal-type diets reduced aerial dust about 50% and tended to lower lung lesion scores in pigs fed fat. Adding fat also lubricates and extends the life of feed-mixing equipment.

**Table 12.** Estimates of Energy Content of the High-Protein Rendered Feeds[a]

| Feedstuff | Mcal/kg | |
|---|---|---|
| | DE | ME |
| Blood Meal, Spray Dried | 2.98 | 2.33 |
| Feather Meal | 2.73 | 2.21 |
| Fish Meal, Menhaden | 3.80 | 3.30 |
| Meat and Bone Meal | 2.54 | 2.28 |
| Meat Meal | 2.81 | 2.42 |
| Soybean meal, 44% | 3.49 | 3.22 |
| Corn | 3.53 | 3.42 |

[a] Values from NRC (1988).

## Growing-finishing pigs

Adding fat to diets of growing-finishing pigs consistently improves feed efficiency and lowers voluntary feed intake. Pettigrew & Moser (1991) summarized 92 experiments evaluating supplemental fat in diets of growing-finishing pigs. On average, pigs fed fat grew 0.04 kg faster each day (78% of the experiments had a positive response), consumed 0.10 kg feed less each day (83% positive responses), and had an improved gain/feed ratio of 0.04 (95% positive responses). Average backfat also increased 0.17 cm (67% positive responses). The degree of response in each trait was dependent on the level of fat inclusion. Daily gains improved up to 5% added fat, and thereafter decreased with increasing fat content. Daily feed intake was slightly increased at fat levels of 3% or less, but decreased at higher levels. Gain:feed ratio and backfat increased consistently as the level of fat increased.

Fat supplementation appears most beneficial when pigs are kept in thermal neutral or hot environments, due to the lower heat increment of fats. Stahly et al (1981) reported that the addition of 5% tallow to diets of growing-finishing pigs improved daily gains 8% and feed efficiency 12%, compared to 1% and 8% responses, respectively, for pigs fed in the winter. Feeding fat in the summer increased metabolizable energy intake over control pigs only 3%, but the lower heat increment of fats would have resulted in considerably higher net energy intakes. This increased energy intake is likely responsible for the 3% increase in backfat noted in the report. Stahly (1984) discusses the effect of environmental temperature on utilzation of fats in detail.

To obtain the most benefit from added fat, concentration of other nutrients in the diet should be expressed as a proportion of energy content. Simply adding fat to an existing diet may result in an amino acid or mineral deficiency due to the lower feed intake of pigs fed fat. Inadequate lysine/energy ratios lower performance and carcass leanness (Chiba et al 1991ab).

The ultimate decision to use fat in swine diets is one of economics and feasibility of handling and mixing fats in a given mill. Adding fat consistently improves feed efficiency, improves growth under the correct environmental conditions, but also lowers carcass leanness due to increased fat deposition. The recent merit buying systems based on carcass leanness suggest that feed cost/lb of gain will no longer be an adequate method of evaluating the economics of fat additions.

## Weaned Pigs

Fats are added to diets of weaned pigs primarily to improve performance. Long-term effects on carcass merit are not a concern. In a summary of 92 experiments, Pettigrew & Moser (1991) reported a small 0.01-kg advantage in daily gains (40% positive responses), a 0.05-kg reduction in daily feed intake (64% positive responses), and a 0.04-increase in gain/feed (71% positive responses) from feeding fats. The response to added fat is less consistent for the weaned pig than for the growing-finishing pigs.

**Table 13.** Reported Energy Contents for Animal Fat

| Reference | Description | DE | Mcal/kg ME | NE |
|---|---|---|---|---|
| NRC (1988) | Tallow | 8.20 | 7.90 | |
| | Lard | 7.86 | 7.75 | |
| | Poultry, fat | 8.64 | 7.98 | |
| Stahly (1984) | Tallow | | 7.89 | |
| | Tallow | | 7.88 | |
| | Lard | | 7.99 | |
| | Lard | | 7.70 | |
| Morgan et al 1984 | Tallow | | 9.27 | |
| Wiseman et al 1990 | Tallow | 8.16 | 7.77 | |
| Powles et al 1993 | Tallow | 7.46 | | |
| | Tallow | 8.08 | | |
| Powles et al 1994 | Tallow | 8.20 | | |
| Noblet et al 1993 | Animal fat | 7.12 | 7.06 | 7.00 |
| Powels et al 1995[a] | Tallow | 8.05 | | |
| | Choice white grease | 8.38 | | |
| | Yellow grease | 8.45 | | |
| | Poultry fat | 8.56 | | |

[a]Based on equations given by Powles et al (1995) for growing pigs and U/S ratios and free fatty acid content reported by NRA (1990).
[b]DE = digestible energy; ME = metabolizable energy; NE = net energy

The ability of the young weaned pig to digest animal and vegetable fat is age dependent. The pig efficiently digests the fat in sow's milk (Frobish et al 1967), but when provided the long-chain fatty acids in animal fats and vegetable oils during the immediate post-weaning period, digestibility drops, then recovers by the end of the first 14 days post-weaning (Cera et al 1988ab). Benefits in performance from adding fat during the post-weaning period reflect these differences in digestibility. Adding 3 to 6% soybean oil did not improve performance of pigs weaned at 21 days during the first 14 days post-weaning, but improved feed efficiency during the 15- to 35-day post-weaning period (Howard et al 1990).

Although young weaned pigs may not efficiently utilize fats during the immediate post-weaning period, diets of weaned pigs typically contain fats to minimize dust and to improve pelletting of phase I and II diets containing milk products. Quality of the fat fed to weaned pigs is important. Rancid fats and fats with high free fatty acid content may lower palatability and reduce growth rates.

## Lactating Sows

Fats are best utilized in the breeding herd by the lactating sows. Increasing energy density by adding fat reduces voluntary daily feed intake, increases metabolizable energy intake, reduces weight loss in the sow, and increases litter weaning weights (Pettigrew & Moser 1991). As with growing-finishing pigs, the greatest response to added fat will likely occur in the summer when heat stress reduces voluntary intake (Schoenherr et al 1987). A large cooperative study (Coffey et al 1994) examined the interaction of energy intake during gestation and energy density in lactation on reproductive performance. Inclusion of 9% fat in the lactation diets improved pig weaning weights 8%.

Feeding high levels of fat to sows just prior to farrowing and during lactation has been shown to increase lipid content of both colostrum and milk by about 2% (Seerly et al 1978), this increase in fat content is associated with increased survival of piglets under certain conditions, as reviewed by Pettigrew (1981) and Pettigrew and Moser (1991). For a benefit in survival rate, adequate amounts of fat must be fed prior to farrowing, and survival rate must be low. Pettigrew (1981) initially reported that feeding at least 1 kg of fat prior to farrowing, and a survival rate of 80% or less (subsequently revised to 70 to 80%) were required to obtain a response to added fat. Survivabilities that low are uncommon in modern farrowing facilities.

## REFERENCES

ARC. 1981. *The Nutrient Requirements of Pigs*. Commonwealth Agricultural Bureau., London.

Batterham ES, Andersen LM, Baigent DR, & Beech SA. 1990. Utilization of ileal digestible amino acids by pigs: lysine. *Br J Nutr* 64:679.

Batterham ES, Andersen LM, Lowe RF, & Darnell RE. 1986. Nutritional value of lupine (*Lupinus albus*) -seed meal for growing pigs: availability of lysine, effect of autoclaving and net energy content. *Br J Nutr* 56:645.

Batterham ES, Lowe RF, & Darnell RE. 1986. Availability of lysine in meat meal, meat and bone meal and blood meal as determined by the slope-ratio assay with growing pigs, rats and chicks and by chemical techniques. *Br J Nutr* 55:427.

Batterham ES & Watson C. 1985. Tryptophan content of feeds, limitations in diets and requirement for growing pigs. *Anim Feed Sci Techn* 13:171.

Batterham ES, Darnell RE, Herbert LS, & Major EJ. 1986. Effect of pressure and temperature on the availability of lysine in meat and bone meal as determined by slope-ratio assays with growing pigs, rats and chicks and by chemical techniques. *Br J Nutr* 55:441.

Bellaver C. 1989. Estimation of amino acid digestibility and its usefulness in swine feed formulation. MS thesis. Univiversity of Illinois, Urbana.

Braude R & Newport MJ. 1973. Artificial rearing of pigs. 4. The replacement of butterfat in a whole milk diet by either beef tallow, coconut oil or soya-bean oil. *Br J Nutr* 29:447.

Cabel MC, Goodwin TL, & Waldrop PW. 1988. Feather meal as a nonspecific nitrogen source for abdominal fat reduction in broilers during the finishing period. *Poultry Sci* 67:300.

Cera KR, Mahan DC, & Reinhart GA. 1988a. Effects of dietary dried whey and corn oil on weanling pig performance, fat digestibilities and nitrogen utilization. *J Anim Sci* 66:1438.

Cera KR, Mahan DC, & Reinhart GA. 1988b. Weekly digestibilities of diets supplemented with corn oil, lard, or tallow by weanling swine. *J Anim Sci* 66:1430.

Chausow DG, & Czarnecki-Maulden GL. 1988. The relative bioavailability of iron from feedstuffs of plant and animal origin to the chick. *Nutr Res* 8:175.

Chiba LI, Lewis AH, & Peo ER Jr. 1991a. Amino acid and energy interrelationships in pigs wighing 20 to 50 kilograms. I. Rate and efficiency of weight gain. *J Anim Sci* 69:694.

Chiba LI, Lewis AH, & Peo ER Jr. 1991b. Amino acid and energy interrelationships in pigs wighing 20 to 50 kilograms. I. Rate and efficiency of protein and fat deposition. *J Anim Sci* 69:708.

Chiba LI, Peo ER Jr, Lewis AJ, Brumn MC, Fritscher RD, & Crenshaw JO. 1985. Effect of dietary fat on pig performance and dust levels in modified-open front and environmentally regulated confinement buildings. *J Anim Sci* 61:763.

Chiba LI, Ivey HW, Cummins KA & Gamble BE. 1996. Effects of hydrolyzed feather meal is a source of extra dietary nitrogen on growth performance and carcass traits of finisher pigs. *Anim Feed Sci Techn* 53:1.

Chiba LI, Ivey HW, Cummins KA, & Gamble BE. 1996. Hydrolyzed feather meal as a source of amino acids for finisher pigs. *Anim Feed Sci Techn* (In Press).

Chung TK & Baker DH. 1992. Ideal amino acid pattern for 10-kilogram pigs. *J Anim Sci* 70:3102.

Chung TK & Baker DH. 1992. Methionine requirement of pigs between 5 and 20 kilograms body weight. *J Anim Sci* 70:1857.

Coffey MT, Diggs BG, Handlin DL, Knabe DA, Maxwell CV Jr, Noland PR, Prince TJ, & Cromwell GL. 1994. Effects of dietary energy during gestation and lactation on reproductive performance of sows: A cooperative study. *J Anim Sci* 72:4.

Commercial source 1. 1995.

Commercial source 2. 1995.

Commercial source 3. 1995.

Commercial source 4. 1995.

Commercial source 5. 1995.

Commercial source 6. 1995.

Conway D, Sauer WC, Den Hartog LA, & Huisman J. 1990. Studies on the threonine requirements of growing pigs based on the total, ileal and fecal digestible contents. *Livestock Prod Sci* 25:105.

Cromwell GL, Stahly TS, & Monegue HJ. 1991. Amino acid supplementation of meat meal in lysine-fortified, corn-based diets for growing-finishing pigs. *J Anim Sci* 69:4898.

Eastoe JE & Long JE. 1960. The amino acid composition of processed bones and meat. *J Sci Food Agric* 11:87.

El Boushy AR & Roodbeen AE. 1984. Amino acid availability in dry poultry waste in comparison with relevant feedstuffs. *Poultry Sci* 63:583.

Ermer PM, Miller PS, Lewis AJ, & Giesemann MA. 1992. The preference of weanling pigs for diets containing either dried skimmed milk or spray-dried porcine plasma. *J Anim Sci* 70 (suppl 1):60 (abstr).

Escalona PRR, Pesti GM, & Vaughters PD. 1986. Nutritive value of poultry-byproduct meal. 2. Comparisons of methods of determining protein quality. *Poultry Sci* 65:2268.

Evans DF & Leibholz J. 1979a. Meat meal in the diet of the early-weaned pigs. II. Amino acid supplementation. *Anim Feed Sci Technol* 4:43.

Evans DF & Leibholz J. 1979b. Meat meal in the diet of the early-weaned pigs. I. A comparison of meat meal and soybean meal. *Anim Feed Sci Technol* 4:33.

Freeman CP. 1984. The digestion, absorption and transport of fat - non-ruminants. In *Fats in Animal Nutrition* (J Wiseman, editor), p 105–122. Butterworths, London.

Freeman CP, Holme DW, & Annison EF. 1968. The determination of the true digestibilities of interesterfield fats in young pigs. *Br J Nutr* 22:651.

Frobish LT, Hays VW, Speer VC, & Ewan RC. 1967. Digestion of sow milk fat and effect of diet form on fat utilization. *J Anim Sci* 26:1478.

Frobish LT, Hays VW, Speer VC, & Ewan RC. 1970. Effect of fat source and level on utilization of fat by young pigs.*J Anim Sci* 30:197.

Goodband RD, Tokach MD, & Nelssen JL. 1994. *Kansas Swine Nutrition Guide*. Kansas State University, Manhattan.

Green S. 1989. A note on the digestibilities of nitrogen and amino acids in meat, skimmed-milk and fishmeals in young pigs. *Anim Prod* 48:237.

Green S & Kiener T. 1989. Digestibilities of nitrogen and amino acids in soya-bean, sunflower, meat and rapeseed meals measured with pigs and poultry. *Anim Prod* 48:157.

Hahn JD & Baker DH. 1995. Optimum ratio to lysine threonine, tryptophan, and sulfur amino acids for finishing swine. *J Anim Sci* 73:482.

Han Y, & Parsons CM. 1990. Determination of available amino acids and energy in alfalfa meal, feather meal, and poultry byproduct meal by various methods. *Poultry Sci* 69:1544.

Han Y, & Parsons CM. 1991. Protein and amino acid quality of feather meals. *Poultry Sci* 70:812.

Hansen JA, Nelssen JL, Goodband RD, & Weeden TL. 1993. Evaluation of animal protein supplements in diets of early-weaned pigs. *J Anim Sci* 71:1853.

Haugen EW & Pettigrew JE. 1985. Apparent digestibility of amino acids in meat meal as affected by manufacturing variables. Minnesota Nutrition Conference.

Howard KA, Forsyth DM, & Cline TR. 1990. The effect of an adaptation period to soybean oil additions in the diets of young pigs. *J Anim Sci* 68:678.

International Association of Fishmeal Manufacturers. 1985. The digestible energy content of fishmeals fed to growing/finishing pigs. Fishmeal Flyer.

Jorgensen H, Sauer WC, & Thacker PA. 1984. Amino acid availabilities in soybean meal, sunflower meal, fishmeal and meat and bone meal fed to growing pigs. *J Anim Sci* 58:926.

Kats LJ, Nelssen JL, Tokach MD, Goodband RD, Hansen JA, & Laurin JL. 1994. The effect of spray-dried porcine plasma on growth performance in the early-weaned pig. *J Anim Sci* 72:2075.

Kats LJ, Nelssen JL, Tokach MD, Goodband RD, Weeden TL, Dritz SS, Hansen JA, & Friesen KG. 1994. The effects of spray-dried blood meal on growth performance of the early-weaned pig. *J Anim Sci* 72:2860.

Kennedy DW. 1995. Personal communication. Arkansas State University.

Kennedy JJ, Aherne F, Kelleher D, & Caffrey P. 1974. An evaluation of the nutritive value of meat and bone meal. 1. Effects of level of meat and bone meal and collagen on pig and rat performance. *Ir J Agric Res* 13:1.

Knabe DA. 1986. Final Report, Fats and Proteins Research Foundation, Inc. Bloomington, IL.

Knabe DA. 1989. Apparent ileal digestibility of amino acids in meat and bone meal. Final Report. Fats and Proteins Research Foundation, Inc, Bloomington, IL.

Knabe DA. 1991. Apparent ileal digestibility of N and amino acids in 22 selected feedstuffs. Heartland Lysine Inc., Chicago, IL.

Knabe DA. 1993a. Apparent ileal digestibility of protein and amino acids in calcium caseinate and four fishmeals. International Proteins Corp, Woodbury, MN.

Knabe DA. 1993b. Apparent ileal digestibility of protein and amino acids in fishmeals. International Proteins Corp, Woodbury, MN.

Knabe DA. 1994. Apparent ileal digestibility of protein and amino acids in dried blood products. American Protein Corp.

Knabe DA, LaRue DC, & Gregg EJ. 1989. Apparent digestibility of nitrogen and amino acids in protein feedstuffs by growing pigs. *J Anim Sci* 67:441.

Liu JK, Waibel PE, & Noll SL. 1989. Nutritional evaluation of blood meal and feather meal for turkeys. *Poultry Sci* 68:1513.

Morgan CA, Whittemore CT, & Cockburn JHS. 1984. The effect of level and source of protein, fiber and fat in the diet on the energy value of compounded pig feeds. *Anim Feed Sci Techn* 11:11.

Noblet J, Fortune H, Dupire C, & Dubois S. 1993. Digestible, metabolizable and net energy values of 13 feedstuffs for growing pigs: effect of energy system. *Anim Feed Sci Techn* 42:131.

[NRA] National Renderers Association. 1990. Rendered Animal Fats. NRA Fact Sheet. National Renderers Association Inc, Washington, DC.

[NRC] National Research Council. 1988. *Nutrient Requirements of Swine,* 9th edition. National Academy Press, Washington, DC.

Parsons CM. 1995. Effect of processing methods on availability of amino acids and energy in animal protein meals. Final Report, Fats and Proteins Research Foundation, Inc, Bloomington, IL.

Peo ER & Hudman D. 1962. Effect of levels of meat and bone scraps on growth rate and feed efficiency of growing-finishing swine. *J Anim Sci* 21:787.

Pesti GM, Faust LO, Fuller HL, & Dale NM. 1986. Nutritive value of poultry-byproduct meal. 1. Metabolizable energy values as influenced by method of determination and level of substitution. *Poultry Sci* 65:2258.

Pesti GM, Dale NM, & Farrell DJ. 1989. Research Note: A comparison of methods to determine the metabolizable energy of feather meal. *Poultry Sci* 68:443.

Pettigrew JE. 1981. Supplemental dietary fat for peripartal sows: a review. *J Anim Sci* 53:107.

Pettigrew JE & Moser RL. 1991. Fat in swine nutrition. In *Swine Nutrition* (ER Miller, DE Ullrey, & AJ Lewis, editors), p 133–146.

Powles J, Wiseman J, Cole DJA & Jagger S. 1995. Prediction of the apparent digestible energy value of fats given to pigs. *Anim Prod* 61:149.

Powles J, Wiseman J, Cole DJA, & Hardy B. 1993. Effect of chemical structure of fats upon their apparent digestible energy value when given to growing/finishing pigs. *Anim.Prod* 57:137.

Powles J, Wiseman J, Cole DJA, & Hardy B. 1994. Effect of chemical structure of fats upon their apparent digestible energy value when given to young pigs. *Anim Prod* 58:411.

Puchal F, Hays VW, Speer VC, Jones JD, & Catron DV. 1962. The free blood plasma amino acids of swine as related to the source of dietary proteins. *J Nutr* 76:11.

Sato H, Kobayashi T, Jones RW, & Easter RA. 1987. Tryptophan availability of some feedstuffs determined by pig growth assay. *J Anim Sci* 64:191.

Schoenherr WD, Stahly TS, & Cromwell GL. 1987. Effect of dietary fat and fiber addition on yield and composition of milk from sows housed in a warm or hot environment. *J Anim Sci* 65(suppl 1):318 (abstr).

Seerley RW, Griffin FM, & Campbell HC. 1978. Effect of sow's dietary energy source on sow's milk and piglet carcass composition. *J Anim Sci* 46:1009.

Sohn KS, Maxwell CV, & Buchanan DS. 1991. Plasma protein as an alternative protein source for early weaned pigs. *J Anim Sci* 69 (suppl 1):362 (abstr).

Stahly TS. 1984. The use of fats in diets for growing pigs. In *Fats in Animal Nutrition* (J Wiseman, editor), p 313–331. Butterworths, London.

Stahly TS, Cromwell GL, & Overfield JR. 1981. Interactive effects of season of year and dietary fat supplementation, lysine source and lysine level on the performance of swine. *JAnim Sci* 53:1269.

Stockland WL, Meade R, & Nordstrom J. 1970. Meat and bone meals as sources of amino acids for growing swine: use of a reference diet to predict amino acid adequacy by plasma levels. *J Anim Sci* 31 (6):1142.

Stoner GR, Allee GL, Nelssen JL, Johnston ME, & Goodband RD. 1990. Effect of select menhaden fishmeal in starter diets for pigs. *J Anim Sci* 68:2729.

Williams CM, Lee CG, Garlich JD, & Shih JCH. 1991. Evaluation of a bacterial feather fermentation product, feather-lysate, as a feed protein. *Poultry Sci* 70:85.

Wiseman J, Cole DJA, & Hardy B. 1990. The dietary energy values of soya-bean oil, tallow and their blends for growing/finishing pigs. *Anim Prod* 50:513.

Wiseman J, Jagger S, Cole DJA, & Haresign W. 1991. The digestion and utilization of amino acids of heat-treated fishmeal by growing/finishing pigs. *Anim Prod* 53:215.

# 10

## Utilizing Rendered Products: Petfood

### Timothy Miller

Archaeological evidence indicates that the first domesticated canid appeared about 12,000 years ago before the advent of agriculture. Our bond with animals of other species has continued, evident in archaeological remains such as the abundant dog and cat footprints in Roman rooftiles and bricks. Now, at the end of the 20th century, some 38% of all households in the United States own at least 1 dog; 32% own at least 1 cat; and nearly half of the cat owners have 2 cats. These 53 million dogs and 62 million cats are the cause of approximately $9 billion annually in US petfood sales plus an equal amount spent on veterinary care. An estimated 15,000 different products are manufactured by more than 3,000 small and large petfood manufacturers.

But, the human pet bond also engenders a unique market. The nomenclature of petfoods in the marketplace is commercial dog and cat foods although the petfood industry includes birds, reptiles, rodents and serpents. Anyone associated with the petfood business should keep the following in mind:

1.  Dogs are different from cats in nutritional requirements.
2.  Dogs and cats do not purchase their foods.

3. Dogs and cats are not raised to market weights.
4. Ingredient prices only affect the size of the petfood profit margin, not its existence.
5. Petfoods are part of the family food system just as pets are part of the family.
6. No pets ever get sick, it is always something they ate.
7. There are no loose stools only diarrhea.
8. Baby pets are babies to their owners and are treated as such, including close inspection of food.
9. Most people do not understand that quality is measured by compliance to specification, not level of expectation. Geo Metro and a Lexus can have the same level of quality; edible tallow and yellow grease can have the same level of quality.

## Nutrients

Proper diet is among the most important considerations in health maintenance and necessitates a knowledge of dietary nutrients and their availability. Nutrients are divided into six basic classes:

1. water
2. carbohydrates
3. proteins
4. fats
5. minerals
6. vitamins

A nutrient is any food constituent that helps support life and accomplishes this function by:

1. Acting as structural components of the body.

2. Enhancing or being involved in chemical reactions that occur in the body (metabolism).

3. Transporting of substances into, throughout, or out of the body.

4. Regulating temperature.

5. Affecting food palatability and, therefore, consumption.

6. Supplying energy.

Nutrients are necessary for health, but their absolute requirements vary. For example, the amount of protein needed varies inversely with the digestibility and essential amino acid content (quality) of the protein. The crude protein of most nonprescription, commercial pet foods ranges from 20 to 50% of the diet's dry matter.

## Water

1. The most important nutrient—a 10% loss of total body water causes serious illness; a 15% loss results in death.

2. At a comfortable environmental temperature the amount of water consumed by mature, healthy, nonreproducing dogs and cats is about 2.5 times the amount of dry matter consumed in food.

3. Water of good quality should always be available to pets.

4. The amount of total dissolved solids (TDS) is a useful overall index to the quality of drinking water.

## Carbohydrates

1. Most food ingredients used in commercially prepared dog and cat foods contain carbohydrates providing energy and affecting gastrointestinal function.

2. Carbohydrates are often classified based on digestibility characteristics—monosaccharides are considered soluble because they require no digestion ("soluble carbohydrates"); carbohydrates comprised of beta monosaccharide units resist the action of endogenous digestive enzymes and are called "insoluble carbohydrates."

4. "Soluble carbohydrates" supply relatively inexpensive calories and comprise a percentage of most pet foods other than those composed entirely of meat, fish, or organ tissues.

4. Carbohydrates fed in excess of the pet's energy requirements are stored in the body as glycogen, or fat, for later use. Excess usable carbohydrate intake results in obesity.

5. "Insoluble carbohydrates" are also known as "dietary fiber" and include cellulose, hemicellulose, pectin, gum, mucilage, and lignin (a noncarbohydrate constituent).

## Protein

1.  Proteins consist of amino acids and function as components of enzymes, hormones, secretions, and structural and protective tissues.

2.  Pets require a dietary protein source since they cannot synthesize amino acids.

3.  Some amino acids are essential in the diet and are called essential amino acids (indispensable)—required by pets for growth.

4.  The quality of a protein varies with the number and amount of essential amino acids it contains. Protein quality is estimated by a method called biologic value—the percentage of a nutrient absorbed and retained.

## Fats

Fats are required in the diet of pets:

1.  For the absorption of the fat soluble vitamins—A,D,E, and K.
2.  To enhance the palatability of the food.
3.  As a source of essential fatty acids.
4.  As an excellent source of dietary energy, yielding approximately 2.25 times more energy than either soluble carbohydrates or proteins.

## Minerals

1.  Minerals are important for a variety of functions in pets and are classified as macrominerals—calcium, phosphorus, potassium, sodium, and magnesium. Their dietary requirements are best expressed as a percent.

2.  Macrominerals function to maintain acid-base balance; osmotic pressures needed for maintaining body fluid balance; cellular functions, nerve conduction, and muscle contraction; structural integrity.

3.  Microminerals (trace) are those for which dietary requirements are best expressed as parts per million (ppm) and include iron, zinc, copper, manganese, iodine, and selenium.

## Vitamins

1. Vitamins are not used as an energy source or for structural purposes; their main function is to regulate and promote a wide variety of physiologic processes. They function as enzymes, enzyme precursors, or coenzymes.

2. Vitamins are classified into two major groups based on solubility—water soluble or fat soluble. The solubility of vitamins relates to how they are absorbed, stored and excreted.

3. Processing and storage of foods decreases their active vitamin content. The least stable are vitamins $B_1$, folic acid, A, E, and K. Manufacturers of quality pet foods compensate by adding vitamins to correct deficits caused by storage and processing.

To the rendering industry these points have significant implications. Both cats and dogs have protein, mineral, and energy needs that can be satisfied by animal byproduct meals and tallow, but those needs and preferences are significantly different. Dogs prefer a higher level of fat added to the base product; cats, however, have little or no response above a threshold lower than that provided by most diets. Both animals seem to prefer high quality fats. (Dogs prefer edible tallow and lard to the inedible products while cats find edible and inedible tallow equivalent if the inedible fat has good quality reflected by moisture, insolubles, unsaponifiables, free fatty acids, color and raw material composition). In this chapter rendered animal fat is implied by the term fat. Other fats are available and used in petfood formulations but the vegetable/legume/seed fats are generally referred to as oils.

Dogs can easily be maintained with good quality protein and proper amino acid balance by a diet in excess of 16% protein. Cats however require essential amino acids (some of which differs from those for dogs) at higher levels than dogs and have a total protein requirement at or slightly above 30%. This remaining protein level seems to be satisfied by any available protein.

In the petfood business the consumer's perception of quality is often sensory. Poor control of input material, storage and transport can result in offensive odors of both fats and meals. These odors carry through to the packaged product which, when opened releases this odor to the unwary consumer. Other perceptions of quality are consumption, palatability, acceptability, and consistency of a product.

For both choice white grease and bleachable fancy tallow, grades are based on physical and chemical limits. Sources are slaughterhouses with on-site rendering, renderers that pick up free fatty acids from slaughterhouses, grocery stores, restaurants, and dead stock. Free fatty acids from grocery stores often include out-of-date packaged meats. The packages often are not emptied so some plastics may be present in trace amounts. The third source is a fat blender. This type operation may render but primarily it blends purchased fat to customer's specifications. A disadvantage with this type of supplier is lack of control over input; an advantage is that the fat is almost certain to meet specifications. Risks can be variable and ranges from palatability and potential for staining. The benefits are delivery, logistics, and price stability.

## THE PROCESS

Rendering is a cooking and drying process. A good analogy is frying bacon. As the bacon fries it gives up moisture and fat to the frying pan and the atmosphere. If it is lightly cooked it is pliable, still contains moisture, and much of the fat and the grease in the skillet is clear and nearly colorless. If it is fried to a crisp the fat level is significantly lower in the bacon, the color is darker, little moisture remains, there are fine particles in the skillet, and the fat is dark. Instead of bacon renderers cooks animal byproducts which have been reduced, pieces smaller than about 2 inches, allowing uniform cooking. This cooking releases fat and moisture from the cells. The cooking continues toward dryness with an endpoint around 8 to 10% moisture. In North America this is done at or below atmospheric pressure with maximum product temperatures from 240 to 280°F. The maximum temperature affects the rendered products: Lower temperatures favor lighter colors both in fat and meal. The fat, with light color contains few insolubles. Lower temperatures also improve digestibility although this is difficult to quantify in repeated testing because input variability of the small quantities used for testing can result in a greater difference. Higher temperature yields a darker product with more fine insolubles. These insolubles eventually settle as sediment in tanks.

The cooked product consists of free fat with some particulates and protein/bone solids with fat entrained. The solids are pressed using a screw press to remove most of the fat. The result is a meal with fat levels of 8 to 11% for red meat and 10 to 14% for poultry. This step depends on several factors, most importantly the amount of ash and secondarily the freshness of raw material. If the ash and bone contents are low then the pressure developed in the screw press will be lower. The tissue will slip and more fat will remain in the meal. If the raw material is not fresh, natural enzymes begin to digest the tissue, also resulting in lower pressure in the screw and in higher fat levels. Usually pressing is done on stream so the temperature is close to that of the cooker discharge and any losses of temperature are gained from the mechanical energy involved in the process. This results in more moisture losses. At this point the fat and meal streams are completely divergent. Fat is pumped to centrifuges for clarification and possibly through additional filtration and finally to storage. Meal in some facilities is cooled before grinding, with the particles that did not pass through the sifter being ground and returned to the sifter. Sifted meal goes to storage for shipping.

The edible and the low temperature rendering systems are similar and significant. In both systems the raw material is ground or, more properly, chopped to allow uniform cooking. The chopped material is cooked to a low temperature, about 160°F, to release moisture and fat from the cells and then pressed to yield a product. The liquid is centrifuged to separate the fat, water, and solids. The fat at this stage can be a final product or can be further processed such as polished or deodorized. The water contains 4 to 6% soluble solids, predominately protein and some fat. This is generally concentrated using waste heat evaporation. The solids are recombined with the press solids and dried at low temperature and reduced pressure. The recovered dissolved solids are usually dried to approximately 20% solids content and sprayed into the drier onto the press solids. The concentrate, liquid meat solubles, is an under-utilized potential source of highly digestible ingredients.

## RENDERERS

Renderers can be divided into 3 broad categories according to the nutrient profiles of their products: packer renderers, collection renderers and renderers.

Packer renderers are part of an integrated slaughter plant usually handling only raw material generated on site and often not handling dead stock from the collection pens. A well-maintained rendering plant of proper size will run nearly synchronously with the slaughter plant so that fresh material will be cooked within hours of death. Customer concerns include: How the guts are handled? Are paunches opened? Do the contents go to rendering? How much hide is rendered (this is a significant contributor of hair)? Are nearly all hair switches (tails) land-filled or rendered? How much further processing is done? Is the predominate raw material bones and guts? This will result in lower protein and higher ash which will give higher phosphorus, which is valuable, and calcium, which is not. The fat from a packer-renderer can rival edible fats in color and odor.

Collection renderer is a somewhat arbitrary category that includes only those renderers whose raw material comes from small slaughter plants with no rendering facility, out-of-date product from markets, bones from butcher shops, essentially no dead stock. This product may or may not be low in protein but will contain almost no hair. The fat from this type of plant will often be very light in color and nearly odorless.

Renderers comprise the most divergent category with one commonality: They are still in business after the adversity of the 1980's, so each plant is doing the best it can with the raw material available. There are no poor quality operations within the context of their raw material base. There is some variation, day to day, but given the quality of material involved that variation is small during times of extreme changes in weather. Dead stock often comprise 20 to 25% of the raw material; extremes of weather that tend to occur in the spring and late fall can push death losses in feed lots from a norm of less than 1% to nearly 2%. This seasonal variation nearly always taxes the capacity of a renderer and results in longer periods between collection and processing. The good news is that deterioration is reduced by the lower temperatures during spring and late fall. The meal quality is normally good but the protein is often higher than normal as is the digestibility. Even the additional manure may not result in significant problems since the bulk of the raw material is unchanged.

## PETFOOD TECHNOLOGY

The formulation and processing of petfoods have evolved as has the rendering process. Pelleting and baking were the predominate processing methods. At first little was known about the effects of ingredient variation and of variation on processing, nutrition, or palatability. Suppliers were evaluated as to price, volume, service, and proximity. As experience and knowledge increased, supplier evaluation shifted to quality. Color and free fatty acid requirements were added to fat specifications for some producers but these specifications were based primarily on trading rules. Likewise meat and bone meal acquired specifications which loosely paralleled industry definitions. Petfood was a small player in the animal byproduct and feed ingredient market. It could not significantly influence these markets.

Recently, phenomenal changes have taken place in pet nutrition, specifically a refining of nutritional profiles, improved dog and cat food testing methodology and nutritional changes within ingredients.

## Extrusion

The application of extrusion technology, specifically to dog food was a watershed event for the petfood industry. The extruder, with continuous short-time, high-temperature, high-pressure cooking of the mixed ingredients produced a "rope" of cooked product which when cut, dried, and coated with fat exceeded the palatability and digestibility of previous dog foods. This new product was sold in grocery stores in 1956 and 1957, and was immediately accepted. Extrusion processing, despite higher product temperatures than those used in pelleting or baking, does not destroy essential amino acids. The extrusion cooking process improved digestibility of grains that had previously required cooking before they could be pelleted, aside from reducing the process steps. Early extruded diets were not significantly different from those of the pelleted precursors. These petfoods were basically mixtures of corn, wheat, oats, soybean meal, meat and bone meal, animal fat and vitamin and mineral supplements with traces of other minor ingredients. Although variation in the fat levels of ingredients and formulations affected the pellet quality and baking properties, the extrusion process was far more sensitive to these variations. Density in this process is the primary manifestation of the cooked product, and density is critical to putting a specified weight of product into a fixed volume package. The identification of this variation and its effect on extrusion brought on new specifications for maximum and minimum levels of fat acceptable for animal byproduct meals as well as in the mixed meal for extrusion.

In 1959 to 1960 extrusion technology was applied to cat food. Initially the diets were very high in solvent-extracted fishmeal to achieve the requisite protein level in excess of 30%. Because of availability and practicality, poultry byproduct meal seemed to be a logical ingredient for the new cat food. To meet the requirements of cats, both nutritional and finicky, a change was required in the way a "petfood grade" poultry meal was sourced and produced. One of the primary changes was in time between slaughter and cooking: increased time increases deterioration which reduces ability to press out the fat. Cats are not accepting of increased degradation of the raw material. Furthermore, reduction of fat in the meal is critical to the extrusion process and density control. This work was based on the batch cooking systems then in place and included methods and timing for introduction of antioxidant as well as the content of raw material and process parameters.

As rendering methods evolved to continuous cookers and low-temperature cookers, processes have evolved to meet those specifications as well as to exceed and define new specifications and products. Such changes include an overall reduction of cooking temperatures, an increase in meal moisture, a reduction of end-point temperature, and overall improvement in quality of meals and fats. This was in part a response to the energy shortages of the 1970s , since the greatest production variable when evaporating water is energy. The attention focused on energy resulted in technological innovation, attention to return on investment and the 1980s term, value added. Many operations split raw material streams to improve quality or to yield another product such as handling blood separately from meat or feathers. Other plants eliminated sources of raw material that reduced overall quality of finished product. The 1980s was also a period of consolidation when many economically marginal plants closed; raw sources were redistributed, often resulting in a better mix for larger plants that could reduce the time between collection and processing.

## WET PETFOOD

In the infancy of the wet petfood industry, raw materials were obtained from the slaughter industry vs. traders and brokers. These raw materials were generally in the form of boxed frozen organ meat. The organ meat was usually condemned, inedible, or excess edible that was taken out of the edible market. There was little rendering competition for these products because of the low fat and high moisture content.

As the demand in the industry developed, many of the traders and brokers set up collection facilities for organ meat to better service the petfood industries. Generally, the collection facilities were near the packers and adjacent to existing freezers. In an effort to eliminate stripping and packaging costs, tub freezing of byproducts was developed. This is a process where meat is put into tubs, racked, and rolled into a holding freezer. The tubs were taken out 24 to 48 hours later, the meat popped out, and then stacked on pallets.

As demand increased and the market for byproducts became more competitive, more efficient production methods were developed. First, fresh chilled bulk was shipped in milk tankers. Second, the first major plate freezing operation was installed in the United States.

The fresh chilled bulk technology uses grinders and sweeps surface heat exchangers. It was a spin-off of the process used for edible comminuted meat. The fresh chilled technology has the advantages of ease of use, energy efficiency, and minimum packaging costs. The main disadvantage is the time restrictions and limited inventory.

The advantages of plate freezers for frozen products are efficiency, ease of use and storage, and reduced packaging costs. Production demands have encouraged the installation of more plate freezers rather than the tub freezers.

The technologies in use today are a blend of old and new. On the fresh usage side, product is shipped bulk in tanker loads plus bulk in 2000 lb. capacity returnable combo bins. Frozen shipments consist of box frozen, tub frozen, and plate frozen.

The product mix has expanded from organ meat to ground viscera mixes to blends of various byproducts to specific analytical profiles. The future desires of the petfood industry in the United States will lean toward fresh byproducts, but the need to maintain inventory will continue the need for frozen product. Export will always demand frozen product.

Expansion of the petfood industry will increase meat demands, both nationwide and worldwide. The market share of canned petfood in the United States is less than dry petfood. Globally, the opposite is true, especially in Europe. Consequently, export meat demands will be greater than those statewide. The one factor that will lessen the impact upon the US rendering industry is the slaughter industries in developing nations. As these industries increase, US export of byproducts decrease. Today, the total usages of these fresh and frozen byproducts worldwide is estimated to be well in excess of 10,000 tons per day.

The rendering industry has viewed wet petfood as a competitor for raw material. While this is true to a certain extent, there will be future opportunities for value-added products for wet petfood. These opportunities will allow progressive renderers to enhance their bottom lines.

## Consistency

Regardless of the product and specification, consistency is supremely important in color, odor, grind, protein, moisture, and temperature. If a product is consistent many customers will find it of use even if those parameters vary from the norm; for instance, meat and bone meal is always 47 to 49% protein and always 5.5% phosphorous. If the product is inconsistent, it will be sold on the spot or secondary market.

## Fat

The selection of fat type is usually dictated by the desired product, projected shelf life, and company's objectives, knowledge base, packaging material selection, animal testing results and economics. Fat is one of the most expensive ingredients used in quantity in petfoods and it is surrounded with prejudice. All participants have objective reasons for the choice and all have another set of prejudicial reasons.

## Packaging Material

Paper fibers wick (absorb) any type of fat, although mobility varies among oils, greases, and tallows. Mobility becomes a minor criterion because of time and temperature. Because the shelf life of petfoods is generally 6 months or longer, the manufacturer must allow for seasonal temperature variation. Distribution areas also require allowance for temperature variation. To help prevent wicking, the paper fibers are treated with a fluorocarbon as they are formed into the web that results in the finished paper. The fluorocarbon bonds to the paper fiber reducing the void between the fibers, and with it the wicking potential.

This reduction of the void prevents wicking and staining so long as the barrier is not compromised and the fat is not too challenging. Compromise may result when the barrier is creased as in the gusset or bottom fold of a bag or box and no bag or box can be produced without a seam. The fat becomes challenging when it becomes molecularly small enough to penetrate the void. Early work identified iodine value and free fatty acid as one criterion and the differentiation of products that had a higher potential to stain their packages as a second criterion. Products with higher potential to stain were said to be critical and required a different specification for animal fat. From this differentiation came the terminology for critical fat and non-critical fat with differing limits for iodine value and free fatty acid. Free fatty acid seems to be the greatest force affecting staining. The acid does not just penetrate the barrier; it seems to open the barrier to the fat molecules. If the fat is sufficiently mobile it can move through the seam and onto the outer plies. An alternative solution to the staining problem is to use a plastic coating, a plastic liner, or a plastic bag to seal in the fat. (However, an improperly selected liner will dissolve in the fat.)

## Color

Generally color of the fat will not affect the petfood color but it is a testimony to the history of the fat. Degradation of the raw material begins at the animalís death and continues through collection to processing. As degradation continues, fat darkens. Excess heating will cause fat to darken. Paunch manure or other sources of chlorophyll are required for green fat. At some level of color companies establish a limit. That limit may be based on established grades, prejudices, or test data.

## Odor

Dogs prefer clean fats and more importantly consumers are not sympathetic to foul odors in their petfoods. Like color, no positive case can be made for an offensive load of tallow.

## Iodine and Peroxide Values

Iodine value measures the degree of unsaturation of a fat. The lower the iodine value, the harder the fat. It reflects mobility to some degree but is best used to characterize the mix of sources in a fat. Very little poultry fat increases the iodine value of a fat. Originally this was a key criterion for segregating critical and non-critical fats. Fats and oils with lower iodine values have higher inherent stability to oxidation than fats with higher iodine values.

Peroxide levels indicate the potential for rancidity.

## Moisture, Insolubles, Unsaponifiables

Moisture and insolubles will end up at the bottom of containers, react, and produce off odors and off flavors. Often the processor with the most challenges producing low insolubles levels does the best job of removing insolubles. Typically inedible tallows will not have detectable levels of moisture and insolubles should be 0.15% or less. Unsaponifiables are not fat. Specifications may list levels of 0.5 to 1.0% as maximums for total moisture, insolubles, unsaponifiables.

## Fatty Acids

Free fatty acids are a good measure of the time and temperature effects from the onset of death until processing began. Generally, palatability increases as free fatty acids decreased; stability to oxidation increases as free fatty acids decrease.

The fatty acid profile varies with the animal's feeding regime, the source of the raw material, the ratio of trim to internal fat, and with the species of the animal. For instance, linoleic acid can be increased by including more poultry products and fat, or it can be increased by increasing seed oils; arachidonic acid is more easily obtained from poultry oil.

## Stabilization

All fats should be stabilized before they are used in foods. Rancidity is to be avoided or minimized. Suppliers use a wide range of antioxidants for this, but the methods and preferences vary from company to company and sometimes from product to product within a company. Adding antioxidant and then relying on the antioxidant to become randomized is inadequate. The antioxidant must be mixed uniformly throughout. The best way for a user to be assured that the load is stabilized is to add stabilizer during unloading. This can be done using a small pump calibrated to deliver the requisite quantity of antioxidant over 75 to 85% of the time required to unload the conveyance. The pump can be turned on and controlled by a timer set to shut down after the appropriate amount of time has elapsed.

## Common Problems

- A common quality problem results from tanks with sludge in the bottom, whether at the supply end, the customer end, or the conveyance tank. Edible quality tallow transported in a tank car with sludge in the bottom can arrive at the customerís facility 10 days later with free fatty acids as high as 7% or greater, with color and with significant odor problems. Part of any Hazard Analysis Critical Control Point (HACCP) plan should be to inspect all conveyances before unloading. Savings from eliminating rejections or down-grading the load only because of the poor condition of the conveyance translate into directly recovered profits.

- Nearly all fats and oils contain some level of moisture and insolubles. The insolubles are generally high in protein and will eventually settle to the bottom of a container. In the presence of moisture and temperature below about 145°F the mix can support anaerobic bacteria and become putrid, contaminating the entire container no matter how large its volume. The easiest remedy is to only use cone-bottom tanks so that all material purchased is used in a timely manner. Slope and flat-bottom tanks should be inspected and cleaned if any sludge is found. Given the increasing problems and cost of sludge disposal, the cost of changing tanks to the bottom-discharge cone type should be reviewed.

- Palatability of fat varies from type to type and source to source with no guarantees from the kennel, but guidelines seem certain:

  +Good quality performs better than poor quality.
  +Mink in any quantity will foul the fat.
  +Cats seem to dislike fat from older dairy cows.

## RED MEAT INDUSTRY

The producers of red meat, for the greyhound industry, are not organized in a structured association, but do work together in a cooperative effort to address industry matters. Approximately 25 producers sell high quality denatured, inedible, raw cattle muscle meat (red meat) to racing greyhounds, breeding stock, puppies, and young greyhounds in training. The producers make farm meat (maximum fat content 7% wet) for racing greyhounds. Both types come from the same high quality carcasses, whose selection is based on fat content of cuts or overall carcass fat distribution.

Annual red meat production is approximately 39,000,000 lbs and is divided equally between track and farm meat: 6 companies produce 85%; 4 produce 75%.

Red meat comes from beef cattle feed lots and dairy areas. These areas are serviced once or twice a day by collectors who quickly transport animals to processing plants.

Plant personnel skin, eviscerate, split, and inspect the hot carcasses. Obvious bruises, injection sites, excess fat, and undesirable portions of accepted carcasses are trimmed and discarded for rendering. The desired carcasses are placed in a high capacity cooler to reduce the internal carcass temperature to 34 to 36°F within 7 to 10 hours.

Of the 40 states that allow red meat production, 35 require state as well as the periodic USDA inspections. These inspections assure the use of proper facilities, handling, selection, and denaturing of red meat products.

A trained employee segregates the chilled carcasses into excellent greyhound or good canner quality. The small percentage of carcasses that meet the greyhound criteria are again trimmed of undesirable pieces of meat and fat.

The carcasses are boned, meat is again selected, ground, denatured, boxed, and placed in a blast freezer. Meat is shipped to dealers by refrigerated vans, and stored in the dealers freezer and then to the customer's freezers.

# MEALS
## Meat and Bone Meal

The generic term meat and bone meal in petfoods is being supplanted by distinguishing terms of the animal's origin. This is partly due to market forces that show preferences for beef, lamb, and even venison. Most manufacturers specify that the product cannot contain rendered pets and certain other sources such as zoo dead stock.

Hair is a major consideration for any producer of petfoods and is perhaps one of the greatest detriments to product quality. Many systems have been devised to remove hair but none result in a significant difference in the appearance of the petfood. The only way to make a significant difference is to minimize introduction to the process, by removing switches, hoof trim, and hide trim.

Digestibility is one attribute of meat and bone meal that is alleged to be decreasing over the last 20 years. One possible explanation is that the recovery of fat has increased and fat is nearly 100% digestible. Another explanation, whether true or not, is the improved removal of meat from the bones by modern packing plants. Many studies are made of ingredient digestibility both in industry and academia. Few of those studies list the raw material source, type of process, temperature of process, elapsed time of process, all specific criteria that define the potential quality of the finished product. If that test of meat and bone meal is repeated later it will not duplicate the previous test simply because the previous test was not adequately defined. If the first test is in early spring or late fall, uses meat and bone meal from a renderer servicing an area with many feed lots, and there has been a significant weather change, the meal will be disproportionately high in protein due to the high level of dead stock, and depending on capacity of the plant cook variation as well as press out could be unusual. If the repeat test is from the same plant the potential for the same material occurrence is minimal, most probably origin and processing data will not be documented and the test results will be compared as "old" and "new" meat and bone meal. If the second test is made using packer material that runs 49 to 50%, the potential for digestibility differences is even greater.

Another possibility for error in comparisons is the evolution of testing methods that affect the results. Results from tests using a "correction diet" to determine the digestibility of ingredients often do not compare favorably with results obtained using a formula with the ingredient treatments as the sole variable.

## Beef and Bone Meal

Beef and bone meal was the original delineation to convey a premoisture, insolubles, unsaponifiablesm image versus meat and bone meal. To apply this term to sourcing required no specific change to the formulas nor to nutrient profiles. Change to the term beef and bone meal was based on the general public image of beef as the preferred food of flavor. This continues today, so that the term has become almost a generic descriptor.

## Lamb Meal

Lamb meal timing and popularity seemingly were meant to challenge the US news coverage of the outbreaks of bovine spongiform encephalopathy (BSE) in the United Kingdom. No sooner was APPI outlining bovine handling procedures for the US renderers than lamb meal usage surfaced in the petfood arena.

The popularity of lamb meal probably originated in California as an answer to a perceived need to find alternative protein sources in petfoods.

sumer that it generally contains much more wool than is tolerated when one compares the level to hair in meat and bone meal. Often lamb meat is not 100% lamb but an analog using other protein meals to extend the lamb.

## Fish Meal

Fish meal, originally a staple of cat diets, has been reduced to a generic meal. In keeping with the trend toward upscale products fish meal use has switched to species nomenclature; salmon, tuna, catfish, etc. In part this is due to the cost experienced in the 1980s and in part to quality problems experienced by some users. Fish solubles also found their way out of the petfood market in the same period and mostly for quality issues. A quick check of petfood labels shows the resurgence of fish solubles to petfoods as a palatability enhancer. Solubles are either used in combination with other protein sources or blended with the digested protein.

## Poultry Meal

Not to be outdone, the poultry segment has split into numerous delineations:

1. Poultry byproduct meal—almost always chicken sometimes with turkey thrown in but could be the reverse.

2. Poultry meal—no byproducts but significant premoisture, insolubles, unsaponifiablesms.

3. Chicken byproduct meal—different than poultry byproduct meal (as beef and bone meal differs from meat and bone meal—"deja vu all over again," to Yogi Berra).

4. Chicken meal—no guts, more glory.
5. Turkey byproduct meal—not only an alternative to poultry meal but an alternative protein source according to some.
6. Turkey meal—see 4 and 5.

7. Low ash poultry meal and derivations thereof—almost exclusively used in cat foods that try to assign stone formation in the lower urinary tract to ash in the diet. The product has a significant premoisture, insolubles, unsaponifiablesm to those using it. This was disproved many years ago, yet like many theories and myths it has a life of its own. This product can result from sorting source material if a plant has such luxury. A separation might be made using gravity tables as used for producing gel-bone if the

in the lower urinary tract to ash in the diet. The product has a significant premoisture, insolubles, unsaponifiablesm to those using it. This was disproved many years ago, yet like many theories and myths it has a life of its own. This product can result from sorting source material if a plant has such luxury. A separation might be made using gravity tables as used for producing gel-bone if the stream is classified prior to grinding. After grinding, air classification is most effective.

It should be noted that cats' requirement for taurine is present in viscera. This makes an interesting paradox about "premoisture, insolubles, unsaponifiables," ingredients requiring "additives" or "chemicals."

Poultry byproduct meal finds wide use in cat foods because its protein and fat levels are higher than most other meals. In recent times digestibility has been emphasized and poultry byproduct meal and poultry products in general have found more application. The reasons for the pursuit of increased digestibility started with an attempt to help consumers comply with curb laws in large cities. Improved digestibility equals reduced output of waste. As pets follow masters, the petfood market follows human consumption trends and the premoisture, insolubles, unsaponifiables product market flourished. What had been a specialized and small market almost exclusively for dogs expanded to the upscale target audience of pet owners. The premoisture, insolubles, unsaponifiables market soon became the growth market of petfoods.

In this arena, digestibility and palatability are key. The implication of high quality is to deny any connection with regular petfoods. The use of byproduct is penalized. Producers use poultry, turkey, or chicken meal instead of poultry byproduct meal. To improve the perception of quality and a premoisture, insolubles, unsaponifiable product, many companies add fresh tissue. This has enlarged the fresh tissue market beyond canned and moist products into dry petfoods. Most fresh tissue used in this market is chicken followed by turkey as a long second.

The petfood market for fresh tissue is strongest in the poultry area with ground chicken free of byproducts being used in both canned and premoisture-insolubles-unsaponifiables dry products. The soft-moist market is declining sharply and accounts for little use of fresh products. Viscera is used both in canned products as is a mix of heads, feet, and viscera. Viscera also is finding a strong market in the palatability additive market, as are giblets and lungs. These products are treated with enzymes to convert the protein to a liquid "digest." The liquid can either be stabilized against oxidation and bacterial growth, then added to the dry products; or dried and the resulting powder dusted on products as a palatability enhancer.

Frozen chicken and the other products, such as giblets and viscera are not the only forms available. These ingredients and blends are also shipped in combos or tankers after being ground and chilled to about 36°F. Use of chilled products requires special sanitation steps as well as logistical safeguards. The penalty for downtime resulting from missed unloading is greater than the savings. The reward is reduced energy costs for both supplier and customer, less the costs of sanitation and handling frozen blocks. Frozen chicken is undergoing a technological transformation not unlike the change in rendering from batch cookers to continuous cookers. Much of this industry has converted to vertical plate freezers, similar to ice makers in a refrigerator. The advantage, aside from labor and sanitation associated with using tubs and blast freezers, is the flat sides and uniformity of both size and weight of the frozen blocks. A plate freezer load can be put on pallets and stacked without becoming unstable as would the tub-frozen blocks which bulge like ice cubes made in a conventional tray.

## Low Ash Poultry Byproducts and Poultry Meal

Originally, low ash poultry byproducts and poultry meal (low ash is defined as 11% ash and below) was developed as a highly digestible, premoisture, insolubles, unsaponifiablesm petfood ingredient in the early 1970s. The method for this varied from raw material segregation at the rendering plant to screening and re-screening at the petfood facilities or blending plants. As the premoisture, insolubles, unsaponifiablesm petfood niche grew, the demand for low ash grew. Concurrently, poultry processing gradually increased the ash content in regular poultry byproducts and poultry meal. These 2 factors caused the supply and demand to diverge. By the early 1980s, the petfood industry required a larger, higher quality, more consistent supply. At that time a process to separate animal protein using air classification was patented. The increased demand was met by technology; meanwhile the old technologies continued. By the mid 1980s, low ash shipments were around 40,000 tons per year.

The premoisture, insolubles, unsaponifiables markets have continued to expand as the ash content of regular poultry byproducts and poultry meal have increased. This has increased the demand for other products such as chicken meal (backs and necks only), comminuted poultry, and spray-dried egg. Air classification, byproduct segregation, and screening continue to be used to the fullest. As demand continues to increase, pricing will drive other products into usage because the supply of quality poultry byproducts and poultry meal is limited by the number of renderers that can produce petfood grade meal.

## Specialty Product Potential

Meat meal, a standard definition, but one that is seemingly without a product, limited by maximum phosphorus but implies a potential of high protein, high digestibility, and unlike poultry products, does not require the descriptor "byproduct" in the name. This could be available as pork, beef, veal, venison meal. Lamb meal is already beyond the expectation of such ethical responsibility.

Inedible fats that have additional refining, clarification, or polishing. At some point edible tallow may find its way back in the human food chain and the gulf between edible and inedible will widen. Much of the palatability differences between edible and inedible may be due to removable elements resulting from rendering entrails.

The mechanical heat resulting from mechanically deboning chicken remains in the residue and little temperature rise is seen in the deboned tissue. Systems using reduced pressure and improved recovery result in a lower temperature residue that when immediately chilled and frozen is potentially equal in palatability to frozen chicken.

## CONCLUSION

The US rendering industry, which supplies billions of pounds of animal proteins and fats yearly to the petfood industry, has developed new products to meet the ever-increasing demand for high quality ingredients. This progressive action by renderers has enabled them to market approximately 30% of their protein products, and approximately 20% of animal fats sold into companion animal diets. Thus, the relevance of the economic and social importance of companion animals to the rendering industry is well established.

The petfood line of business is a way for the rendering industry to derive added value from its operations and diversify away from pure commodity markets.

The 3 major petfood products produced by the packing rendering industry are mechanically deboned beef, mechanically deboned chicken, and lean chunk beef. The annual volume sold to petfood companies is undetermined. It is believed that the product with the largest sales volume is mechanically deboned beef with mechanically deboned chicken the next largest, followed by lean chunk beef.   These products are typically packed and frozen in 50-lb blocks.

The typical chemical analysis of each product would be:

Mechanically deboned beef
>Moisture—68 to 72% maximum
>Protein—12 to 14% maximum
>Fat—15 to 20% maximum
>Ash—4 to 6% maximum

Mechanically deboned chicken
>Moisture—66 to 70% maximum
>Protein—12 to 16% maximum
>Fat—16 to 20% maximum
>Ash—2 to 4% maximum

Lean chunk beef
>Moisture—68 to 70% maximum
>Protein—16 to 20% maximum
>Fat—8 to 12% maximum
>Ash—1 to 2% maximum

The red meat petfood business has matured as demand for cattle meat has declined in recent years. In addition, the supply of meat depends on weather conditions year to year, as well as season to season.

The petfood business requires considerable investment in equipment and inventory to collect and process the raw materials, and to store the product from season to season to assure a steady supply for customers who require meat year round.

Overall retail petfood sales continue to increase yearly. American pet owners spend more than $155.00 per household per year on petfood. In 1994 dog food sales increased 3% and cat food sales 5%. The total combined annual sales rose to $8.7 billion. Business trend analysis projects that petfood sales will grow by 4.5% annually between 1995 and 2004.

# 11

# The Fats and Proteins Research Foundation

**Gary G Pearl**

The rendering industry's benefits to world health and economics are measured in the hundreds of millions of dollars annually, yet rendering remains the "Invisible Industry." While rendering, the first recycling industry, may be unseen, it is not unseeing. Imagination, insight, foresight, and vision have been required to guide renderers as they have invested time and effort in scientific research to develop new products and to refine processes and products.

The Fats and Proteins Research Foundation, founded in 1962, evinces the industry's commitment and dependence upon research. It is the only independent research organization dedicated exclusively to rendering. As a process, rendering has existed for thousands of years; and as an industry rendering has existed for well over 150 years. Nevertheless, dictionary definitions of rendering tend to be absent or vague and inaccurate; and other references yield equally limited information. (This is testament to the continued invisibility of an industry that is fundamental to the well-being of the industrialized world.)

In 1901, *The National Provisioner* (1981) reported that Professor Plumb of Purdue University had observed an accelerated growth rate when animal proteins were used to supplement corn rations fed to pigs. Plumb's was one of the earliest reported animal nutrition experiments. Other researchers added dried blood to tankage to enhance growth. This discovery led to the development of digester tankage, which was associated with a dramatic decrease in the time required for swine to reach market or slaughter weight, and revolutionized the feeding of pigs. These successes spurred research on the use of animal byproducts for animal feeding, as well as basic animal nutrition in all species. It was quickly realized that the so-called value-added products could result from ancillary recycling of heretofore discarded materials.

William H (Bill) Floyd, a broker in San Francisco, born in 1845, described those involved in rendering "as hard working, self-made, each possessing a damned good business head with a common solution to common problems philosophy." The formation of the Fats and Proteins Research Foundation illustrates this mettle. The formation and initial funding of the foundation can be credited to the foresight and vision of 2 men: Robert J Fleming (National Byproducts, Inc) and Charles L Haussermann Jr (Darling–Delaware Company, Inc). Bob Fleming presented the concept for such a foundation as early as 1959. Minutes of past meetings show the commitment of these 2 men in developing a high quality, ongoing research program for the industry.

At this time Myer O Sigal (G Bernd Co) was president of the National Renderers Association (NRA), and the research functions and initiatives were under the coordination of the NRA's Research Committee. Gene Hopton (Inland Products Inc, Columbus, Ohio) chaired that committee and later became president of NRA. During the formative stages of the Fats and Proteins Research Foundation, the NRA Research Committee continued to function while organizational meetings were conducted to enumerate the wants and needs of the industry. The Fats and Proteins Research Foundation was formally chartered as a nonprofit, non-lobbying foundation on June 20, 1962. The organizational meeting of the first Board of Directors of the Fats and Proteins Research Foundation was held at the Edgewater Beach Hotel in Chicago, Illinois, at 12:30 pm on June 20, 1962. At a previous meeting of the Board of Directors of the National Renderers Association, 11 directors had been elected to guide the foundation's formation. They were:

Allen Berne-Allen
RJ Fleming
Stanley Frank
John Hough
Gene Hopton
Lloyed Hygelund
Nelson Morris

Roger Morse
Howard Norton
Myer Sigal
Dean Specht

RJ Fleming was elected chairman. The first motion was to employ Earl Meisenbach as counsel; the second was to file the Articles of Incorporation and Bylaws in the State of Illinois.

In other business, Mr Fleming recommended establishment of a Standing Committee to be known as the Research Committee whose function would be to act as the technical steering committee of the foundation, considering all possible research fields and projects, appraising all research proposals, reviewing and controlling all projects in progress and advising the Board of Directors on technical matters relating to research. At such time as the Foundation employed a Technical Director, he or she would chair the Research Committee. Meanwhile, Mr Fleming appointed 11 persons to serve on the committee. They were:

Gene Hopton, Chairman
Allan Berne-Allen
Fred Bisplinghoff
John Christian
Robert E Crohan
Stanley Frank
AJ MacGregor
William R Malloy
John Quinn
Kenneth Reinhart
CH Skinner

The meeting adjourned at 1:00 pm. Formation of an organization that offered "common solutions to common problems" required a mere 30 minutes.

The Foundation shared offices with the National Renderers Association in Chicago, without charge, and moved with the NRA when they relocated in the suburbs of Chicago. The foundation's first 4 addresses were:

30 North LaSalle Street
Chicago, Illinois

2250 East Devon Avenue
Des Plaines, Illinois

8800 Governors Hill Drive
Cincinnati, Ohio

7150 Estero Boulevard
Fort Meyers Beach, Florida

Currently, the headquarters offices of the Fats and Proteins Research Foundation are at:

R.R. 2, Box 298
Bloomington, Illinois  61704

Dr DM Doty, from the American Meat Institute Research Foundation, was employed as the first technical director, joining the Fats and Proteins Research Foundation. Dr Werner Boehme succeeded Dr Doty, and continued in the position until December 31, 1982. In 1980, the Foundation added a new position to the staff, executive director. David L Gilcrest was employed in that capacity to take charge of the day-to-day operations. (This staff position title was later changed to president.) This change allowed the technical director to devote full time to the industry's research initiatives.

Fats and Proteins Research Foundation technical directors and presidents are:

Technical Directors
1962–1979     Dr DM Doty
1979–1981     Dr Werner Boehme
1981–1985     Dr JD Shroder
1985–1993     Dr Hank Fuller
1993–          Dr Gary G Pearl

Presidents
1980–1985     Mr David L Gilcrest
1985–1988     Dr Larry Davis
1988–1993     Dr Fred Bisplinghoff
1993–          Dr Gary Pearl

Robert J Fleming served as chairman of the Board of Directors for 8 years. He was an avid supporter and a tireless recruiter, and at the 1970 annual meeting he was recognized with an official resolution on behalf of the foundation for his vision and leadership. Mr Fleming's tireless efforts to address financial concerns and for individuals to serve as "mendicants" is ever-present throughout the records of the Fats and Proteins Research Foundation.

During the 1960s, prices for animal fats decreased dramatically, reflecting decreased demand.  Oils from the soybean, sunflower, cottonseed, peanut, coconut, rapeseed, and olive emerged as strong competitors to animal fats for soap manufacturing and other chemical industrial uses.  These changes emphatically illustrated the necessity to find new uses for animal fats.  The industry focused on funding research that would broaden its product base.  Throughout the Fats and Proteins Research Foundation's history, soliciting research funding and support has been a primary function.  But it was CL Haussermann Jr who recognized the need for an endowment.

During 1972 and 1973, Mr Haussermann initiated a major fund-raising campaign to establish an endowment for the Fats and Proteins Research Foundation.  Through the efforts of Mr Haussermann and his task force, nearly $1 million was generated.  This visionary effort has allowed the Foundation to persist during turbulent times and to assure that long-term projects will be completed.  It is important that we continue to fund this endowment.  Thus, fund-raising for supporting the research initiatives of the Fats and Proteins Research Foundation continues to be a vital part of the success of the Foundation.  The Foundation has operated with funding derived from solicitation rather than an established dues structure.  The records document many examples of "evangelistic" techniques of those responsible for generating funding for the Fats and Proteins Research Foundation from the industry participants.

In Dr Doty's February 2, 1968, "plea presentation," he aptly articulated the importance of funding research as an industry to accomplish collectively what would be impossible on an individual basis.  His presentation is included in the addendum.

To supplement Dr Doty's solicitation endeavors, Mr Lou Ziegler, a retired Faber Industries Inc executive from Peoria, Illinois, was employed to solicit contributions.  Mr Ziegler is remembered for performing his "evangelistic functions" in one of the finest Mercedes Benz cars ever made.  Many other pleas followed.  On April 24, 1980, Dr Boehme presented a "solicitation and appeal for contributions," to the NRA Area IV meeting attendees at Hilton Head, South Carolina; and again, on August 23, 1980,  to the NRA Area V meeting attendees at the continental Plaza Hotel, Chicago.  Dr Fred Bisplinghoff will be remembered for his dramatic presentations, the dramatics reportedly reducing their presenter to tears and perspiration.

A modern example of the industry's aggressive response to specific funding opportunity is the biodiesel and alternative fuel initiatives developed in early 1992.  When the possibilities of using rendered fats and used cooking oils became evident to Gerald Smith Sr, of Valley Proteins, he started a Biodiesel Funding Campaign, which has permitted the Fats and Proteins Research Foundation and the industry to research and cooperate with allied groups in the development of biodiesel. The ultimate role of biodiesel in fulfilling the world's demand for ignition energy is not yet clear. However, a very optimistic projection would be that biodiesel may have a significant and integral part of the total future fuel usage and, likewise, that animal-derived and recycled rendered fats will be the feedstock that permits the production of biodiesel in quantity.

These examples illustrate the commitment of the Foundation's members, but of more significance, it also illustrates the generosity of the entire industry to have responded to those past please for monetary support during "thick, thin, and extremely thin" times. Suffice it to say that the Foundation has not only existed but has prospered as evidenced by the image it has developed and maintained as a research organization. It has remained financially strong; the original Haussermann Fund is still invested to assure extended life of the organization. The rendering industry by its aggressive approach to solving common problems with common solutions has attended to its duty. Monetarily the rendering industry has funded the Foundation without the establishment of a dues structure, checkoff system, or government subsidies but by its attitudinal traits of earning it the old-fashioned way. Mr David S Evans, the current (1994 to 1996) Foundation Board Chairperson and CEO of CBP Resources in Greensboro, North Carolina, has been quoted as saying, "When research dollars are most needed, the industry will hunker down and somehow in total will generate them for the needs expressed."

## RESEARCH SCOPE

The scope of the research involvement has been as broad as the budget allowed. Readers interested in obtaining Foundation funding are encouraged to pursue this possibility. Priority is given to projects with the greatest potential to enhance the utilization or value of rendered animal products. The Fats and Proteins Research Foundation funded many of the studies cited in references in other chapters of this book. The *Director's Digests* published by the Foundation list project applications and results. This assemblage shows the diversity of studies with which researchers are diligently seeking answers to hard questions.

Early accounts refer to numerous non-nutritional studies, including waterproofing concrete, using fat in Portland cement, and chemically modifying animal proteins into structural plastics. Currently underway is a project to evaluate the efficiency of various animal protein meals as soil amendments for managing populations of soilborne pests including weeds, nematodes, fungi, and bacteria. Using hydrogenated tallow as an environmentally-friendly baled hay preservative awaits commercialization following more than 3 years of research.

Processing technology and the influence of cooking time and temperature on the nutritional value as well as biosecurity of animal rendered protein ingredients have been routine objectives for research projects.   Priority continues to be given to projects that address improving bioavailability and uniformity of nutrients.   Nutrition-related subjects have predominated the listing of completed projects for both proteins and fats.

Nutrition is the process of furnishing the individual cells with that portion of the external chemical environment needed for optimum functioning of the many metabolic chemical reactions involved in growth, maintenance, work, production, and reproduction.   Nutrition encompasses the procurement, ingestion, digestion, and absorption of the chemical elements that serve as food.   Knowledge of the basic functioning of the nutrients in the animal's body and the interrelationships among various nutrients has been acquired in very small increments, and the task is by no means complete.   The volume of publications on nutrition of domesticated animals equals that of research in other areas.

There are virtually millions of references dealing with nutrition-related research on animals.   Although records do not allow for an accurate count of all the foundation has sponsored, the Fats and Proteins Research Foundation can be credited with involvement in very few.   However, nearly 300 *Director's Digests* articulate the findings of either single or multiple related projects.   The majority of these research projects were completed by university scientists.   Cooperating researchers are encouraged to publish our work in peer-reviewed journals and to present their findings at scientific symposia and conferences.   Fats and Proteins Research Foundation grantees in actuality are spokespersons for rendered animal products and the industry.   It would be so gratifying to list these devoted scientists and researchers individually.   With the fear that the listing could not be complete, suffice it to state that every grantee who has ever acknowledged the Fats and Proteins Research Foundation in their manuscript has been individually important and valued in the success of the Foundation.

Authors of several chapters of this book are recipients of Fats and Proteins Research Foundation grants.   Past and current projects involve virtually all species, all products produced by the rendering industry, and all disciplines of use or potential use.   Evidence of the vast scope of projects is found in the titles, which include words such as beef, growing pigs, dairy cattle, broiler, beef calves, catfish, single-cell protein, turkeys, piglets, ruminants, pets, horse, layers, sows, racehorses, poultry, light growing steers, Western Hemisphere shrimp, growing turkeys, laying hens, nursery pigs, early weaned pigs, segregated early weaned pigs, feeder pigs, dogs, adult cats, high-performance horses, salmonid fish, high-producing dairy cows and high-lean pigs.

The Fats and Proteins Research Foundation has addressed biosecurity issues, both perceived and real threats, objectively and persistently with clear-cut science based on practical experience, investigation, observation, and principles. *Salmonella,* foreign animal diseases, scrapie, anthrax, and pseudorabies are examples of past biosecurity research involvement. The Research Committee structure as established in the Foundation's charter still exists. This Committee is composed of 12 industry, academic, and end user nutritionists and veterinarians who meet formally biannually to evaluate and establish research project priorities. A 20-member Board of Directors determines final project approvals and funding. The mission and focus of the Fats and Proteins Research Foundation are specific:

To provide for an institution which will direct and manage the process whereby research is initiated, prioritized, approved, conducted, and completed, results disseminated and funded on any issues relating to the rendering industry and to cooperate where appropriate with any other institutions with similar goals.

The Fats and Proteins Research Foundation continues to focus on new utilizations and improvement in existing products. The Foundation's success has been formidable. It is recognized as the research organization for rendered animal products throughout the world.

The breadth of research involvement—both practical and exploratory, both nutritional and non-nutritional, both fat and protein, both negative and positive results—have been too all-inclusive to summarize in a single chapter. To single out only one specific product and only one specific use is unfair in quantifying success. Nevertheless, an example is feeding fats. In 1962, when the Foundation was formed, only 300,000 lb of feeding fat were used by all of animal agriculture. The ensuing basic research, followed by applied research and its implementation into practical feed formulations via a dedicated product awareness program, resulted in growth that approaches 4 billion lb, its present annual usage in the United States. This accomplishment was not made possible through a single project by a single scientist with a singe one-time research investment. Nor does it assure that the market is preserved and the task completed.

Feeding concepts that have benefited as well as contributed to the increased usage of feeding fats have included fats as an economical energy source for poultry while improving egg weight and production. The use of fat in late gestation and lactation swine diets improves pig weights, piglet survival, and reproduction. The supplemental use of both fat and undegradable intake protein results in persistent milk yield in dairy cows. Research has consistently demonstrated improved daily gains, feed utilization, and carcass characteristics from supplementing finishing cattle diets with fats. Animal fats provide required fatty acids and enhance palatability when in pet foods. Ancillary properties, such as controlling dust in feed and ingredients, enhance pelleting efficiencies and extend the life of feed-handling equipment—valuable assets to the use of animal fats in animal rations.

Animal husbandry and its component parts continues to change at unprecedented rates. Each faction of the industry is rapidly becoming more consolidated and decision makers fewer in number. What required decades to accomplish can be reversed by the decisions of a few. Unfortunately, all decisions are not based entirely on science or logic, and it is very difficult to satisfy emotions with facts. Long-term decisions can, however, best be directed by credible science, unbiased interpretations, and commitment to responsiveness to the wants and needs of the customer (decision maker).

The Fats and Proteins Research Foundation has been blessed with consistent leaders who appreciate the importance of research in the maintenance and growth an industry. At the risk of redundancy, comments from several of the past Board chairmen follow:

Mr David Evans, currently the Fats and Proteins Research Foundation chairman:

> The Fats and Proteins Research Foundation is an essential part of the future of the rendering industry. Through the Foundation we develop windows that allow us to find future opportunities that will improve the state of the industry. Research is food for growth and improvement, the absence of which would assuredly limit success for all renderers. We must continue to look to the future. We must continue to support a proven and worthy engine for research: The Fats and Proteins Research Foundation.

Mr Dennis Griffin, President and CEO of Griffin Industries in Cold Springs, Kentucky, and Chairman of the Board, 1992 to 1994:

> The research wing of the rendering industry is the Fats and Proteins Research Foundation, most commonly called FPRF. It has been most informative and helpful to us through the years, guiding us in our search for new products and new uses for our existing products. Griffin Industries have continued to be active in the Fats and Proteins Research Foundation, volunteering our time and financial support. I feel that this research organization is very important to us as we move toward the 21st century. We always want to be current on nutritional uses for our animal proteins and to maintain awareness of the technological advances on new products.

Mr Greg Van Hoven, President of the Van Hoven Company in St. Paul, Minnesota—like so many in the rendering industry, a multi-generation, family-owned business—and Chairman, 1990 to 1992:

Since my earliest years with Van Hoven Company, my Dad always stressed the importance of our participation in a focused, industry-wide research program dedicated to identifying new and expanded market opportunities for our products.

We believe that projects funded by the Fats and Proteins Research Foundation over the past thirty years have contributed significantly to the success we enjoy today—as a company and as an Industry.

Likewise, we view our current investment in the Fats and Proteins Research Foundation as the foundation upon which tomorrow's successes will be made possible for ourselves and for the next generation of Van Hoven employees.

Mr Eddie Murakami, Vice President at Baker Commodities Inc, Los Angeles, California—with James Andreoli as President, Baker has long been a committed supporter of the Fats and Proteins Research Foundation, both with personnel and monetary resources—and Chairman, 1988 to 1990:

At Baker Commodities, Inc. we think highly of research because it is the basis for growth and without growth we cannot survive.

Baker has been a long time member of the Fats and Proteins Research Foundation. We strongly support this organization for its research efforts for the rendering industry.

Mr Frederick S Wintzer—a personal mentor for me when I joined the Fats and Proteins Research Foundation—President of GA Wintzer & Son Co, Wapakoneta, Ohio, until his retirement in 1995, and Chairman, 1976 to 1977:

The Fats and Proteins Research Foundation defends our place in existing markets and helps us to develop new products for new markets. Specialty products, were derived directly from FPRF research, made up 39% of our sales last year. The importance of the Fats and Proteins Research Foundation to the success of our company cannot be overstated.

All chairpersons have been consistent in their enthusiastic support of the research mission of the Fats and Proteins Research Foundation. Each made a significant contribution in pursuit of that mission. To complete the record I list the other past Board Chairmen:

Stanley Frank, Carolina & Southern Processing Co, Greensboro, North Carolina, 1975 to 1976

Robert N Peterson, Peterson Manufacturing, Los Angeles, California, 1978 to 1980

George Theobald Sr, SERCO, now the Florida Transport Co, Miami, Florida, 1981 to 1982

Charles L Tocalino, Modesto Tallow, Modesto, California, 1982 to 1984

Jack Barensfeld, 1984 to 1986

Warren J Alcock Jr. 1986 to 1988

Unfortunately on August 14, 1986 a flood destroyed many of the records filed at 2250 East Devon Avenue, Des Plaines, Illinois.

Research and Development is and has been an integral part of each incremental expansion of the industry.   More and more renderers are coming to the realization that the past is just that—the past—and they can only continue in business and prosper by implementing change to adjust to the demands of today's society.   Certainly the current dependence upon research will not be altered by a mere flight of ideas. The Foundation, as does its members and their needs, continues to change.   In nearly every thriving industry or successful company a focused research and product development program that responds to customer needs and wants is fundamental.   Conversely, the de-emphasis or lack of research is a commonly seen in regressing industries.   The future will only exacerbate these facts.   It will become difficult to survive in an environment of science and technology without the basics of research.   The implementation of new technology is now occurring at an unprecedented pace.

New industries within the food-producing sector are developing with regularity.   An emerging industry that already has a significant presence in the United States and the world is that of aquaculture.   "Farm raised" fish and shellfish are only one example of the changes occurring in our food supply production systems.   It should not be forgotten that rendering and its recycling of a major portion of all animal products determined to be inedible for humans are feedstuffs for those same animals; animal agriculture could be extremely vulnerable.   This partnering function has afforded a symbiotic relationship that has resulted in the most economical and high quality meat in the world.

## CONCLUSION

It has been said that the only constant is change.   And this axiom holds true for the rendering industry.   New challenges will surface in the coming decades as agribusiness consolidates and humans grasp more and more resources to sustain a burgeoning global population.   Finding solutions to new problems or opportunities is an ongoing quest.   As Francis Bacon once opined, "He that will not apply new remedies must expect new evils."

Change also tends to precipitate nostalgia.   Though memories are nice, it is not only those memories that provide benefit to an organization;

dreams and visions of the future are more important. Benjamin Franklin had it right, "We must all hang together or assuredly we shall all hang separately." What Franklin knew and most of us should remember is the strength of neighbors and the value of numbers. It was with just such thoughts that the Fats and Proteins Research Foundation was formed.

One of my favorite memories of life on the farm is of butchering day. Although too young to be of any material assistance other than being a "go-fer" and being in the way, the day was an important day and a neighborhood festival. Each neighbor had a specific specialty within the process, such as scalding, scraping, cutting, sausage seasoning, or ham curing. The process could only be done on what seemed to be the coldest, most blustery day of winter. It was, therefore, a real pleasure to be near the cast iron kettles over the open wood fire. The kettles had been filled with fat chunks dissected from the lean cuts of meat, from which the lard would be extracted via a press when the steaming potion had been heated for the required length of time. To this day, the cast iron kettle, the long-handled paddle, and the lard press are some of my most prized possessions passed down from my father and grandfather. This very basic and early introduction to rendering, an industry that at the time certainly was not considered a very important part of my later life, can be described as warm, important memories.

Just as the past of the Fats and Proteins Research Foundation can remain a warm memory for the successes that it has achieved for those of us who have had some involvement or influence, it is the dreams for its future from the new generation of pioneers who surface as leaders that will determine its destiny and success. In only my short tenure as an "honorary renderer" I have no doubt that all of the dreams and visions can be fulfilled for another 34 years. But I still yearn to again sample the fresh, warm cracklings from the lard press while being warmed by the open fire.

# ADDENDUM

# A tribute to Mr. Robert J Fleming, 1970

We are indebted to Bob for the concept and the form with which he has brought into being the Foundation and its structure.  The breadth of the concept is sufficient to serve all companies in our areas.  He exhibited the patience, the guidance which has made possible the stability, the growth and professional competence and direction which has characterized our development.  His business statesmanship has a force for unity in our total organization.   The same statesmanship won worldwide recognition for our association eliciting great prestige for NRA with the Government, the scientific community and all phases of industry.

Be it therefore resolved:  That the Fats and Proteins Research Foundation and the National Renderers Association extend to Robert Fleming our highest commendation and thanks for so fine an accomplishment, and that the official records shall so show.

## Dr Doty, February 2, 1968:

FPRF, organized and incorporated in 1962, strives to initiate and conduct research activities that will develop new and expanded uses for fats, proteins and related materials throughout the world.  The Foundation's purpose is to pool the research resources of the rendering, meat packing and related industries so that we may accomplish collectively what would be impossible on an individual basis.  But the future of the Foundation depends upon your help and your support—and your future may well depend upon the Foundation.  If you are not an FPRF member now, become one and give your support to the vitally important activity of the industry.

## Dr Boehme, April 24, 1980:

Over the years, the rendering industry's collaborative effort to maintain a productive level of research led to the establishment and growth of the Fats and Proteins Research Foundation. Its objectives have been to expand the uses of tallow and the other products of our industry. This continuing effort for more than seventeen years, since the Foundation was established, has given us the renown as the worldís foremost center of animal byproducts research.  No other scientific entity has taken such an active part in animal byproducts research, and FPRF is the only organization that monitors new developments of importance to the rendering industry throughout the worldís scientific and patent literature.   These efforts and your support of them have helped to maintain the profitability of the rendering industry and have led to great changes in the uses of tallow and meat meals since the decline of the soap business in the late 1940ís when the synthetic detergents appeared in the marketplace and with disastrous effects on the demand for tallow.  As an example, the use of tallow in animal feed, now its largest single use, is the direct result of an intensive research program sponsored by our industry.  Our Board of Directors has enthusiastically supported the research program and has urged that it vigorously be expanded because it is clearly a successful undertaking.  This expansion, however, has greatly increased expenditures beyond income.   Income from industry solicitations has created an annual deficit that is rapidly depleting the reserves, principally the Haussermann Fund.  It has recently been stated by Earle Barnes, President of Dow Chemical Company, that "Research is not an option open to us, like white sidewall tires.  It is a necessary component of our business and as integral to our operations as the wheels on axles are to an automobile."  Research is a long-term investment and you have supported it in the past because it is benefiting the rendering industry.  Now, more than ever, in the face of increasing competition and rising production costs, we will need more research to assure our profitability over the long term.  If you still believe, as Mr. Barnes does, that research is not the white sidewalls of our industry but is as vital as the wheels on our cars, I know I can count on your continued support and a substantial increase in your contributions.

# 12

# North American Perspective of Rendering—21st Century

## Fred Bisplinghoff

In the book, *The Invisible Industry,* Frank Burnham opened the last chapter, "Focus on the Future," with the following paragraph:

> A period of major transition, transition that is far from completed, is perhaps the most accurate way in which to describe what has occurred and what will continue to occur in the rendering industry during the latter half of the twentieth century.

One major transition that Burnham alludes to has been ongoing and is continuing at a modest pace. We have experienced a significant reduction in the number of independent rendering establishments with a commensurate increase of packer and integrated poultry renderers. When *The Invisible Industry* was written in 1978, more than 600 independent rendering plants were processing 60% of the North American raw animal byproducts, while today fewer than 200 independent facilities are processing less than 30%.

The numerous changes currently taking place in all facets of the rendering industry make accurate depiction of the industry in the 21st century a formidable challenge. Zack Stentz stated in the *Meat/Poultry Magazine* in their "The Next 40 Years" edition:

> The most difficult story to write is one set 40 or 50 years in the future. Place the action 200 years in the future and you can say pretty much whatever you want without any fear of being proven wrong in your own lifetime. Set a story 5 or 10 years in the future, and you merely take one or two current trends and magnify and extrapolate them.

Predict the rendering industry in the 21st century?  That's a tough assignment.  To prepare for this difficult task, I asked leaders in all segments of the rendering industry to share their ideas and projections on several subjects that will contribute to shaping the industry in the next 20 to 40 years.

## TRENDS FOR RAW MATERIAL AVAILABILITY & WHO PROCESSES THE BY PRODUCTS?

If the pool of raw material is to grow, the livestock and poultry population must increase, and this depends, to a large extent, on the eating habits of food consumers all over the world.

Over the next 10 to 20 years, consumers will continue to have the opportunity to be more informed, so they can make "educated" decisions about what foods to buy.  Certain articles in the popular press would have you believe that a significant number of consumers will be vegetarians by the year 2000.  Less meat consumption equates to less livestock and poultry in the 21st century.  Harry Balzer, Vice President of the NPD Group, a Park Ridge, Illinois firm that follows American eating habits, comments, "People are moving away from anything that requires cooking, and during the past 10 years consumers have moved away from certain 'ingredient' items, such as bacon."  Results of a recently released study, commissioned by the National Live Stock and Meat Board, uncovered several interesting facts about American eating habits. *Eating in America Today: A Dietary Pattern and Intake Report,* 2nd edition (EATII), provides current information available about American food consumption habits, and information about what consumers are actually eating compared with their attitudes toward food.

Daily, consumers are eating a variety of foods.  Within the Meat Group of USDA's "Food Guide Pyramid," which depicts food groups along with recommended servings, meat (beef, pork, lamb, veal, processed, and variety or other meats) represents about half of all consumed foods within the Meat Group, at 3.4 oz consumed.  On average, the population eats 1.3 oz of eggs, dry beans, and nuts, 1.2 oz of poultry, and 0.5 oz of fish and seafood per day.

Many vegetarians are vegetarians in name only—they are not eating that way.  EATII compares people's self-reported dietary preferences with their actual food intake.  The study compared meat-eaters to 2 types of self-classified vegetarians; meat-avoiders (people who say they make an effort to not eat meat), and vegetarians (people who say they are always on a vegetarian diet).

When the diets of all study participants were analyzed, despite claims to the contrary, fewer people were true vegetarians when it came to consumption.

Fewer than 1% of the respondents actually ate no meat during the 14-day recording period.  Even though meat-avoiders and vegetarians say they do not eat meat, on a daily basis they actually consume an average of 2.3 oz of meat.  Meat-eaters consume only 1.2 oz more meat per day than meat-avoiders and vegetarians.

Consumers are continuing to eat not only poultry, but beef and pork as well.  The EATII study found that what we think we eat is vastly different from what we really eat.  The National Restaurant Association reports that the proportion of vacillating patrons—those who "talk the talk" of good nutrition, but do not necessarily "walk the walk"—has consistently grown over the past decade, from 27% in 1996, to 32% today.  Those who do "walk the walk" have dropped from 39% in 1989, to 31% in 1994.  The balance (37%) are the unconcerned.

Table 1 outlines the trends in per capita consumption of red meat, poultry, and fish from 1970 through 1993.  Most renderers are aware that red meat per capita consumption dropped from 131.7 lb (beef, veal, pork, and lamb) in 1970 to 112.0 lb in 1993.  The per capita consumption of poultry went the opposite direction, as it moved to a level of 61.2 lb in 1993 from only 33.8 lb in 1970.  The increase in per capita consumption of fish and shellfish was surprisingly low; it increased from 11.7 lb in 1970 to a high of 15.6 lb in 1989, but subsequently dropped to 14.9 lb in 1993.

**Table 1.** Changes in Food Consumption, 1970 - 1993
(All quantities are in pounds per capita unless otherwise indicated)

| FOOD CATEGORY | 1970-74 | 1993 |
| --- | --- | --- |
| Red meats | 130.2 | 111.9 |
| Poultry | 34.1 | 61.1 |
| Fish & shellfish | 12.1 | 14.9 |

*Source*: US Department of Agriculture

There is some good news in the beef picture:  1994 was another good year for beef production.  The beef total for 1995 is likely to top 1994's record of 24.4 billion lb by 1%, with beef output running nearly 4% over year-earlier levels during the first quarter of 1995.  Per capita consumption will not change much in 1995, but zoomed nearly 2.5 lb higher in 1994.  This is not surprising, considering the success of restaurants like Outback and Lone Star that feature red meat items.  Tables 2, 3, and 4 give USDA's 10-year baseline projections for beef, pork, and chicken production, respectively.

USDA projects a 5% increase in broiler production in 1995 following a gain of 7% in 1994, but expects a slowing of poultry expansion over the next 10 years.  Pork production will grow modestly through the period, with a small cyclical downturn in 1998 and 1999, as small producers are forced to leave the industry.

Exports will absorb much of the increase in production of beef and poultry. In 1994, beef exports grew an impressive 24%, and USDA anticipates another 9% increase in 1995, to 1.7 billion lb. Poultry meat exports have increased at a rapid pace, with growth predictions of from 2.83 billion lb in 1995 to 3.66 billion in 2005. Exports of all meats will continue to expand, which will support current US slaughter levels.

**Table 2.** Baseline Projection for Beef Production

| Year | Commerical Production (billion pounds) |
|------|----------------------------------------|
| 1995 | 24.465 |
| 1996 | 24.807 |
| 1997 | 25.342 |
| 1998 | 25.465 |
| 1999 | 25.524 |
| 2000 | 25.709 |
| 2001 | 25.709 |
| 2002 | 25.755 |
| 2003 | 25.922 |
| 2004 | 26.072 |
| 2005 | 26.289 |

*Source*: USDA baseline projections

**Table 3.** Baseline Projection for Pork Production

| Year | Commerical Production (billion pounds) |
|------|----------------------------------------|
| 1994 | 17.648 |
| 1995 | 18.425 |
| 1996 | 18.852 |
| 1997 | 10.019 |
| 1998 | 18.970 |
| 1999 | 18.936 |
| 2000 | 18.938 |
| 2001 | 19.012 |
| 2002 | 19.193 |
| 2003 | 19.415 |
| 2004 | 19.620 |
| 2005 | 19.797 |

*Source*: U.S.D.A. Baseline projections

USDA's baseline study shows turkey production climbing from 5.29 billion lb in 1995 to 5.97 billion lb in 2005. The devaluation of the Mexican peso will curtail US turkey meat exports in the short term by as much as 15 to 20%, but the baseline report has turkey meat exports growing from 280 million lb in 1995 to 435 million lb in 2005. A conclusion we can draw is that the US rendering industry can expect a slower, but steady growth of poultry raw material, and a modest increase in beef and pork raw byproducts. This conclusion leads to the question, "What are the long-term raw material projections for the poultry, red meat, and independent rendering industries?"

**Table 4.** Baseline Projection for Young Chickens

| Year | Federal Inspected Slaughter (billion pounds) |
|------|-----------------------------------------------|
| 1994 | 23.806 |
| 1995 | 25.050 |
| 1996 | 26.306 |
| 1997 | 27.197 |
| 1998 | 28.066 |
| 1999 | 28.939 |
| 2000 | 29.834 |
| 2001 | 30.767 |
| 2002 | 31.732 |
| 2003 | 32.701 |
| 2004 | 33.667 |
| 2005 | 34.631 |

*Source*: U.S.D.A. Baseline projections

As mentioned above, there has been a drop of nearly 70% in the number of independent rendering plants in the United States in the last 20 years. Mike Rempe, of Excel Packing Company, says that the same trend is taking place in the meat packing industry. In 1976 there were 217 large cattle plants (killing more than 50,000 head/ year), which accounted for 75.6% of the slaughter. In 1989, there were only 96 large beef plants, which slaughtered 89.7% of the kill. Today, IBP, Excel, and Monfort account for 75% of the US cattle slaughter. Similarly, for pork, 116 plants slaughtered more than 100,000 head/year, 84.7% of the kill in 1976. In 1989, only 77 large pork plants were doing 91.9% of the kill.

The above statistics highlight the dilemma regarding one of the principle remaining sources of raw material for the independent renderer, the small- and medium-sized packer, and niche market value-added meat processor. There has been a gradual decline in these facilities, and most renderers agree with Dennis Mullane of Taylor Byproducts on this group's ability to survive. Mullane believes these slaughterers and processors will have real obstacles in the future because:

- Cost to process and slaughter will increase, necessitating volume increases.

- Capital requirements due to additional USDA regulations will force older facilities to upgrade.

- The market niche that these specialty processors developed will attract large packers, thereby increasing competition.

Other packer-renderers interviewed agreed that unless these companies have a solid niche or specialty product line, chances of survival long-term are questionable. Large packers will continue to build portfolios of value-added products (through acquisitions and research and development), and moving into these niche markets will be part of their strategy. Most independent renderers agreed with the packer-renderers' assessment of the small packers' future, and are only optimistic about those that have creative and aggressive marketing programs and continue to monitor the needs of the marketplace and then develop quality products to fill these needs.

Before boxed beef, Benny Schwartz's Supermarket at University and Glenn in Peoria, Illinois, would generate more than 5,000 lb of fat and bone trimmings for a Monday morning pick-up—and, many independent renderers can top this story. But the gradual erosion of products at supermarkets has not only increased hauling costs, but has hindered the renderer's ability to produce quality tallow. Also, the proportion of trash (plastic, cardboard, cans, etc) and spoiled goods (chickens, sausage, etc) to good product has lowered the overall quality of the finished proteins and fats. David Evans of CBP Resources summarizes the problem in this way:

> The quality and quantity of route material has been seriously affected by the conversion of almost all suppliers (grocery stores, small meat vendors, etc) to boxed beef.
>
> Generally, the volume is about 20% of historical numbers, and a drum contains about 15% trash, 30% rejects and returns, 30% poultry and fish, and 25% red meat.

The problem is only exacerbated by the trend to more closely trimmed beef cuts and case-ready products prepared at the packing house. Mike Rempe of Excel notes that the original specifications for beef cuts, when boxed beef started in the 1960s, was 1 inch of fat on the beef cut. This was then trimmed at the retail store or purveyor's, and some went into ground beef, with the remainder to the local renderer. Consumers do not want fat on their meat in the case, so the new specification is 1/4-inch trim, and the desired ground beef is now 80 to 85% lean, versus the old standard of 70%. Rempe estimates that 30% of the beef cuts that Excel ships are close-trimmed, and that within 3 to 5 years they will be nearly 100% close-trimmed beef. This will increase the edible tallow per head yield from the present 50 to 60 lb/head to 65 to 85 lb/head.

Bill Combs of Monfort believes that genetic improvements will lead to less fat and more lean and lighter bone structure of cattle. Combs, Dale

Graham of IBP, and John Hendricks of Moyer Packing agree that further processing at the packing house will continue. While the industry will have "near case-ready" products, and later, "case-ready" products, the genetically engineered animal will be more totally used in the process. Combs and Graham predict that lean recovery efforts will accelerate due to the difficulty in finding labor and the economic necessity to recover more protein. Some material will end up in hamburger, the balance in the "value-added" area and made into fat-reduced beef and partially defatted chopped beef.

The packer has to overcome some shelf-life problems to produce the consumer-acceptable tray-ready product, but John Hendricks referred to new technologies on the horizon, such as modified atmosphere packaging (MAP) which is intended to give the meat a familiar appearance in terms of packaging and color. All of the trends to increased amounts of tray-ready beef and pork and improved value of trimmings mean less raw material for the independent renderer.

As the livestock population stabilizes and animal husbandry improves on the large cattle and swine production units, fallen animal tonnage will gradually decline. It was generally accepted that disease control, with corresponding higher death loss in large confinement operations, would be a major stumbling block to the development of these farms. Extensive strides in vaccines and other innovative disease prevention methods have reduced the death loss on large units to below those experienced by small producers of over 20 years ago. Hot summers and sudden cold snaps used to produce large numbers of "deads," but with improved and properly ventilated housing, these summer and winter peaks are decreasing each year.

The major change renderers will experience in fallen animal pick-up service in the future is the increased numbers of collection centers, which large swine producers and county governments will establish to prevent the spread of disease and to ensure proper disposal of dead animals. With the producers delivering the animals to the center, the renderers will enjoy reduced collection costs.

Charging for dead stock pick-up service used to come and go with the rise and fall of animal protein markets. Free dead-stock service, even in pet-food operations, will be very rare in the next 20 years. Charging for this service is probably the forerunner to charging for all straight truck pick-up services (grocery stores, lockers, etc).

Poultry renderers agree with USDA's growth projections, and they forecast moderate increases in raw material tonnage for both integrated and independent poultry renderers.

All poultry renderers alluded to the trend of losing formerly inedible parts to edible markets, such as foot pads (exported to China), and the mechanically deboned meat from deboned frames being used in stock solutions. Offsetting this loss of raw material is the increased tonnage from further processing of poultry parts.  Doug Baskin of Tyson Foods related how the skin and bones that used to go to the landfill via the kitchen are now being recycled.  This is a good-news–bad-news story: fat yield has increased due to skin and leaf fat going to rendering, but ash content of the poultry byproduct meal has increased correspondingly which, in some cases, makes it unacceptable as a premium priced pet-food ingredient.

Tommy Bagwell of American Proteins, Jack Smith of Sanderson Farms, and Baskin foresee fewer small poultry processing and poultry rendering plants.  Environmental and high capital costs of poultry rendering are cited as reasons small poultry processors and renderers will find it diffi-cult to stay in business.  David Evans of CBP Resources estimates the add-on environmental costs to a poultry rendering plant can be as much as 35% of the cost of the plant.  The overhead of processing feathers and the high environmental capital and operating costs mean that most poultry and turkey slaughterers do not have sufficient volume to make rendering cost-effective.  Bagwell of American Proteins believes that as long as the independent poultry renderers can accumulate enough vol-ume to realize economies of scale and strive to service the needs of the poultry processors, they will continue to have a major role in poultry ren-dering.  In general, poultry processors have not adopted in-house render-ing, where they have had the option of more cost-effective large-scale toll rendering.

Other than poultry byproducts, kitchen grease is the only bright spot in the raw material picture for the independent renderer.  The rendering industry is processing more than 2.3 billion lb/year of kitchen grease, and many renderers have experienced increases in volume of more than 10% yearly for the past 15 years.

The maturing of the fast-food and family restaurant industry, coupled with more consumers eating less deep-fried foods, has resulted in many kitchen-grease processors recording no growth or single-digit volume increases.  Renderers in the few areas of growing population are report-ing continued double-digit increases in tonnage.  James Andreoli of Baker Commodities, Inc, foresees a gradual growth in volume at most of Baker's plant locations.  Andreoli notes that, in spite of the tremendous growth of fast-food outlets, when a particular chain goes out of business, another franchise enters the area and subsequently the availability of grease increases.  Most renderers agreed with Andreoli's opinion that the industry will employ more efficient and sanitary collection techniques over the next 10 years.  Where climatic conditions permit, renderers are using sophisticated pumping equipment, and this trend will continue.

New groups of entrepreneurs regularly enter the kitchen-grease collec-tion arena.  Some pay for the material, others provide only pick-up service, and a few steal the grease which is usually located in an acces-sible area.  Thieves have been caught, but the one prediction that le-gitimate renderers can be assured will come true, is that the theft of kitchen grease will continue into the 21st century.

# RENDERING TECHNOLOGIES OF THE FUTURE

Dennis Griffin of Griffin Industries foresees new rendering technologies in the future. He says, "Better processing methods, which will include enzymatic reduction and lower temperature processing, will give renderers improved finished products." For the next few years, Griffin foresees only modifications to the present systems to improve their wearability and energy utilization.

James Andreoli of Baker Commodities agrees with Griffin that renderers need a more efficient method to process raw materials. Since competition from producers of other fats and proteins determine finish market prices, a concern of renderers is how much of the increasing collection and production costs can be passed on to raw-material customers.

Many renderers think they have reached the limit of major new technological advances. They concede, however, that they will modify existing systems to improve capacity, save energy, and improve finish product quality. Their opinions were probably reinforced by the fact that very few new systems were introduced in the past 25 years. It is interesting that the latest rendering systems appeared at approximately the same time. Continuous processing in heated shell and paddle cookers, disc cookers, and vacuum slurry systems energized the rendering industry in the 1960s and 1970s, and many renderers expected further developments. When microwave cooking was exhibited during high oil and natural gas prices, it seemed to some that their wishes had come true. Because they could not cope with the inconsistent nature of the raw material, or compete with lower energy costs, microwave processing and enzymatic rendering disappeared from the scene. In the Fats and Proteins Research Foundation—sponsored enzymatic rendering study, the researchers could not identify the proper proteolytic enzyme or design an energy efficient method of drying the hydrolyzed protein.

As they say, "what goes around comes around," and today we see renewed interest in enzymatic rendering and microwave processing. Whether these systems will be perfected over the next few years remains a question, but environmental issues will drive the development of more sophisticated and larger capacity systems. In the near term, there will be continued building of high-volume plants using continuous cookers, modified low temperature, and slurry/vacuum systems. The common denominator among all systems will be more computerized controls. Greg Van Hoven of The Van Hoven Company anticipates more and improved heat-recovery systems, utilizing waste heat to evaporate moisture from increased levels of lower-yielding raw material.

As mentioned above, most renderers believe the industry will increase their utilization of computerized control systems, thereby reducing reliance on human input and the inconsistencies associated with operator performance. But, Dennis Griffin thinks that too much computerization will remove the common sense element from the equation. Griffin proposes more employee training and motivational programs so the skilled operator can control the system.

Looking ahead 20 to 40 years, the industry will have one large independent rendering plant processing all available raw material from a large geographic area. This plant will have at least 2 systems, one for high-quality raw material and the other for low-grade products. Increased amounts of end products, both domestically and overseas, are moving into the animal food markets. This indicates that the animal food nutritionists will exert additional control over finish material prices, by determining the inclusion level of the end product in all types of animal diets.

However, these quality-concerned nutritionists will also create new opportunities for value-added products.

The industry will always be able to sell end products at a price, but that price will force higher pick-up charges to raw material suppliers. And this could enable outside recycling companies, for instance garbage collectors, with ample capital for research and development, to enter raw material markets. It is imperative that the rendering industry create new markets for all grades of finished products. The most economically feasible and logical method to accomplish this goal is for the industry to contribute a larger percentage of their sales dollars to research.

## WILL PROPERLY PROCESSED & NEW PRODUCTS BE PROFITABLE VENTURES ?

Since the introduction of the wet rendered cooker, the rendering industry, for the most part, has been production driven. "Push it through and lower the processing per-unit cost" has been the driving force for over a century. Higher temperatures equate to lower moisture content of greasy cracklings, which leads to:

- less pressing problems (fines, etc.),
- less stressful operation of the system for the operator,
- increased throughput, and
- sometimes setting a production record.

Many renderers are beginning to train their management and operating personnel to be concerned about end product quality. Hopefully, in the future, rather than asking production questions, the plant superintendent will ask:

- "Are you sure we avoided overheating the protein, to prevent destruction of some of the heat-sensitive amino acids, and reducing the availability of what was left?"

Until 20 years ago, if end-product quality was stressed, it was directed toward fat products. Fat customers set strict fat-quality specifications, and the supplier was penalized if they were not met. This has not been the case with the renderers' protein products until the past few years.

Renderers who promote protein quality have been called star gazers by other renderers who reasoned that no matter how renderers processed their raw material, there would always be a market for their protein products, even if modest discounting was necessary. Just as many young community leaders are becoming concerned about the environment, many young nutritionists are concerned about the quality of protein ingredients. Not cut from the same mold as their predecessors, they are insisting on stricter specifications. In some cases are willing to pay a premium for properly processed animal proteins and blended material. The leaders of this charge for improved animal protein quality are the nutritionists of premium low-residue companion animal rations. They insist on highly digestible protein ingredients with acceptable protein efficiency ratios, for example, spray-dried eggs, low-ash poultry byproduct meal, chilled and frozen ground poultry viscera, poultry byproduct meal, and sometimes good quality meat and bone meal.

Most interviewees agreed that the quality trend will continue into the next century, and quality of end products will influence their decisions when purchasing new processing equipment. They recognize that the inconsistencies of the raw material cause problems for renderers, but admit that renderers will have to produce properly processed and more consistent products in the future. To improve quality, renderers suggest:

- Improve the quality, safety, and consistency of our end products by educating our suppliers and our own personnel, that the rendering industry produces food (not feed).

- Users of our products will continue to set higher standards and will develop more sophisticated technologies to measure the value of the products. Technical research and quality control programs will become increasingly more important to the renderer.

- The microbial quality of our products has long been under attack; pressure from the government (and we know it may not happen otherwise) will force the industry to comply with standards.

- All segments of the industry should support the Animal Protein Producers Industry and Fats and Proteins Research Foundation so these organizations can assist us in producing safe and improved finished products.

- Microbiological quality of rendered proteins is one of our major quality problems. Our government must allow renderers to use chemical antagonists that are proven to be effective and safe.

- Product quality must be improved. But the market must pay for the additional cost associated with the improved production technology, product handling for better microbiological control, and quicker laboratory analysis of product quality.

- The feed industry is showing a willingness to pay more for a higher quality product despite the availability of cheaper, but energy-inferior alternatives.

Greg Van Hoven of The Van Hoven Company summarizes many of the thoughts expressed throughout this section regarding future attitudes toward quality:

> I believe the industry is divided between those that believe profitability is driven by raw material and plant costs alone, and those that believe profitability is driven by innovation, quality, and new product development. I think both of these philosophies will probably succeed during the next 10 years, but those that embrace the latter will be far more successful beyond 10 years.

## ENVIRONMENTAL REGULATIONS NEXT CENTURY AND HOW TO COPE WITH THEM

Every renderer has had to come to grips with expanded and more restrictive environmental regulations over the past 20 years. The majority of the renderers responding to a recent survey agree that this trend will only accelerate into the next century. Many renderers think that, in the next 5 to 10 years, complying with environmental regulations will be the industry's area of largest capital expenditures. Doug Anderson of Darling International sees an ever-increasing pressure to bring the industry closer to the food industry than the garbage business.

> Renderers tend to focus on government regulations and the officials enforcing the laws. But if we look at what is driving the increase in regulations, we find neighbors, concerned citizens within the rendering communities, and career "green" activists. Most renderers realize that they must actively become acquainted with and involved with these people and attend and speak at environmental meetings. At both the national and state levels, the national association (the National Renderers Association) can represent the industry's position and negotiate acceptable standards.

Tommy Bagwell of American Proteins agrees. He expresses his company's position in this way:

> We will experience more regulations in the future and they are being driven from both the government and citizen level. Being an activist today is a common practice for many people, and they consider any environmental intrusion unacceptable. This will, of course, require rendering technology to continue to advance to become more and more environmentally sound. Our experience with government officials at the state and local levels has been very good. Our company takes a pro-active approach of trying to head off problems before they become real and encourages meetings with environmental regulatory authorities.

One very important aspect of government relations is allocating the time and having the patience to educate the local enforcement officials. Jack

Smith of Sanderson Farms relates the frustration of working with some environmental officials.

> We hardly have time to get our permits satisfied until they usually are asking for more difficult standards for the next year. . . . The attitude of government officials is sometimes difficult to understand. The rules are changing before the regulation books (that explain them) are printed and in the officials' hands.

Smith finds many officials willing to assist renderers, but they do not know how, and many times do not have the resources to carry out their plan. Doug Baskin of Tyson Foods agrees with Smith, that many times these officials do not understand the rendering process, or the impact of the decisions they make. He adds, "Without proper training and knowledge, they can cause complications for renderers."

When David Evans of CBP Resources looks ahead to environmental challenges in the future, he sees the government continuing to follow the demands of the public, since a politician views the public's opinion as more important than either science or government–industry cooperation (for the good of the public). John Hendricks of Moyer Packing Company sees a small bright spot in the next century. He thinks there is a chance of fewer regulations, and he thinks that enforcing agencies will have a more rational approach (risk basis versus public opinion basis) in dealing with industry.

On another positive note, Andre Couture of Sanimal Industries views the increased environmental expenditures as an asset to the established renderer: "Tougher future environmental regulations is one of the greatest assets of independent renderers." His explanation is, "The tougher they get (and they will), the harder it will be to build a new rendering plant. Time will always bring more value to a rendering site if volume holds."

As stated before, the renderer who is willing to maintain proper local, state, and federal relations, to communicate with local officials, and to make the necessary capital expenditures will be operating a successful rendering plant in the next century. In summary, over the long term, a rendering company's governmental and public relations will be only as good as the amount of effort renderers are willing to put into it.

## WHAT LIES AHEAD FOR THE INDEPENDENT RENDERER?

After reviewing the data on the raw materials that will be available for independent renderers, it is quite logical to ask what lies ahead.

All contributors agreed that there is excess production capacity, and when combining this factor with decreasing raw materials and increasing environmental expenditures, consolidation is certain to continue in the independent rendering industry. Dean Carlson of National Byproducts maintains that consolidation of the independent rendering industry will accelerate over the next 10 years, from the slow pace of the past 5 to 8 years. This will primarily be due to the decline of raw material, the excess production capacity, and the effect of environmental costs and other economic conditions, such as finished product prices. Carlson recognizes that several of the family independents are quite strong, but that they will need to evaluate their investment in this industry, compared with alternatives.

Andre Couture of Sanimal Industries envisions the industry 10 years from now declining from approximately a dozen large independent rendering companies today to no more than 6. Couture thinks there are too many plants, and that the potential for synergies through buy-out is still tremendous.

Greg Van Hoven of The Van Hoven Company, a family independent renderer representing one of the few remaining family renderers, views further consolidation differently. Van Hoven estimates that the present pace of consolidation, which has slowed in the past few years, will slow even further. He thinks the independents that remain are financially strong. Many of the family independents have second, third, or fourth generation operators active in the business, with powerful emotional ties. Most of the companies have relatively young owner-managers, who are deeply committed to their careers, the organization's future success, and continuation of tradition. Van Hoven believes that for these persons, the value of their stake is very high, certainly higher than a bargain hunter is willing to consider. The Wintzer brothers of GA Wintzer and Son, along with Gary Baas of Inland Products, agree with Van Hoven and see their businesses expanding, rather than being auctioned off.

Doug Anderson of Darling International addresses this topic from the perspective of a company that purchased a long-time independent rendering plant in 1995. Anderson agrees with Carlson and others, that government regulatory enforcement will have the biggest effect on the smaller independents who choose to retain their capital and not comply. Anderson suggests that strength and price can be advantages, as well as disadvantages for the independents. He also believes that a pivotal issue is the amount of reinvestment required of these independents.

After analyzing the renderers' viewpoints, all seem to be on target. The strong family independents who are experiencing adequate raw material volume and have the mechanical expertise and the capital to upgrade their production facilities and who meet new environmental regulations, will be a force in the industry for many years.

The family and corporate independents who, through no fault of their own, have seen their red meat raw material volume plummet and are facing serious competition in the limited-growth restaurant grease business, will seriously consider selling their operations (at a proper price) before making large investments in new rendering processes and pollution control equipment.

# CHALLENGES THE NEXT 10 to 20 YEARS

Participating renderers were asked to list the 3 most important challenges facing the rendering industry over the next 10 to 20 years. Since the problem of raw material availability differs significantly between the poultry and packer renderers versus the independent renderers, their responses to the above question are separated.

## Packer and Poultry Renderers

- *Environmental regulations proposed by OSHA and similar governmental agencies* (6 renderers). Previously, the effect of this area on the independent renderer was stressed, but renderers in this category have a concern for the survival of many small- and mid-sized packing plants and poultry processors, due solely to environmental problems.

- *Tighter nutritional standards and competition from alternate feed proteins and fats* (5 renderers). Most of this discussion has been on quality, addressing improving animal proteins, but Mike Rempe of Excel thinks there is a major challenge in upgrading fat quality to compete with the old and new vegetable oils that are being improved by utilization of modern refining technologies.

- *Microbial acceptability of finished proteins* (4 renderers). But, note that independent renderers were challenged only by bovine spongiform encephalopathy (1). When reviewing the comments on the financial effect of producing microbiologically acceptable products in the future, most independent renderers assumed it would be accomplished or resolved in a timely manner. The packer and poultry renderers saw this problem as very difficult to overcome and were perplexed with the cost of accomplishing this task.

- *Hiring and training people to manage and operate facilities* (3 renderers). Finding trainable plant personnel was mentioned as the most significant challenge by several renderers. As plants become more automated, they require personnel with higher skill levels to operate the plant and to maintain the sophisticated equipment.

The industry has made dramatic improvements in plant working conditions over the past 20 years. However, unless renderers have in place an effective and ongoing employee training program, they could experience above-average labor and management turnover, operator miscues, absenteeism, etc, which could drive up operating costs to a non-competitive level.

- *Ability to change fast enough to meet challenges and to establish satisfactory public relations* (2 renderers). Many renderers are hiring PR firms to assist them in communicating with their neighbors, customers, and communities in their marketing area.

- *Developing export markets* (2 renderers), *achieving breakthroughs to find acceptable food use for edible tallow and lard* (1 packer), and *availability of competitively priced energy and the efficient utilization of eₓergy* (1 packer renderer).

Developing export markets is covered in another chapter, but think how effective the industry could become if all renderers would work together within some type of national organization, so that they could cooperate and share ideas on how to compete in the world marketplace. The canola people speak with one voice. The palm, soy, and other major oil-producing groups are not splintered into 5 or 6 different organizations. Domestic and export marketing initiatives, government relations, and food safety are important to every renderer. Developing a strategy so renderers can all work together as a team, as they do in improving the microbiological quality of proteins (Animal Protein Producers Industry), is a major challenge of the rendering industry in the 21st century.

## Independent Renderers

- *Diminishing raw material base and developing strategies to assist suppliers in competing and maintaining a profitable business* (7 renderers). Independent renderers are worried about the repercussions of less tonnage, such as higher operating and collection costs, having to alienate long-time customers due to implementing pick-up fees, and the inability to comply with governmental regulations from a smaller raw material base.

- *Environmental regulations and profitably operating a rendering plant while maintaining good relations with their neighbors* (5 renderers). Typical of this group were expressions such as, profitably operating rendering facilities in a manner that will enable peaceful and harmonious coexistence within the communities where we operate; keeping your neighbors happy and dealing successfully with environmental demands; and operating in harmony with various relationships (environmental, agricultural, labor, etc).

- *Where will the people come from to operate the facilities?* (3 renderers). This problem was mentioned many times by both groups in answers to other questions. Dean Carlson of National Byproducts articulated the problem in this manner, "The ability to attract and hire employees for all levels of employment in our industry is, and will continue to be, a major challenge." David Evans of CBP Resources said simply, "Giving your employees the resources so they can be productive and happy is a challenge. Employees must be made to realize they are important to the success of the operation, and if it is successful, they will be fairly rewarded for their efforts." Training and effective communication are "musts" in maintaining proper employee relations. All employees, from the president down to new hires, must become renderers, understand their assignments, be familiar with the objectives of the company, know the purpose of the business, and know how their roles fit into the big picture. Several renderers ranked as the number 1 challenge hiring effective plant operating personnel over the next 20 years.

• *Producing quality products* (2 renderers), *ability to produce value -added products with a changing raw material mix* (2 renderers), and *maintaining competitive plant costs with higher labor and other costs charged against lower raw material tonnage* (2 renderers). These challenges are all related to the raw material dilemma. Independent companies producing top white and extra fancy tallow for the export market will have to become magicians if they are to produce these grades with less shop fat and bones in the coming years. Additional concerns mentioned were.

• *Fear of bovine spongiform encephalopathy being diagnosed in North America* (1 renderer), *availability of quality livestock for suppliers* (1 renderer), *just surviving* (1 renderer), and *improving our public relations image on a state and national level* (1 renderer). Dennis Griffin of Griffin Industries expresses his company's goals for good public relations as, "Making society understand the necessity of our function, and better educating our children as to the needs and benefits of not only our industry, but all of agriculture."

Possibly renderers believe that if each company will address the public relations issue in its community, the state and national situation will take care of itself. Griffin wants the industry to respond to the challenges from the far left liberals by stressing the importance of the meat industry, promoting the need for grassroots farmers, and educating the people about where food products really come from—which is NOT the supermarket.

The emphasis all renderers placed on environmental regulations and the importance that independents gave the reduction of raw material was expected. The fact that so many renderers mentioned the necessity of improving the nutrient value and consistency of finished products was encouraging. The industry is beginning to realize that raw material cannot just be "cooked," but must be processed with the objective of producing end products having the highest possible nutrient value and purity. Dennis Mullane of Taylor Byproducts suggests that renderers focus on the consumer of rendered products, the cow, chicken, cat, dog, pig, and soap-using human. Renderers can sell products to feed mills and meet the nutritionists' specifications, but if the products are not palatable or fail to elicit the expected response in the animals, they will be removed from the ration or reduced to insignificant levels.

Another positive movement taking place also relates to product quality. More renderers are adding part-time or full-time nutritionists to their staffs. This indicates a real concern in improving communication with food company professionals to gain information to assist plant personnel in producing value-added and superior end products.

## 21ST CENTURY PROFITABILITY

The packer-renderers know they are in a low-margin business, and to a great extent their profitability depends on the supplies of animals. Recognizing that cattle and swine cycles will continue to be part of their future, they must concentrate on controlling costs and being innovative. When packers look to future profitability, they see that they must:

- Stay lean and improve productivity.
- Add more value-added products.
- Ensure that these products are viewed as healthy and convenient.
- Develop innovative domestic and export marketing program.

William Combs of Monfort offered these thoughts on the long- term profitability outlook:

> The red meat industry will remain a low margin, but profitable industry. The competition between the majors is incredibly intense. This kind of competition is driving many efforts that are and will bear fruit in the form of better operating efficiencies, product acceptance, and superior products as a whole. Many of these 'innovations' will bring beef and pork into an improved competitive position, relative to poultry.

All packers agreed that rendering is becoming a more visible segment of the packing business, and top management, even though they are not knowledgeable in rendering, are becoming aware that receiving the highest return on the drop is important. Dale Graham of IBP expressed it this way:

> Meat packers that thought of rendering as a necessary evil have gone the way of the dinosaur. Those that remain and those that will prosper into the future will maximize return in every aspect of the business.

Poultry renderers all agreed that for the most part, profitability has been good, and the industry will continue to grow and prosper through the end of this decade. Tommy Bagwell of American Proteins thinks that, at some point in the future, the profitability of the poultry industry, which has been reinvesting in capital assets, may result in overgrowth and over capacity, which will lead to consolidation. Doug Baskin of Tyson predicts that companies that realize they are not chicken or poultry companies, but food companies, will survive. Baskin thinks diversification is the key to 21st century profitability.

Poultry tastes good and is a great converter of feed, but these assets have sometimes been used against poultry as supermarkets use it as a loss leader to draw customers to their stores. This contributes to consumers' believing that chickens should always be cheap. Jack Smith of Sanderson Farms commented on comparative meat values from when he was a 12-year-old cutting meat in 1958 to today: "Chicken was selling for 24 to 29¢/ lb, and bone-in rib eyes were 89¢/ lb. Today, chicken is from 49 to 55¢/ lb, and cheaper on sale, while bone-in rib eyes are $2.99/ lb, on sale."

The pork and beef industries, plus true vegetarians, are all taking aim at the chicken people, but it will still be the best-value meat into the next century. The efficient, large poultry rendering plants will be significant contributors to poultry profitability.

Every independent renderer interviewed agreed that with good strategic planning, the industry will prosper in the future. Some of the comments that illustrate the adjustments and changes that independents think are necessary for survival and profitability are:

- Consolidate operations in low volume and highly competitive areas. Lower operating costs.

- Become more market-driven, investing more dollars in research and development.

- Maintain plants properly, be lean, and operate efficiently.

- Improve ability to adjust to swings in finish material prices.

- Do not get greedy with the fewer and larger customers. Recognize that one of their alternatives is to build their own plant when renderers underprice their raw material.

- If customers are profitable, they will allow renderers to get good prices. If suppliers are profitable, they will allow renderers to obtain raw material at the right price. If neither of them is profitable, consolidation will escalate.

Most of the above have been discussed, but the repetition of these challenges illustrates the importance they play in the future of the owners, managers, and employees of approximately 200 independent rendering facilities.

# SUMMARY

Summing up what the 21st century holds for renderers from the vantage point of 1996:

- *Packer-renderers will process more of the available red meat animal byproducts and will place greater emphasis on edible and inedible rendering.* In the next 20 years, they will make a significant penetration in the poultry and independent renderers' value-added products markets.

- *Poultry renderers will continue to lead the way in building large volume plants, utilizing the latest technology , and processing different grades of raw material separately.* They are part of a value-added product industry and will use these skills to continue to upgrade their high protein feather meal and poultry byproduct meals.

- *All renderers will spend more time and money on hiring and training plant personnel.* Competent plant superintendents, maintenance personnel, and systems operators will be much in demand.

- *Environmental regulations may not be as serious a problem in the next century as in the past 20 years.* New control technologies, less governmental interference or regulations, and sound management that puts their companies in front of the problem rather than having to catch up will lower the cost and stress of this challenge. Improved community relations is in vogue today.

- *The rendering industry, with the assistance of the Animal Protein Producers Industry and the insistence of the FDA and customers, will deliver animal proteins with a maximum 10% salmonella incidence level to their customers.* This will be accomplished by the use of chemical antagonists, active HACCP programs, and heat sterilization in rare cases. Feed companies, using proper pelleting and cooling technologies and HACCP programs, will deliver a less than 5% salmonella incidence product to the farm. Red meat and poultry carcasses will be treated, at the processing plant, to destroy pathogens. Irradiated red meat and poultry will be prevalent in supermarkets.

- *Strong family independents will focus on quality management and value-added niche markets.* Most will purchase other rendering plants over the next 10 years. Surviving multi-plant companies and strong family independents will actively pursue the independents who decide to sell for all of the previously mentioned reasons. There will be fewer than

100 independent rendering plants in North America in the 21st century.

- *Other than poultry independents, there will be less raw material available to the independent rendering industry.* This will accelerate consolidation in certain geographic areas, but many renderers will diversify into allied recycling areas. The reluctance to utilize dehydrating technology will diminish, and those who risk the investment will reap the rewards. When 1 independent rendering plant can process all of the raw material in a large metropolitan area or state, the other rendering sites and equipment could be converted to municipal sludge, manure, food waste, etc dehydrating facilities. This will be a major charge-for-service industry.

- *Surviving independent renderers will be charging all customers for collection services, other than very large accounts.*

- *Renderers will increase support for the Fats and Proteins Research Foundation and other rendering research organizations.* Information from these groups will demonstrate the importance of proper processing of raw material, and renderers will produce a more uniform and consistent product for all their customers. Pet food companies and progressive feed manufacturers will pay a premium for selected, properly processed and blended animal proteins.

- *"Food" will replace "feed" in renderers' vocabulary, and "inedible" will never be used in the 21st century.*

# GLOSSARY

**Animal fat**—An aggregate term generally understood to be fat from mammals.

**Bleachable fancy tallow**—Primary beef tallow defined by hardness, moisture, insolubles, unsaponifiables, free fatty acids, fatty acid content, and color.

**Byproduct (raw)**—All discarded material from animals or poultry and other sources that is processed in a rendering plant.

**Centrifuge**—Machine using centrifugal force to separate materials of different densities.

**Choice white grease**—A specific grade of mostly pork fat defined by hardness, color, fatty acid content, moisture, insolubles, unsaponifiables, and free fatty acids.

**Cooker, batch**—Horizontal, steam-jacketed cylinder equipped with a mechanical agitator. Batches of raw material are cooked according to a repetitive cycle.

**Cooker, continuous**—A cooker used in continuous rendering where the flow of raw material through the system is essentially constant.

**Cracklings**—Solid protein material discharged from screw press after removal of liquid fat.

**Crusher**—Machine containing blades or knives that grind raw material to uniform size.

**Edible**—Fats and proteins produced for human consumption which are under the inspection and processing standards established by the US Department of Agriculture, Food and Safety Inspection Service (USDA/FSIS).

**Edible grease**—Lard, the process and parameters of which are the same as for beef but with pork as the raw material.

**Edible tallow**—Exclusively beef, this product is rendered from fat trimmings and bones taken from further processing at a slaughterhouse. Because of the associated processing and the limits of raw material, the product of light color and low moisture, insolubles, unsaponifiables, and free fatty acids. The tallow may be further refined, polished, and deodorized to become a cooking fat. The petfood industry generally uses the crude product not shipped under seal. This often is referred to as technical tallow.

**Fat products**—Tallow and grease.

**Feather meal**—Protein product also known as hydrolyzed poultry feathers.

**Grease**—A fat product with a titer less than 40.0°C.

**Hydrolyzed**—Subjected to chemical reaction with water to break down the indigestible protein of poultry feathers into a digestible form.

**Independent rendering plant**—Obtains its byproduct material from a variety of sources which are off-site or separate from the plant facility.

**Inedible**—Fats and proteins produced for animal and poultry consumption or for other non-edible uses.

**Integrated rendering plant**—Operates in conjunction with a meat , slaughterhouse, or poultry processor whose byproduct materials are processed on-site.

**Meat meal**—Dry rendered protein product from mammal tissues with 4.4% or less phosphorus.

**Meat and bone meal**—Dry rendered protein product from mammal tissues with more than 4.4% phosphorus.

**Offal**—All material from the animal's body cavity processed in a rendering plant.

**Percolating pan**—A tank with a perforated screen through which the liquid fat drains freely and separates from the tankage.

**Pressure leaf filter**—Machine for removal of solids from liquids where a filter cloth mounted on a series of leaves or plates can accumulate a solid cake as pressure is applied continuously.

**Primary treatment**—Waste water treatment for removing suspended and floating material. Examples of primary treatment include mechanical skimmers and air flotation cells.

**Rendering, dry**—The process of releasing fat by dehydrating raw material in a batch or continuous cooker.

**Screw press**—Machine used to separate fat from tankage continuously by applying the required pressure with a rotating screw.

**Secondary treatment**—Waste water treatment for removing organic treatment matter by biological action.   Examples of secondary treatment include activated sludge systems and lagoons.

**Tallow**—Animal fat product with a titer of 40.0°C or higher.

**Tankage**—Cooked material remaining after the liquid fat is drained and separated.

**Tertiary treatment**—Wastewater treatment for removing nitrogen, phosphorus, or other pollutants below   concentrations achievable through primary or secondary treatment.

**Titer**—An analytical measurement used to indicate the hardness or softness of fats, and expressed in degrees centigrade.

**Wet scrubber**—Pollution control device for contacting air exhausted from rendering plant with a water solution containing deodorizing chemicals for odor removal.

**Yellow grease A or B; no 1, no 3 tallow**—These result from the poorer pork and beef sources of raw material.  Free fatty acids range up to 35%, and color can be as high as 37 FAC.  Often referred to as feed fats, they come from spent frying oils and animal fats.  They may be animal or vegetable.

# INDEX